W9-BYJ-116

ATLANTIC HIGH

Atlantic High

A CELEBRATION

William F. Buckley, Jr.

Photographs by Christopher Little

LITTLE, BROWN AND COMPANY · BOSTON · TORONTO

C

A portion of this book appeared originally in *The New Yorker*.

Published by arrangement with Doubleday & Company, Inc.

BP

*Published simultaneously in Canada
by Little, Brown & Company (Canada) Limited*

PRINTED IN THE UNITED STATES OF AMERICA

FOR

Charles W. Wallen, Jr.

Felix cui litteris suis faveat

ACKNOWLEDGMENTS

I am grateful to my companions from whose journals I quote. I have integrated in the text parts of articles previously published in *Motor Boating & Sailing, Ambassador, Esquire,* and *National Review.* Portions of this book were published in *The New Yorker.* One section of it was written, absent the profane interpolations, by Plato (the *Euthyphro*).

Samuel S. Vaughan, Publisher at Doubleday, was at all moments encouraging, in some indispensable. For their editorial suggestions I am indebted to Betty Prashker, Reginald Stoops, and—especially—Sophie Wilkins. Alex Gotfryd, the art director of Doubleday, is responsible for the imaginative presentation. Frances Bronson, Dorothy McCartney, and Susan Stark corrected a thousand errors and produced three drafts. Chaucy Bennetts did a superb job of copy editing. Joseph Isola did the proofreading. My thanks to them.

And for the singular photographs, my thanks go to Christopher Little. The photographs that accompany the first two chapters were not taken by him, as is mortifyingly self-evident.

The most marvelous thing that happened to boats and boat life in 1981 was the publication of "*Sailing* (sā'ling): 1. *n.* the fine art of getting wet and becoming ill while slowly going nowhere at great expense." This "dictionary for landlubbers, old salts, and armchair drifters" was written and illustrated by Henry Beard and Roy McKie, and published by the Workman Publishing Company in New York. Here and there I cite Beard-McKie *aperçus*, with subversive admiration.

In sailing there is a term called "lift" which is both technical and po-
etic at once. It describes the moment of acceleration in a sailboat—the
moment when the sails harden against the wind forcing the keel side-
ways against the water, and the boat begins to slide forward, faster
and faster, until you can suddenly feel what William Buckley meant
by the title of his sailing book Airborne. *How something moving so*
slowly—about the pace of a moderate jog—can impart such exhila-
ration in this moment is probably unanswerable. Hang gliding, drop-
ping in a parachute, doing barrel rolls in a light airplane—the thrills
are easy to understand. But at seven miles an hour the moment of lift
in a sailboat is just as much a leap off the earth.
   Airborne.

From "Setting Sail"
By Tony Chamberlain
Boston *Globe*, July 20, 1979

Prologue

It was 11:30 at night and I was sprawled in the recesses of an armchair, in the living room of the hotel suite, doing a little listless reading, a glass of vodka and grapefruit juice at hand (the ingredients are packed by my wife when I tour); heavy with the fatigue that always hits after your hosts have finally returned you to your quarters—after the reception—after the question period—after the speech—after the dinner: a fatigue to which you don't want instantly to surrender by sleeping, because the sweetness of decompression is too keen. You are *alone!* You aren't *talking!* You will be able to sleep seven hours, before rising to go on to the airport for the next engagement. The telephone rang.

"This is Christopher. Christopher Little. Gee I'm *terribly* sorry to ring you so late—"

Christopher regularly apologizes when he calls, as if his presence were somehow burdensome. In fact it brings pleasure.

"Apologize to me?" I said. "God," I looked at my watch, "it's *two-thirty* in New York! You *are* in New York?"

"Yeah. I know. But the editors of *People* are going wild. They want just *one* line from you—there isn't room for more than *one* line—on why you did it again."

"Did what again?"

"Sail across the Atlantic."

"What do they have surrounding the blank line?"

"Shall I read you the whole thing?"

"Shoot."

"The big headline says, 'WILLIAM F. BUCKLEY, JR. BRAVES THE HIGH SEAS, IN HIS FASHION, WITH CHAMPAGNE & SCARLATTI.'"

I groaned, but not noisily—and anyway, it was largely my fault. Nobody *made* me mention champagne or Scarlatti.

"Then they have the lead, in italics. It says: '*William F. Buckley, Jr., 54, is well-known as a conservative (TV's "Firing Line") and best-selling author* (Who's On First). *His reputation as an adventurer is less appreciated. Last month he set out from the Caribbean island of St. Thomas to sail the Atlantic with four friends, four paid crew members and one intrepid photographer, Christopher Little—*'"

"Who said you were intrepid?"

He laughed. Christopher laughs like a shy teenager, at once appreciative and self-effacing. "You did, in the story."

"Okay. Go ahead."

"'—*aboard the 71-foot ketch* Sealestial. *It was Buckley's second such crossing; the first was the subject of his 1976 book,* Airborne. *Why would he try it again?*'—that's where they need the line."

"What comes after the missing line?"

"'*After 30 days at sea the* Sealestial *landed in Marbella early this month. Before beginning a book about the voyage—*Atlantic High, *to be published by Doubleday next year, with photographs by Little—Buckley wrote this account of the trip for* People.'" Christopher paused. "That's it."

"Say: '*Buckley answered, "The wedding night is never enough."*'"

Christopher laughed. But he'd have laughed if I had said, "'Buckley answered, "Toasted Suzy is my ice cream."'" Christopher is that appreciative, but it pays to remember that he maintains very high standards. He is too nice to kill anyone; that apart, he is the kind of person about whom you would say, "Christopher Little would kill to get a good picture." It would have been totally accurate to say that Christopher Little damn-near killed himself to *get* some of the pictures he took. So I asked, cautiously, with that inflection of genuine curiosity necessary so that you don't give the impression you are asking for praise, "Do you think it's okay?"

"Yeah," said Christopher. Then there was that little social maneuver by which one treads cautiously away from any suggestion of sycophancy. "I think they'll like it."

Of the six (all told) who shared the whole or a part of the passage, I knew Christopher least well. I had set out to get a professional photographer, and he came to mind. His father and my brother had been classmates at Yale, colleagues at the Yale *Daily News,* and lifelong friends. But my first meeting with Christopher had been professional. He was assigned by *Time* magazine to photograph me in connection with the publication of one of my books. I found him charming, obviously intelligent, easily amused, handsome like his Danish mother. When his father Stuart W. (Stu has only the single affectation that he insists on the use of his middle initial) wrote a book about Joseph Papp, I was invited to the book party at the apartment of the Littles. There I had a chance to chat with Christopher and observe him in relaxation. Then there was yet another professional photography session, in what connection I don't remember.

I called my brother's charming and indiscreet daughter and told her I was looking for a photographer, but that since said photographer would be a member of my party, he had to be *just right,* because you don't set out across the sea to eat ninety consecutive meals across the table from someone who isn't *exactly right.* Priscilla, who had known Christopher since childhood, said he was splendid in every way. But Priscilla is only twenty-three years old, so (uncharacteristically) I decided to be a little more thorough, and called Christopher to ask if he would come around, as I wanted to talk to him about something.

The meeting was at my apartment on Seventy-third Street. Christopher was instantly disarming. "Look, Mr. Buckley [he said], I have to level with you. Priscilla confided to me over the phone what this is all about. I went out ten minutes later and found a copy of your book *Airborne.* I finished it at five this morning. I've always wanted to cross the ocean. I want to go on *this* trip, desperately. I will take the best pictures you ever saw."

I took the precaution of asking him for a portfolio of pictures and, during the weekend, I and Pat (wife) and son (also Christopher) viewed them, and were much taken by them, as I had been by him. The subject of remuneration came up and I asked him to let me know what his fee would be. As so often happens in tender social situations, the subject of money gets picked up like a dead mouse, the breath held until the creature is dropped in the garbage. Weeks went by, and three times I had to press him. "After equal amounts of thought and procrastination," he finally replied by mail, "I've arrived at some figures which seem to make sense." I was greatly disconcerted, not to say astonished, at learning that he intended to shoot a total of 270 rolls of film, or 9,720 pictures. I replied, "I now wish your letter had been delayed even further. . . . I find the figures too high, but it grieves me terribly to argue with you (or anybody) about money. . . . I'd be sullen, but not mutinous, with a total bill, including expenses, of [I gave a figure]; but I would be extremely unhappy if you were unhappy. . . . What shall we do?" To which he replied, "We are in complete accord on at least two points—our enthusiasm for this grand project and our aversion to arguments about money. I accept your counteroffer without a trace of rancor. I hope this letter resolves our business and leaves us free to enjoy a venture which, frankly, is the most exciting single project of my career." Was ever a partnership better launched? Only the champagne was missing, but there would be time for that. . . .

"How's everything else?" I asked on the phone.
"Great. When are you getting back?"
"Friday."
"The magazine will be out Monday. I might have a copy for you on Sunday."
"Terrific."
"Thanks again. Sorry about the hour. But that's the way they work down here at deadline time."
We said good night. I thought, How *quickly* conventional habits are resumed. At eleven-thirty at night during the preceding month, far from being asleep, I was on watch duty. That was my one great big perk. I always took the watch from 8 P.M. to midnight, the dream watch. To be sure that's when, as navigator, I'd work out the star sights. But it meant you could sleep the night through, barring a difficulty the watch captain didn't want to take responsibility for: I was the captain, and always on call. Eating supper at seven tends to leave you undisposed for sleep at eight, though the two crew members (one chief and one Indian as we called them) who had the watch from midnight to 4 A.M. usually

were asleep, if not by eight, by nine or a little later, unless their spirits and stamina were especially high—there were even nights when the midnight watch slept not at all before going on duty, electing instead to read in the saloon, or play a little poker. Much depended on how greatly they had exerted themselves during the day.

The duty roster, by sailboat standards, was close to hedonistic: four hours on, eight hours off. The roster was systematically interrupted, in order to effect social rotation. To arrange this may strike you as easy, but that is only if you fail to reflect that chiefs and Indians are not interchangeable parts. There must be one chief on watch, which meant me, or Reggie (we've sailed together twenty-five years) or Danny, who is a chief though only in his late twenties, like Christopher (Christopher is an Indian because although he has sailed, he is not in Danny's league, Danny having for four years skippered my yawl, taking out charter parties, and sailed and raced with me since he was thirteen). Van is an Indian, even though he is my age and has sailed with me practically since our college days together. There is something about Van, who is omnicompetent as a banker, and as a human being, that resists that incremental effort to dominate the art sufficient to earn a chief's star; and besides, he would laugh right through the graduation ceremony, causing shambles. Although Tony is younger even than Christopher and Danny, he is a chief, having spent most of the two years after he finished Harvard racing sailboats, including a transatlantic race. He is a seasick chief the first day or two of any leg, but shrewd, and sound of judgment, quiet-spoken, happier at the helm when it is winding up and the waves have hit their stride, even than when eating, though it's close.

So then, why do it again? I had given the *People* people a flip reply, but the metaphor is not inept. Sailing satisfies, for some people, a certain quiet lust. Sailing across the Atlantic is both an elemental and a social experience. There are those who like to do it alone, even as there are mountain climbers who want to do it alone. I admire them, but disdain that masturbatory lust—you plus the sea plus the vessel are less than you plus the sea plus the vessel plus one or more companions. At one point during the crossing Danny evidently felt he had to *say* it, and did so even to an inanimate logbook: *"This is one hell of a sleigh ride, Santa. Speed 10.15. Winds now gusting to 45 knots!"* Would Danny have felt the same satisfaction if he had had only the logbook to speak to? Since first setting down my thoughts on the matter I have read Philip Weld's enthralling book *Moxie*, an account of his single-handed race from Plymouth to Newport (a coincidence: our passages were simultaneous) in which among other things he condescended to set a world speed record for single-handed Atlantic crossings. He is so persuasive on the distinctive pleasures of a solitary passage that he very nearly takes you into his net. . . .

But then I return to my log, and read Tony's entry when risen at 4 A.M. to relieve the predecessor watch.

"Very cold and wet. Reg and Christopher somewhat happy and extremely exhilarated."

An experienced logbook reader, who is also an experienced friend of the principals, will know that that entry suggests ever so lightly that the oncoming chief detected, in the watch he was relieving, both natural, and synthetic, stimulants to the spirit.

How to substitute for such exchanges? It is required that you have aboard companions who take, and give, pleasure from refractions of every kind. Without them we lose what the social scientists so regrettably term the "interfaces." My conviction—though, after reading Philip Weld, no longer dogmatically pronounced—is that the entirety of the experience grows out of the sea and the shared experience, the operative word here being "shared." Because, without my companions, it would not have been possible to say that when, finally, after twenty-eight days, we tied in to the slip at Marbella at midnight, I knew what (usually set in other contexts) goes by the name of the repose of the soul.

Book One

1

~~~~~~~~~~~~~~~~~~~~~~

Owning boats is costly in a second sense of the word. You can't rusticate them—as you might, say, an atelier. I have a little such studio, and when I reach Switzerland I am fifteen minutes separated from cruising speed rpm. The paints are all there, the dust on the canvases can be made to disappear in seconds. The brushes, cleaned, are good again this year and will be, a dozen years down the line. (My painting companion in Switzerland is David Niven, and today he uses the identical brushes he bought in Hollywood before the Second World War. When he told me this he rejected my flattering suggestion that perhaps they really dated back to when he had gone 'round the world in eighty days.) Everything, put simply, is just sitting there—canvases, turpentine, linseed oil, easels, sketch pads.

Boats require constant tending. I speak now of wooden boats and steel boats, not having experienced the others, though I flatly doubt the chimera of the "maintenance-free boat" even if you stick one in hermetically sealed glass. (Beard-McKie—"*Outfitting:* Series of maintenance tasks performed on boats ashore during good-weather weekends in spring and summer months to make them ready for winter storage.")

Foremost to worry about when owning a boat ready to go to sea is, of course, the expense. But if you seek to mitigate this burden by chartering out your boat, administrative burdens are added to economic burdens. A week seldom goes by without a problem of personnel; or another requiring a decision whether to replace this or that piece of equipment, revise that insurance policy, accept a charter that wishes to leave the boat in Haiti. . . . Was it worth it all?

I resolved, the summer after sailing my *Cyrano* to Spain (on an unforgettable cruise), to probe whether the same spirit that had taken us airborne across the Atlantic could be recaptured. So I reassembled most of the crew. This time I would take her to Mexico. During that trip I decided that on its completion I would experiment with a crewless boat. I would cut expenses by paying a splendid Cuban-American carpenter, who had done work on the boat in preparation for its transatlantic adventure, to spend a half day per week aboard, running the motor, turning on the lights, doing a little varnishing—that sort of thing. I would stop offering the boat for charter on a daily, weekend, or weekly basis, as I had been doing for nine years. That had required maintaining full-time a captain, cook, mate and steward. I would offer it fully staffed, but only for charters of ninety-day duration or longer. I talked to Reggie about it during the Mexican trip. We would see.

I kept a brief journal of that cruise.

There is something especially alluring in sailing to a *foreign* country. But no foreign country is finally exotic if its natives speak English: Thus a trip to Bras d'Or Lake in Cape Breton, though there is much to be said for it, is not quite the same thing as it would be if M. Lévesque and his Parti Québécois practiced a little irredentism and recaptured Fort Louisburg. One of the charms of the Leeward Islands is the need to accommodate to a different language virtually every time you throw out your anchor. Sailing to Europe meets all the tests, but is something of an enterprise. Sailing to Yucatan is less than a transatlantic labor. Indeed, Miami-Yucatan is less than Newport-Bermuda. But you achieve the feeling of having slipped away to a remote and thoroughly foreign country, and as a matter of fact you have.

4

When you dwell on the distance between the Dry Tortugas (the final U.S. departure point) and Mujeres Island (the nearest Mexican point of land)—290 miles—you need to fight the feeling that your outing has been on the order of driving from San Diego to Tijuana. It is more than that for several reasons. Not the least of these is that lying in wait for you if your attention flags, just a few miles to the south, for over one half the distance, is the dragon Fafnir, guarding the forbidden treasures of Cuba. How far offshore from Cuba, I asked my friendly patron at the State Department, must I stay?

"They assert three miles of territorial sovereignty, and twelve for customs," I was told; but it does not do to tease them in the matter, as Lloyd Bucher, commanding the *Pueblo*, did the North Koreans. On *no* account slip past the twelve-mile limit.

"What happens if you do?"

There's the rub. *Anything* can happen. One day a little Cuban coast guard vessel will politely usher you back out of Gulag waters. But another day the same vessel will take you to port, seize your boat, and submit you to a large dose of the People's Hospitality, for days, maybe even weeks, depending on the temperature of international relations and the caprice of the Maximum Caudillo. The mere presence of Castro over one hundred miles or so of coastline is bracing, in the morbid sense that the Berlin Wall is bracing.

Although determined that on setting out from Miami aboard my beloved *Cyrano* the ship would be totally equipped for the journey, foreknowledge that we would be passing by Key West encouraged a kind of nonchalance inappropriate to the preceding excursion one year earlier when the identical crew, save one substitute, set out from Miami bound for Marbella in Spain. This time we knew, subconsciously, that any egregious act of neglect could be corrected ninety miles down the road. I had my ritual bout with technology, which struts its imperfections with special flair aboard *Cyrano*. This year it was the single side-band radiotelephone. This wonderful machine we had used with extravagant delight going across the Atlantic. But no sooner had the vessel returned than the telephone company announced a new rate structure. The rate had been a dollar or two per call plus the local rate, so that a casual phone call from, say, Longitude 25° to Longitude 75° was something of a bargain. No more. The item escaped our attention until, after our Christmas cruise, the telephone bill came in, which I returned to the phone company with a cheerful note suggesting they oil their computers and send us a fresh bill.

The awful news transpired by return mail. The rate is now a flat five dollars *per minute*, and that's how much it is even if you are only just out of reach of the VHF channel, say thirty miles out of Miami. Hardly the way to encourage the diffuser graces of rhetoric. I put in a call to the vice president of AT&T in charge of extortion, and was dismayed to learn that the new rate schedule had indeed been approved by the FCC, upon presentation of the financial records that documented the loss sustained by the company on its high-seas operations. Moreover, said the telephone company official icily, the ocean telephone business is not a government-protected monopoly. Anyone can get into the act, and in fact a station in New Orleans, WLO, has set up an antenna, and we were welcome to hire *its* facilities if we wanted to, and found them cheaper. Accordingly, I had given instructions to install a WLO crystal.

By the time we finally told the technicians (there were two) who had fussed over the installation for four hours, "Never mind, please just let us begin our trip," they had mutilated our beautiful telephone, so that a) the emergency antenna would not transmit on the crystal that goes to the Coast Guard, b) five of the crystals never worked again, and c) we never did raise WLO.

The other problem was the air conditioner. The heat in Miami in early June can be fearful, and in 1976 was. *Cyrano*'s professional captain accosted the problem by the simple expedient of telling me that the air conditioner was working just fine, putting up his hand against the grille, where the milk-warm air dribbled out, and then withdrawing it sharply, as if taking care to guard against frostbite.

A word on the subject: A passage to Yucatan in June is a passage into the hottest latitude on earth, and if you are disinclined to suffer from oppressive heat, you should either not go in that season, or else you should equip your boat with air conditioning— which isn't that expensive these days. The idea of an air-conditioned sailboat, I judge from published comments about my previous book, *Airborne*, strikes some as indefensibly ostentatious or effete, raising the question: Why? Protection against the weather is, after food, the most elementary biological need. It is as perplexing to me that a sailor intending to spend time in the tropics should not wish to air-condition his boat as it would be should he not desire his boat to be leakproof. Sure, the generator presents a problem; but so does one's preference for a boat that doesn't sink. It is one thing to say that a particular sailboat is designed in such a way as to make it impossible to adapt it to air conditioning: that is good, plain, responsible talk, to which the good, plain, responsible reply is: Don't sail in that sailboat to Yucatan, especially not in June of 1976.

One day, diligent in my pursuit of navigational precision in order to keep a safe distance from the Cuban shore, I brandished the sextant for the noon sight and found myself contorting my body in order to keep the sun on the horizon. I looked reproachfully in the direction of my son at the helm, expecting to see him chatting away while the boat (we were under power, no wind) did lazy figure eights. But he was grimly engaged in keeping his course, and I found myself examining my sextant, wondering why the sun was executing circles around the horizon mirror. That is the generic reflex, like kicking your television set when my friend Howard Cosell gets out of hand. But my eyes suddenly focused on the altitude registered on my sextant and calculated it was ninety degrees! I looked at the almanac and, indeed, the sun at that moment was—*directly overhead!* Since there was no wind, and the humidity, not unexpectedly, was high, we could lay claim, however fleetingly, to being located on the hottest latitude on earth at the hottest moment of the day. I went below, closed the hatch, turned on the air conditioner, and recorded the event.

The passage from Miami to Key West is insufficiently celebrated. It is the ideal way to prepare for an ocean voyage. What you have is about ninety miles of water protected from the ocean by a string of shoals and beaches, assuring you lakelike security from swells and waves—but a stretch of water open enough to receive the full stimulus of the wind. Since going down Hawk Channel (as they call it) the course sets off to the south, then eases off toward the west-southwest like a slow golf slice, you are nicely situated when the wind blows from the east, first to proceed closehauled, then gradually to relax the sails. It is a dream sail, permitting you to stop anywhere, throw out the anchor, and declare this your own private, landlocked sanctuary.

We left Miami at 11:30, ran aground smack in the middle of

Stiltsville Channel at 12:15, called the Coast Guard at 12:16, which appeared (most obligingly as always) at 12:30, in a large whaler under the command of a bright and energetic young man who, however, was visibly embarrassed inasmuch as, after attending to our needs, he had to call the Coast Guard himself a) on our radio, because his didn't work, to report b) that his motor now didn't work. We kept him company until a mother ship arrived.

There were no other problems, but when two days later we weighed anchor to pull out of Key West, we got no farther than 100 yards when a furious rain squall broke over us, cutting visibility to zero. We quickly dropped anchor and waited the forty-five minutes until it passed. Then, preparing once again to pull away, we were arrested by an electric bullhorn from a police car on shore calling my name—was "Mr. William Buckley" aboard? An emergency telephone call! A dramatic political interruption! At the pay station I learned that Ronald Reagan, running hard against Gerald Ford for the Republican nomination, had in the preceding twenty-four hours been made to sound as if he proposed to send the Marines to Angola and Rhodesia. An expert on the Rhodesian situation, a friend who gave my name, had proffered his aid. Question: Is he an okay guy? Yes, I said to Reagan's aide, cleverly concealing that what was on my mind (it is ever so at sea) was not civil war in Rhodesia, but: Would there be a succession of squalls during the night?

Negative. And so we slipped out of Key West, and up the northwest channel toward the departure point for Dry Tortugas, the air conditioner in perfect working order, the crew flaunting its sea legs, the sky turned prussian blue. We dropped the anchor and cooked dinner, the stars coming out, a profusion of diamonds on a jeweler's velvet, and a fresh wind came down from the northeast. At ten we set out for Dry Tortugas, due west sixty miles, the spinnaker up, coming in at dawn to the gloomy, isolated fort, most famous for having infamously detained the wretched Doctor Mudd to whose house, craving medical attention, the crippled, anonymous assassin hobbled haphazardly a few hours after firing a bullet into the head of Abraham Lincoln.

From Dry Tortugas to Mujeres Island on the northeast of the Yucatan Peninsula the distance is, as I say, only 290 miles, the course 226 degrees. But in order to pursue this route, it would be required that you head directly into the Gulf Stream, which races

In the background, Dry Tortugas, the ancient federal prison and southernmost U.S. outpost. Background, Cyrano. *Foreground, Danny Merritt, with walkie-talkie, taking soundings in tortuous southern channel and escorting the mother ship through.*

up the Yucatan Channel and eases northeast, swirling around Cape San Antonio at the western tip of Cuba. Accordingly, it is advisable to cut your losses and sail south, say toward Bahía Honda, 100 miles away. From there to Mujeres Island it is about 220 miles, so that you have gone thirty miles out of your way but you avoid (at seven knots) a set (that is, a geographical slide) of as much as 100 miles. It is unfortunate that the winds are characteristically from the northeast so that you can't even count, as a reward, on gliding home after working your way there; indeed, on the return passage *Cyrano* had miserable northeasterlies, with squalls and winds up to fifty miles an hour, heavy rains, and entirely too much togetherness with supertankers coming down in the opposite direction.

Christopher T. Buckley (son) at the wheel of Cyrano, *returning to Miami from Yucatan, in a squall, the wind northwest, the current southwest. (Beard-McKie—"Current: Tidal flow that carries a boat away from its desired destination, or towards a hazard.")*

Twenty-three hours after sailing our leisurely way from Tortugas, we descried the mountain tops of the western Sierra range. During the day we groped against the current in a windless overcast, straining by a radar that worked only intermittently to define the Cuban coastline. That night, still without wind, the radar suddenly elected to work brilliantly, and I put *Cyrano* on autopilot and, with my son, went forward into the huge, sybaritic cockpit and lay back on the settee that sprawls over half the area when the dining table is down, the autopilot controls in my hand.

Outside it continued to drizzle. Inside it was dry, the radar blipping the little clusters of rain squalls, and with the autopilot we did what we could to maneuver around them, like a jet pilot operating in extreme slow motion, at 1/100th a jet's speed. Occasionally, responding to the pressure of my thumb, the boat would turn left provocatively toward Cuba, and we would watch the radials studiously; just before hitting twelve miles, with a switch of pressure the boat would turn east, even as the jaws of Castro's radar, in our fantasy and perhaps in fact, were readying to close down on us. A few hours of that and we slipped away from the dreary Cuban coast and trudged in lifeless water across the Yucatan Channel. Whenever gloom began to set in, I would console myself by reflecting how acutely unhappy I'd have been if it had been a race and we were forced to wallow in such a current during that long, dull, windless day.

Just after midnight Reggie came up triumphantly from his solitary confinement next to the Loran, at whose side he had imposed on himself a sentence to sit until the Loran yielded one coherent reading. (A Loran is designed to tell you, by radio triangulation, where you are.) This reading was quickly validated when we discerned lights, first the flashing white off Contoy, then the Cancún light. Between them lies Mujeres Island, where we docked at eight in the morning after one of those endless approaches to which this sailor will never become accustomed (you see the light, and expect within an hour to arrive at its source—which may be four hours away, given wind and current). The delay presaged the world of *mañana*. We were definitely in Mexico.

Mujeres is a Mexican version of one of the Greek islands. There is a combination of bustle and indolence. We were perfectly introduced to the bureaucracy when the customs officer asked for a form apparently procurable from U.S. Customs, notifying foreign governments that a U.S. vessel is leaving home waters without stigma. In the absence of this form, Immigration announced, we would be fined eighty dollars. This elicited a gasp of indignation—which, one gathers, is a typical reaction because the official retreat was instantaneous. In lieu of paying eighty dollars we might type out, in *quadruplicate*, the name and document number of the vessel, the names and home addresses of everyone on board, and a flight plan of sorts—where in Mexican waters we intended to sail. A half hour later I had done this on my little portable, and Danny, age twenty-five, had taken it to Immigration and in due course returned to say that I would need to re-execute the form, in a specified format—the surnames of the crew must appear in CAPITAL LETTERS. So I fished back out the three sheets of carbon paper and began again, painstakingly. I sent Danny with the freshly typed forms, and in twenty minutes he was back again. I would need to type them yet again, this time omitting the names of any Mexican ports save the port immediately after Mujeres.

A year earlier, at an aerie in Switzerland, I had been introduced to the Honorable Miguel Alemán, former President of Mexico. We conversed in Spanish, and he asked how was it I knew the language. I replied that among other things I had once lived in Mexico. "When?" he asked. Why, while he was president.

"You don't mean it!"

"Yes, 1951."

"What were you doing in Mexico?"

Well, I was in the CIA, and my boss was Howard Hunt. . . . I have had *extensive* experiences in Mexico, and have learned that the moment comes when you have to call a halt. So I accompanied Dan to Customs, and said that rather than complete their forms in quadruplicate one more time I would simply leave Mexico there and then, return to the United States, and perhaps write about my experiences. An urbane native, sitting on a chair to one side of the inspector, commented that Americans were hardly in a position to complain about immigration and customs formalities, given that he had once spent seven hours in detention in Miami pending the validation of *his* papers. I told him I thought that regrettable, and refrained from suggesting that there is more contraband traveling into the United States from Mexico than in the other direction, and the tension broke when the inspector said, Well, he would probably be fined for his permissiveness, but I was free to go my way; he would accept my forms, but of course I now had to present my clearance to Immigration. Where was that? At the airport. Thither we went, the rest of the crew having gone off to a restaurant for lunch.

At Immigration we reported to the designated window, at one side of which hung a large government poster with the words *En Mexico creemos en el valor de una sonrisa. Séamos amables con los turistas.* (In Mexico we believe in the value of a smile. Let's be pleasant to the tourists.) The problem was that no one was there to be pleasant to us. But, in due course, someone arrived, stamped one copy of our form for us, one for himself—forms no one would ever again consult—and we went off to a prettily situated but pretentious French beach restaurant, where we ate a hugely expensive, utterly forgettable lunch under a thatched roof on the beach, looking out over the Yucatan Channel.

The waters around Mujeres Island are brilliantly blue. To the south, the new resort of Cancún is opening up, with its Atlantic City-sized beach. We spent most of the day trying to diagnose our generator's problems: It had blown a head gasket. We resolved, rather than expose ourselves to the vagaries of local labor, to persuade our mechanic in Miami to take the hour-and-a-half flight to Cozumel. When he arrived he told us we were lucky indeed he was a friend of *Cyrano*'s, otherwise he would charge us what *others* would charge us for making the trip. His continence was revealed in his bill, in which he charged $18.50 per hour for three twelve-hour days. He arrived late in the afternoon of day one, and left in the morning of day three. Subsequently the generator needed overhauling. But we were hanging in there—just barely—as far as our air conditioner was concerned.

The night before leaving for Cozumel, we pulled out of the commercial dock at Mujeres and followed the shoreline to the north, searching out the lee, to drop anchor and have dinner. This we did opposite the Zazil Ha Hotel, and I do believe I never saw, anywhere—not in the Bahamas, not in the Antilles, not in Greece—such a feast of blues. As the sun went down the sky turned white, then mother-of-pearl. Off to one side was a shipwrecked shrimp boat. It caught the sun, and the rusty hull turned golden.

We ate the fish Reggie had caught late that afternoon, and then, with the cassette player beginning with Mozart and regressing to rock as the younger generation quietly asserted itself, we played poker. After our game Christopher and Danny took the dinghy into town, a diversion which, begun at 11 P.M., seemed barbarous enough. But when at 1:30 they returned and, instead of going to sleep, began a fresh game of cards, the captain, owner, and father of one of the delinquents announced huffily that if they were not wide awake at 8:30 A.M. we would eschew a visit to Cancún, where I knew they wanted to go. What sanctions does one have left, attempting to govern a twenty-three-year-old boy? Deprive him of a visit to Cancún! Pass the word along.

Cancún is not easily visited by boats drawing six feet. It has the air of an island not *quite* ready to receive the hordes of pleasure-seekers. Two days later, while we were on the island of Cozumel fifty miles to the south, Henry Kissinger, decompressing from a state visit with President Echeverría, stopped over at Cancún for the weekend, and apparently recovered quite nicely. It is a pity, after five years of Echeverría, that all of Mexico couldn't have had a weekend at Cancún.

The passage to Cozumel was downwind, and we hoisted the gollywobbler for the occasion. The younger generation groans when the seizure comes on me and I order the gollywobbler hoisted. This is because raising that sail requires slightly more coordination than is easily accomplished by young men who suddenly find their hands unoccupied by a) a cigarette, and b) a bottle of beer: destroying their equilibrium.

In any event, the sail was splendid, and it was nice to reflect that we were gliding down the gold coast of the Mayans. We tacked downwind, carefree and gay, and a couple of hours after dark we approached Puerto Abrigo. This is done with trepidation, because so far as I know there is no proper chart of the island of Cozumel. And so, over a period of one hour, we glided north, and then south, attempting to find the telltale harbor channel lights. Finally we radioed the local coast guard and asked for instructions. These came in in very rapid Spanish (one assumes they had heard the request before), and the distances were given in terms of hotels. "Proceed four and a half hotels south, approach the shore, and you will see a green and red light." There is ambiguity as to whether a particular building is a hotel or merely a brummagem profile of one. So, finally, we dispatched the whaler with the younger generation, with instructions please to find the channel entrance. They were equipped with the newest of *Cyrano's* accessories, a walkie-talkie; and, *mirabile dictu*, it worked. In due course they beckoned us to the dimly advertised passage, which requires you to enter, and then quickly U-turn into the docking area. This, once found, was entirely satisfactory, equipped with power, water and fuel—and our impatient diesel mechanic, in from Miami, waiting to fix our generator so that we could face the tropics with equanimity.

Christopher Buckley, grown haggard after the exertion of lifting the gollywobbler.

Cozumel would be the end of the line for most of us. I admire those who can combine cruising with sight-seeing. This requires not only a flexible schedule, but skill in adapting to two kinds of living simultaneously. I am, on land, a Stakhanovite sightseer, but I do this listlessly off a sailing boat, preferring perfunctory visits in the lands and islands I visit. We did poke about in Cozumel, but the archaeology is not particularly interesting. To visit Yucatan properly you would need to recross the strait and go inland, which Christopher and the return crew went on to do. We were satisfied to cruise about the island on motorbikes. If you do this, do not fail to stop for lunch at the Faro (the lighthouse) on the southwestern tip. There is an old couple with two or three little grandchildren. Their kitchen is inside a withered old tent where charcoal burns, and when the mood is upon them (at first they declined to prepare lunch for us), they will come up with fresh fish, and with the best tortillas and tacos I ever ate. The Faro is situated close to the Palancar reef, to which we sailed the next day, giving Danny and Christopher a couple of hours in what is reputedly as splendid a diving area as you can find in the Caribbean. I hadn't yet experienced scuba diving. Unhappily, the day was sunless, so that the colors were gone, and when this happens underwater it is as if the sunset were rendered in black and white. In Cozumel there is nightlife (C and D reported); but, truth to tell, sailing to Cozumel is more interesting than visiting in Cozumel. The passage is the thing, surely, and the passage to Yucatan is worth making—indeed, it can be exhilarating. But be careful that you do not run into Cuba, or succumb to the heat. And come armed with the archaic form from Customs, U.S.A., and listen to the old sailors describe, from their wheelchairs, the difficulty in making out the harbor entrance of Cozumel.

When *Cyrano* got back to Miami, I put my plan into effect. Widely did I advertise my beautiful schooner's availability for ninety-day charters. To this day I am stumped as to why I was unsuccessful. In Florida, in the wealthier ports of the inland waterway, primarily those that stretch north from Fort Lauderdale to Palm Beach, there must be a hundred thousand waterfront homes occupied by people who could have handled the tariff and would have got in return a perfect inland pleasure boat, for retired grand-father and grandmother to cruise (an experience unduplicatable, as far as I know) in the late afternoon and early evening during the Christmas season up and down the waterway, at rpm about 1,000—you cannot even hear the motor, and you are sitting in your wide, open, shaded, tranquil cockpit, parading like an electric canoe past forty miles of Macy's windows. The gentry in those parts have an unadvertised convention of celebrating the spirit of Christmas with competitively ingenious lighting on their lawns, porches, chimneys. A million colored lights, in ten thousand configurations. It is enough to make children, and non-children, wild with delight. And then (my *Cyrano* brochures advertised) when the gamy generations came to visit, sons and grandchildren on vacation, the boat was ready to go. Go where? Well, actually, go anywhere. Certainly fifty miles across the Gulf Stream to Bimini, or to the enchanting Cat Cay. And east from there, a day and one half to Nassau, and down the Exuma chain; then back again, returning the vessel to the old folks, until they migrated in April, or whenever, back to Long Island, or Lake Forest, return-ing the boat to the owner.

Nobody, but nobody at all, elected to hire himself these delights; so my wife and I and friends did, a half dozen times dur-ing the ensuing two seasons. But then the day came when our treasurer, Mrs. Flynn, asked me for—yet more money. There was nothing coming in, she reminded me. By chance I had just finished commissioning a major overhaul, directed primarily at getting *Cyrano*'s eccentric electrical system into absolutely reliable order, and endowing her with cold plates that permit you, after only one or two hours' service of the generator, to keep things ice cold all day long. Supervising the operation was a young man of great experience who had served as a professional boat captain. It was while he had the boat in Savannah, where the work was being done under his supervision, that I made the decision that has been made by thousands of grown-up men, backed into stoicism. The only way to go was fast, and so I called a broker. In two weeks he had a likely buyer, a gentleman from El Paso, Texas, and San Diego, California.

Since it is one of my purposes in this book to share practical as well as idiosyncratic experiences, permit me the suggestion that when you sell your boat, if you are especially attached to it, you make it a rule to establish no social contact *whatever* with the buyer. In this case the buyer was instantly recognizable as the self-made man—because he so proclaimed himself. You ask for X. The broker says that he has a buyer who is extremely interested, but is willing to pay only X minus Y. You think a while, measure pride and obstinacy against prudence and convenience and, depending on the mood, tilt one way or the other. On this occasion I was taken up with so many preoccupations extrinsic to sailing or haggling that I said, Okay, I'll go with X minus Y; but remember, I get to keep the radiotelephone (value $5,000).

A few days later the purchaser is on the spot at the boatyard in Savannah, his surveyor poking his ice pick into my *Cyrano*'s bottom to confirm what I had always known, that no sounder ship had ever been crafted, and the broker advises me over the telephone to Connecticut that the purchaser insists on talking to me. Against my better judgment I take the phone. He is the preternatural bargainer, who cannot sleep at night unless, during the day, he has shaken someone's resolution to his own commercial advantage. He *had* to have the radio, he argued, affecting bonhomie, and adducing coy reasons why the radio was of little use to me without a boat to put it in. I told him I retained a perfectly satisfactory yawl. The broker came back on the telephone. I came close to calling the whole thing off, but decided instead to do a little bargaining of my own, so I fired my aesthetic Big Bertha. You see, the saloon of *Cyrano* was lit by a soft shower of multicolored lights that refracted off three original oil paintings by Richard Grosvenor, from whose fingertips the roiling seas come as water from a faucet. The effect of the lighting was spectacular and moved a thousand people, over the years, to near speechlessness with pleasure. Okay, I said to the broker, tell him he can have the radio, but I get to keep the oil paintings. I felt as though I were offering him the Sistine Chapel without the ceiling. The broker warned that the buyer was a man of mercurial temper and mountain-hard resolution. I replied that he could have God or Mammon, but not both. Fifteen minutes later the telephone rang, and I cannot remember a moment of greater dismay. "He says sure you can have the paintings. He was going to take 'em out anyway, give them away, and put up some nice brass lamps."

That was not quite the end of the transaction. When the boatyard gave over the bill to my young captain, he was appalled. He figured it to be about three times the justified amount. "They know you have to turn over the boat by the first of August to the new buyer unencumbered, so they're just holding you up." For instance, he said, there was an item: eight hundred dollars to varnish and paint the whaler. "It couldn't have come to more than two hundred in time and materials." What to do?

I called my friend back at 8 P.M. and, fortunately, found him in a plucky mood. Would he arrange, with two or three companions, to slip aboard sometime between midnight and dawn and sail the boat out of Savannah Harbor, northeast thirty miles to Hilton Head in South Carolina, removed from Georgia jurisdiction?

"Then we can quarrel over the bill at our leisure, without jeopardizing the deal."

My friend was indignant enough to take to the idea ("even though I've got to live here in Savannah after *Cyrano* is gone"). He rounded up three spirited friends and, armed with a bottle or two of liquor to guard against the terrible early morning cold in Georgia in midsummer, they tiptoed on board, loosed the lines, and floated out with the tide before turning on the engine. By dawn they were ten miles from the most irate boatyard owner-pirate on the East Coast. I worried when, by noon, I hadn't heard from them. I called the Coast Guard, and learned they were safe: they had simply run aground coming into Hilton Head. I served notice on the boatyard owner that I was willing to go to arbitration, but that I would subtract from any final figure the cost of my legal defense. We settled. At about one half. At that, he took me for two or three thousand.

This wasn't the very first time I'd had to deal stealthily with boatyards. Three summers earlier, the Westerbeke engine in my yawl, *Suzy Wong*, committed its ritual annual suicide. (I'd had six new or totally rebuilt Westerbekes in fourteen years.) The local yard quoted a figure to rebuild her, and Reg suggested we get a competitive bid from a yard in Long Island, just by La Guardia Airport. Danny got someone to tow the boat over, and exactly one week later I was advised by Mrs. Flynn a) that the engine had been rebuilt; b) that the bill was for $2,100 (approximately the price quoted by my home yard, to which I'd have preferred to give the business); and c) that the money would have to be paid in cash before I could reclaim the boat.

I react adversely to ultimatums. The boatyard owner, without any commission whatever (he had been asked, merely, for an estimate) had undertaken to do the work, setting his own price. That was on Friday. On Sunday morning Danny, Christopher, and I drove to the yard, parked at a safe distance, and having established that there was no watchman on duty, vaulted the fence and approached *Suzy Wong. My* boat was secured to two huge eyebolts on the slip by a chain led around the mainmast and the aftermast and padlocked in place.

We went to City Island and there made arrangements to charter a whaler that would take us over water to the boatyard at three that afternoon. We arrived with a basket of tools, and instructed the skipper in which direction to head. We tried to look innocent, but we correctly surmised, later, that it was he who, on getting back, called the yard, and then the police.

Bounding onto the slip, my son Christopher unsheathed a hacksaw and I was astonished at the ease with which it sawed through the heavy steel links, understanding finally the old business about the hacksaw in the cake being the key to instant manumission for the prisoner. I dove down to start the engine, only to find it cleverly immobilized. One or two vital parts were missing. So who needs an engine? I asked. And Danny and Christopher, thoroughly in the spirit of the heist, repeated, "Who needs an engine?"

We raised the mizzensail, slid the boat out into Flushing Bay, headed her into the wind, raised the main, then the genoa, and three hours later, the two forward sails down, we coasted into the slip at Stamford for a perfect landing.

I wrote out the script for our Mrs. Flynn because, after all, when you go to all that much trouble, you should get some amusement from it. Anticipating what the boatyard owner would say turned out to be as easy as expected, and Mrs. Flynn reported that the script had proceeded as perfectly as if rehearsed.

"Mrs. Flynn? This is John, at John's Yard. *Suzy Wong* has been stolen."

"No, Mr. John, she wasn't stolen. Mr. Buckley went and took her away yesterday."

"That's stealing."

"No, Mr. John. There's no such thing as stealing your own property."

"But he owes me my bill!"

"Who commissioned the work?"

Splutter at the other end. Followed by, "I'm going to call the police."

"You do that, Mr. John. You tell the police Mr. Buckley stole his own boat."

Further splutter.

I offered arbitration, but Mr. John said he would prefer eleven hundred dollars. With arbitration there is always the risk that you will be paid what you deserve to be paid. Technically nothing, but what the hell, okay $1,100.

In any event, the new owner took possession of *Cyrano*. When she was last sighted, I should add, she was a part of the entourage of *Freedom*, our winning 12-meter sloop in the 1980 America's Cup Races, parading back into Newport from the race course, and in all honor I must report that Reggie, who espied her from a distance, reports that she looked like a million dollars. Dear old money-guzzling *Cyrano* belongs to someone who can make her look like a million dollars, so that her raiment will reflect her inner nobility.

2

~~~~~~~~~~~~~~~~~~

After losing *Cyrano*, we took to chartering boats for our own use. In the Caribbean, with Dick Clurman and his wife Shirley, regularly at Christmastime; and, occasionally, in the spring. In the Aegean, with Van Galbraith and other friends, and family. It was the third time out in the Caribbean that we came on *Sealestial*. Six weeks earlier we had joined a couple in the Fiji Islands. I kept a journal.

Saturday [October 21, 1978]. But yesterday was Thursday, the international dateline having been traversed, and by the ache in our bones and spirits yesterday seemed a week ago, a thousand hours having been spent in the cramp of the economy section of a jumbo jet filled SRO. For my wife Pat and me the ordeal, if not, exactly speaking, intolerable (as a historical fact, we survived it), was only just short of that. We cannot imagine surviving what our companions went through. Barbara, Bindy, Vane, and Drue are the stuff that made possible the Battle of Britain. *They* had flown from London nonstop to Los Angeles where we, after spending a leisurely day there, met them at the International Airport. A mere one hour after they landed we were all off on the 747 to Hawaii, seated cheek by jowl. I longed for the arrival there on the assumption that the great plane would immediately empty, leaving us room to stretch out on the next leg. Surely not *everybody* flies on to Fiji, I thought smugly; to which the reply is: Nowadays practically everybody *does* fly on to Fiji, notwithstanding that Fiji is as far from Hawaii as London is from New York. Exactly as far south of the equator as Hawaii is north of it. If you leave the main island of Fiji (there are about 300 islands in the 250,000-square-mile island group) and head straight south, you will eventually hit Auckland. For those who care about these matters fastidiously, a nice way to remember where Fiji is is as follows: What meridian lies exactly opposite Greenwich, England? 180 degrees west longitude, obviously. What is one tenth of 180 degrees? Eighteen degrees. And indeed, that is the southern latitude that runs through Fiji, which gives you the coordinates. I thought it would be amusing to feed into my Hewlett-Packard 97 computer (about which more in due course) the question, "How far is it from Fiji to London?" and, "What course would one give to the navigator starting out?" I tapped the data into my little machine, only to have it—after struggling fitfully in a paroxysm of flashing, hiccupping figures—stop dead with the word, in red-light tracery, ERROR. I could not understand this, and so tried again, only to be accosted once again with ERROR. It struck me that this is a pretty abrupt way to talk back to a purchaser, in a competitive market, of a machine that costs $750—a machine, moreover, designed and sold by terribly polite people. I reflected on it, and then programmed the query again, but this time using 179 degrees west longitude instead of 180 degrees as the starting point, and the answer, after orderly gyrations, calmly popped out 8,789 miles at 001 degrees azimuth. The problem was that the machine had been asked to settle the question whether, in going from Fiji to London, you should head north or south, the distances being unequal. The machine, uninstructed in the matter, declines to assert itself.

Before trying out the 179 degrees alternative, I thought to consult with Vane—we were all seated about a table in the hot noon sun, by the swimming pool, ordering sandwiches and drinks, having slept for three or four air-conditioned hours in the luxury of the Regent Hotel at Nadi, where the planes fly in. I had had no experience of Vane (pronounced VAH-nee) at this point, other than our sleeping on each other's shoulders during the cattle run from Los Angeles, and clearly he thought to apprise me once and for all of a difficulty that has plagued him over the six decades of his hyperactive life.

Although a stout Croatian nationalist who deems himself a Yugoslav patriot first, last and always, and would gladly have hanged Tito on a sour apple tree to prove it, Vane is British to his fingertips, to the elocutionary demisemiquaver, having been schooled in the U.K. right through Oxford and lived there much of the time, with homes in Monte Carlo and Majorca. His manner —kind, courteous, witty, unobtrusively emphatic—goes naturally with his well-set aquiline features, his graying, disciplined hair. Vane is a man accustomed to coping authoritatively with every sort of difficulty, from double agents to Fiji waters; the problem is that his air of competence inspires everyone, on the slightest acquaintance, to take their problems to him. Why did a computer decline to give a civil answer? How does one insert a film into a recalcitrant camera chamber? Why did the outboard engine suddenly refuse to start? As a miserable matter of record, Vane explained to me, he is totally incompetent in all mechanical matters. He is quite certain—he is excited now, as he spins out his complaint while sipping his Punt e Mes—given the relative progress of the forces of evil over the forces of good, that before his exquisitely toned body (he jogs morning and night) finally collapses from natural decrepitude, he will be had up before some Bolshevik firing squad, the leader of which, looking quizzically at the newly issued rifles, will approach Vane while tied to the stake and say, "I wonder, sir, would you mind telling us just exactly how these weapons work?"

Ah, but in one discipline arguably mechanical Vane knows all. He is certainly the equal of the best scuba diver in the world, and unquestionably the finest teacher of the art/science. So I had been told by the organizer of this whole enterprise, Jack Heinz, common friend of everyone present, who had been detained one day by the death of a friend whose funeral took priority. I had prepared for this sailing-scuba diving expedition in the Fijis by spending one hour in a swimming pool in Puerto Rico with a fine instructor eloquent on the disadvantage of drowning while under water. I made a note not to irritate Vane with any further questions that presumed technical knowledge on his part. Indeed, probably I carried my attentiveness to sycophantic lengths when, after Bindy asked Vane to pass over a spoon, I pointed to one lest Vane, in his helplessness, not know to distinguish a spoon from a fork.

It occurred to me, after the hamburger and beer had slightly revived us, to look about and see what it is about Fiji that hits you right away. Answer: Nothing. The Regent Hotel could be a super-luxury hotel in any tropical area anywhere in the world. The air is about what you would expect for spring in the tropics. We would learn something extremely important, which is that although most of the books tell you that the rains and the clouds come to Fiji only after the first week or two in November, those books may be statistically correct but are by no means to be counted on. Nadi is at the west end of the big island (Viti Levu); Suva—which is the center of all boating activity, and where you start from when you head out to sea on a charter boat—is about 100 miles away, to the southeast. There it rains 40 inches per year. And most of that rain is during the three or four summer months, beginning in November. During the ten October days we were with the party, we had spotty sun for only two or three days. I read a lot about Fiji—to be sure, a lot of it in travel bureau prose. ("*Stretches of Uncrowded White-Sand Beaches . . . Palm Trees . . . Inviting Lagoons . . . The Fijian Format for Rediscovering Yourself . . . You are fifteen miles due west of Nadi International Airport. You have just moved onto an idyllic South Sea island with picture-postcard white-sand beaches and bending palm trees. You strip off your city clothes and dive into the sea . . . and here you are. Suspended in the silk-warm water . . . motionless.*") But nothing to suggest you might find yourself motionless because if you move without moving the umbrella along with you *pari passu*, you will be deep in silk-warm water even while standing at a street corner one mile from the beach.

But our spirits were very high. Later in the afternoon we would take the island-hopper (a Viscount turboprop, if memory serves) for the trip to Suva, put up at the Tradewinds Hotel overlooking the yacht basin, and set out to sea the next day, after Jack joined us. From our hotel rooms we had the first glimpse of the great

Tau sitting in her slip, awash with the usual swirl of children, electricians, plumbers, banana vendors, each in some way umbilically related to any large boat at the outset of a charter.

She is a great ketch, designed by her architect-owner Captain Philip, who also built the Tradewinds Hotel. The dimensions (90 feet overall; mainmast of 110 feet) are noble. But, even taking into account the drizzle's dampening effect on the spirits, one must be frank: The boat's topsides are painted in two shades of brown, what must have been the finalists in a worldwide contest to select the most emetic pigment imaginable. I do not know which was the winner, which the runner-up. And then aft, commencing at about amidships, a strange structure which we ended up referring to as "the spare garage." It was wonderfully useful for laying out all our scuba gear, and would have been indispensable for storing, say, five thousand cans of tuna fish. It was not useful for much more, having only church-pew benches in it, suitable for convoying prisoners to penal colonies. There were of course many other factors to be considered in judging *Tau*, but to these we were not to be introduced until the next day when, formally, the charter began, in a drizzle, with Jack—but without Jack's bags, which had been lost by Pan American, which had lost them undoubtedly because Pan Am was preoccupied with looking for the lost bags of Jack's wife Drue, which had been lost on our trip from Los Angeles. But we set out to the mouth of the harbor, and we were happy in the spirit of those who come together to begin an enterprise in the distinctive unity only a boat imposes.

Monday. Jack's bags arrived, along with a few delicacies carried aboard by a half-dozen porters, and we were ready to go. One should know, in sailing the Fiji Islands, that the distances between islands are not inconsiderable. More like the Antilles, say, than the Virgins or the Bahamas. The winds are as one would expect, ranging from northeast to southeast—I had consulted a weather chart in a think-session with Jack at which, during the summer, we made a major mistake.

I shall try to remember to tell my grandchildren that just as, in order to fall, one must first rise; so, in order to travel downwind, one must first travel upwind. We are now all agreed that it would have made sense to ask the skipper to deadhead *Tau* east—perhaps as far as Tonga (500 miles); certainly as far as Mbalavu (150 miles). Because what lay ahead was a lot of very uncomfortable sailing, concerning which a few generic remarks.

During the initial trip to the island of Ovalau, sailing on the wind, the *Tau* ripped its mainsail, depriving us of practically all lateral stability. No effort was made to mend it while under way, and it transpired that the captain, a man of great resourcefulness and, even at age seventy-two, resolution, had never heard of such American commonplaces as sail tape. We departed without spare battens and without adequate stitching paraphernalia; so that when, the following day and thereafter, we hoisted the mainsail, it was reefed, the tear having ripped the bottom one third of the sail. The broken battens were never replaced, so that the noise of the flapping leech was almost always with us during the windward passages.

Having chartered a dozen boats and chartered out my own schooner, I take leave to express a rule of thumb. Boats longer than about fifty feet are thought by owners or captains to be, in fact, motor sailers. The *Sealestial*, as we will see, is a noble excep-tion. Experience teaches us that ninety percent of the time the boat is moving, the engine will be on. Sometimes the engine is required merely to move: I have traveled on boats the profiles of which would appear to qualify them to race out of Cowes or Newport, but when the sails (usually with some reluctance by the captain) are hoisted, suddenly—nothing very much happens. A decade's accretion of big propellers, huge water and fuel tanks, and myriad heavy, comfortable junk have all but immobilized them as sailboats that will cruise at eight or ten knots. Typically, after your first attempt to sail, the captain waits patiently for ennui to set in among the charterers. In my case this happens quickly, and thereafter the sails are used primarily for the purpose of steadying the boat. In the case of the *Tau*, with its huge masts, one would have expected a moderately zippy performance under sail. We got nothing of the sort when on the wind. The genoa was cut like a bikini, and if we relied on canvas to get us anywhere, these words would have been written at the other end of the inter-national date line.

Probably the principal fault is the charterer's. He tends to ask for mutually exclusive amenities. He wants both spacious state-rooms *and* sportscar performance, sailwise. He wants scuba diving equipment for six people (our situation) and 12-meter performance under sail. The postwar designers have done a great deal to achieve livability in small (forty-foot) racing sailboats. But the difficulties increase geometrically, and those who charter a sailing boat of ninety feet expecting both to sail and to luxuriate are going to do one or the other—almost inevitably the latter, since that turns out to be the preference, given the alternatives, of those who charter huge sailing boats.

However, the captain or owner is not absolved from respon-sibility. He should frankly acknowledge the limitations of his ves-sel, if only to tamp down the revolution of rising expectations. Of course, there is no organic reason for failure to carry extra battens, or sail tape, or stitching gear.

An appropriate moment, as I think back on that first day's sail—in the drizzle, and against the seas to Levuka Harbor—to define a rule I have finally decocted, and wonder that it has not been formulated before:

The sea, if you leave aside for a moment the factor of vicissi-tudes, which obviously overrule even the most elaborate fine-tun-ing, is an invitation to tranquillity. I lay it down as an unchallenge-able, uncontradictable proposition that there is an irreconcilable incompatibility between very loud noise and tranquillity. One can, of course, get used to anything. In *My Sister Eileen*, where the play's two principals lived in a basement apartment next to the Third Avenue El in New York City which before it was torn down used to roar by every seven minutes with a noise the designers of the Concorde would have pronounced intolerable, the author-director managed a marvelous manipulation of the players and the audience by causing the actors, every seven minutes for about ten seconds, to raise their voices to screaming pitch, as though nothing unusual had happened. After a while the audience almost failed to notice the difference, much as one gets accus-tomed to the background noise on an old record, training the ear to hear only Caruso.

But on the other hand noise is noise, even as ugliness is ugliness. There are instruments that measure, with scientific exactitude, decibels of sound. Since this is the season for constitutional amendments, I propose one that would require every charter spec sheet to give out the decibel level, at engine cruising speed, 1) in each stateroom; 2) at the cockpit; 3) at the doghouse; 4) in the main saloon. The prospect of a five-hour run from one Fijian island to another under power in hostile sea conditions to a significant degree varies in the intensity of discomfort with the volume of engine noise. I know one or two people whose conversational patter has made me long for the relief of the robust noise of passing subways; but there were none such aboard the *Tau*, and when the engine operated, which was most of the time during the eastward passages, communication was virtually excluded in the principal areas of social congregation, and inflected conversation could only have taken place in the crow's nest. I found that most of my companions sought out narcotic relief, either in escapist literature, spirits, or sleep: not infrequently all three, a useful progressive curve. Why is it, on cruises, that one tends to nap in the afternoon? An odious bourgeois indulgence. We tell ourselves it is the wind and the salt and the exuberance of corporal health. *I* say it is probably nature's reaction to an unnatural licentiousness at lunch, a guard against the possibility of boredom during a long day; and —I say this with utter gravity—a means of attempting to solace oneself against a grinding, encephalophonic engine noise which, however we adjust to it in the manner of our sister Eileen, insinuates its insidious vibrations into our nervous system leaving us, at the end of a day's experience, with the ocean's equivalent of jet lag. A kind of noise jag.

Tuesday. A great day. Unforgettable. Where oh where have I been? Why did nobody tell me? (Everybody did, for years, but I did not listen.) The divers were convening for the first plunge. But to begin with, Vane would check me out—to see what I could handle after my hour in the swimming pool. I proudly displayed the gear I had bought on leaving New York. To wit: 1) a knife; 2) a snorkel tube; 3) a face mask; 4) an inflatable life vest; 5) flippers; 6) boots for the flippers; 7) an underwater watch; 8) gloves; 9) defogging liquid; and 10) an illustrated textbook called *Safe Scuba*. Vane cast an eye on it all and told me he thought the flippers exaggeratedly big, made to go with the boots, which were unnecessary; he would lend me some appropriate flippers. The vest was okay, though he didn't believe in them. The face mask leaked and the purge mechanism, through which one blows out water that gets into the mask, didn't function. The gloves were adjudged too coarse for flexibility. I didn't need the watch, but I did need a depthometer, which Vane provided, and a spear gun, ditto. My knife was fine, and it turned out that the book, when Bindy finally opened it one evening, was good for hours of entertainment.

Vane took me down, in stages, to seventeen feet, after first lecturing me sternly on the point that there is no such thing as a macho diver; there are only bright and stupid divers, the latter defined as those who continue to go deeper even after feeling pain in their ears. You "clear" your ears (there are technical ways of saying all this) by applying pressure, over the rubber of the mask, to close your nostrils and then attempting to blow through your nose. Either you do, or you do not, experience instant relief. If you do, proceed on down. After another ten or fifteen feet, the pain will resume. Clear away. And proceed. *Don't Go Down Farther Than 120 Feet.* Because below that depth odd things happen to the nitrogen content in your blood, to dissipate which your rise to the surface has to be achieved more gradually than your tank's capacity makes possible. When you do rise, do so gradually. It is a good idea, while ascending, to breathe out. When there is no breath left, pause, inhale, and then resume the ascent while exhaling. At the surface a dinghy that has been carefully following you by tracing the wake of your bubbles will be waiting. Its pilot will lift the tank off your back, collect the other paraphernalia and—perhaps a little chilly, but certainly greatly exhilarated—you will reboard the master vessel, maybe with a fish or two in Vane's pouch.

Except that my mask leaked a bit, I found it as easy to habituate myself to underwater life as I would to get used to a freshly discovered Mozart symphony. The pleasure of the weightlessness . . . of three-dimensional movement . . . the disappearance of gravity . . . the lights in greater, more playful variety than ever seen before . . . the underwater life which, observed behind the glass of aquariums, seems menacing and slimy, now suddenly friendly, frisky, endearing (though Vane pointed at a crevice in a shoal, shaking his fingers and forming an M with the two thumbs and index fingers—all of which was later explained to me as the means of warning against a moray eel he had spotted). We descended to 120 feet, and I never felt more carefree, even while observing, more frequently than my experienced companions, the gauge that indicated how many of the precious thirty minutes of air were left to me.

The Fiji Islands are famous for the opportunities they give you to dive. I wish I could successfully transcribe the formulae by which Vane led us, day after day, to the wonder spots, but one could as easily explicate the dowser's art. He did require, I remember, that the water be deep, preferably over 100 feet. The tide should recently have come up against the reef structure, which is something like an underwater Gothic cathedral. That is where the fish collect, individually and in little and great schools: It was nothing to see ten thousand fish of one hundred distinct species and sizes during a single dive. The whole thing has only one disconcerting impediment, that it is impossible to smile. If you smile, alas, you drown; so that nothing is permitted to be wrenchingly funny, or wry. But the impulse to smile, as one would at a spectacular sunset, or burst of wildlife, or during an aria splendidly executed, requires concentration to overcome, particularly when there are comic encounters, as when your rump backs into something and you wheel about convinced you have backed into a shark. Nothing is less sharklike than Bindy (Viscountess Lambton), whose rump it was, though probably she is bigger than any shark, like Kirsten Flagstad. She is the original earth mother, with a whimsical rolling laugh that chokes off the words that are constantly amusing her and, through her, you. On Sunday she accompanied me to Mass at Suva because, she said, although not a Catholic she thought it would be good to pray for the new pope designated as such the previous day. I told her that was a very nice thing to do, that I had to confess the unlikelihood that I would go to Mass specially to pray for the new Archbishop of Canterbury, and she said I most certainly should, since the poor man has few enough people praying for him these sad, schismatic days.

The beautiful Bindy requires the coordination of two men to hoist her on board the dinghy, but whole armies would disengage for the pleasure of serving Bindy, who only yesterday could have posed for the most convincing statue of Brünnehilde ever struck.

She saw that I was cold and, after the first day, gave me her spare wet suit, greatly increasing my comfort. And, as soon as we got back on board, she would make up for all the laughter we missed during the two half-hour dives Vane permitted us every day (more than one hour out of twenty-four in the deep does something, once again, to the nitrogen content of your blood, which needs rebuilding). It was Bindy who said to me innocently, a book on her lap during the cocktail hour, "What is an irresponsible flake?"

"A *what*, Bindy?"

"An *'irresponsible flake.'* That's what it says here." She showed me page 146 of *Safe Scuba*, under the heading "Selecting a Buddy."

I was introduced to what is the most hilariously periphrastic English in print. The co-authors must, between them, have attended at least five teachers' colleges to achieve their prose style. "Most often, we have little choice with regard to the selection of a buddy," you read on, "in many cases we may be married to our buddy, or involved in a similar relationship to marriage, or we may be assigned a buddy by a divemaster on a boat, if possible, regardless of how our buddies are selected it is an extremely good idea to know the person with whom you are going to dive. You should know your buddy's character patterns and diving skills. If your buddy is an irresponsible flake on the surface, the chances are excellent that the same idiotic behavior patterns will continue underwater."

I told Bindy that honest injun, most people in America don't talk that way, and took the book from her. There are acres and acres of the same kind of thing. The authors' intention, clearly, is to persuade anyone who wants to scuba dive that he (or as *they* would put it: "he or she, as the case may be") should spend dozens of hours and thousands of dollars in instructions. My very favorite passage deals with the rather simple question: Can you swim? ". . . failure of a swimming test may not demonstrate the student to be in poor physical condition, but only that the student lacks effective swimming skills. The swimming does not necessarily demonstrate that the diver will function well in the sub-aquatic environment. Mental conditioning, cognitive and affective, and proper habit patterns may be far more relevant to learning diving skills and surviving in the open water than physical condi-

Returned from a half hour's dive, at right Vane Ivanovic. Note spareness of frame and of gear. Jack Heinz, note latter. Bindy Lambton, note none of the above (but see text). Bindy is not a flaky buddy.

tioning as the prime criteria in dive student selection." All that and one mashed potato will get you two mashed potatoes. But I had already resolved never ever to do anything, in the sub-aquatic environment *or* in the super-aquatic environment, to permit Bindy to think of me as an irresponsible flake.

Wednesday. The captain and crew got up early and powered the *Tau* northeast sixty miles to the island of Taveuni, which is the third largest island in Fiji, and said by some to harbor the most spectacular diving and snorkeling reef in the whole area. It is the Somosomo Strait, and of course Vane led us unerringly to a spot that could not have been more enchanting. In the late morning we dinghied out on the *Tau*'s Zodiac, into which the sea-skittish Drue was coaxed on the solemn promise, reiterated by all hands, that Zodiacs have the distinctive feature of being *absolutely unsinkable*, a proposition Drue finally came to believe until, a few days later, the Zodiac sank in front of her eyes. disappearing into the vasty deep without so much as a gurgle of resistance, leaving Captain Philip in great distress.

We went ashore in part to ogle at Fijian life, little of which we had observed. We found it to be exactly as described by *National Geographic*—men and women of all shapes and colors, pleasant, a little lethargic, that admixture of Polynesian, Micronesian, Melanesian and, finally, Indian (the Indians immigrated halfway through the nineteenth century as indentured laborers, the tending of agriculture being unappealing to the native population). They are now a peaceable race of people, and it requires an exercise of the imagination to recall that on his famous voyage from the *Bounty* to Timor in 1789 (3,600 miles in an open longboat) Captain Bligh did not dare to pause in these islands, so notoriously were the natives given to killing, and then eating, uninvited guests. The natives are cheerful, apparently unexcitable, notwithstanding the sweat they work up in their nightclub acts when imitating the frenzied manners of their forefathers. They have been self-governing since 1970, after ninety-six years of colonial rule by the British who had the uncommon good sense to leave 82 percent of the land in native hands. I am not qualified to say whether the 600,000 Fijians are competently governed, but whatever evidence there is of commercial sloth, justice is certainly swift. On Tuesday we read in the local paper that three men had been convicted the day before of raping a young woman of eighteen, receiving sentences of from two to four years of hard labor. The rape had occurred the preceding Saturday. Earl Warren never sojourned in Fiji.

Through the town of Waiyevo, on the western shore of the island, the 180th meridian runs, and the spot on the roadside where this happens is of course properly designated, with wooden signs tapering in opposite directions, one of them marked "Today," the other, "Yesterday." We did a great deal of picture taking, in

At Waiyevo, WFB and wife Patricia, though within two feet of each other, are separated by a calendar day and are standing on different hemispheres.

every conceivable pose, one foot firmly planted on Tuesday, the second on Wednesday—that sort of thing.

It reminded me of an experience a half-dozen years earlier at the exact geographical south pole when an escorting colonel, in the fifty-degree-below-zero cold, asked whether I would like to have my picture taken while standing on my head, making possible a postcard depicting me as carrying the world on my shoulders. That being a characteristic personal burden, I readily assented and was lifted by my boots by an aide. At exactly which moment my brother Jim, then the junior senator from the State of New York, in a fit of chauvinism fired off a firecracker which was programmed to waft to earth in the form of the New York State flag, which he would photograph and send out to his constituents. Unhappily the firecracker went instead directly to my nose, so that there exists only a picture of me standing on my head, being bloodied by the flag of New York State.

No such infelicity marred our picture taking this time around, though I was later advised by an obstinately literal historian of the area that the official boundary marking the international date line was, in answer to a local provocation, made to jag eastward, then south, then west, and back to the 180-degree mark so that the whole of Fiji might repose, unconfused, in the eastern hemisphere. All that bureaucratic geographical commotion was in retaliation against an ingenious Indian vendor whose shop straddled the date line and who got around the sabbath laws by selling from the eastern end of his shop on the western Sunday, and from the western end of the shop on the eastern Sunday. That is the kind of problem the UN was born to solve.

We returned to the *Tau* undecided whether to stop by at the neighboring islands of Nggamea and Lauthala, which are owned respectively by the American tycoon Malcolm Forbes and the Canadian-born actor Raymond Burr. Everyone knows Malcolm Forbes, whose hospitality is in any case widely advertised. The closest tie any of us had to Raymond Burr is that I had patronized his hotel in the Azores during a transatlantic crossing in 1975. I pronounced this an attenuated relationship, whereupon we all decided that in any event we really did not want to visit anybody at all, so we read, and had our wines, and chatted, and listened to beautiful music from the cassette deck I had so thoughtfully provided, and went to bed in high excitement, because the very next day we would visit the fabled Wallangilala.

Thursday. Wallangilala even Captain Philip had never visited. It is a perfect coral crescent. More accurately, a mile-wide coral necklace, with three beads missing at the top, through which you enter. The inside is ringed with white sand, with palm trees on the eastern end. It has a voluptuarian appeal for anyone who cares at

The Tau: *Sailing in the Fijis. The 110-foot masts are of equal size. The length overall, 90 feet.*

all about, or for, the sea. Its stark loneliness in the South Pacific is itself striking. The perfect protection it gives from wind or, rather, from the seas—the height of the coral is insufficient to block the wind—might have been specified by a civil defense engineer. The water is every shade of Bahamian blue; the diving and snorkeling could consume days. There was only a single other vessel there, a 45-foot ketch owned by an oil rigger who works six months of the year in the North Sea, accumulating enough money to sustain him the other six months of the year in Fiji, where he cruises with his wife and child, endlessly, from island to island, disdaining, except in extreme circumstances, the use of his engine, thus doing little to consume the mineral he is paid so handsomely to make available to others. At dinner that night we resolve that now that we have reached the easternmost part of our itinerary, we shall insist on using only the sails as we proceed south to the Lau group of islands. We retired with that vinous determination, which tends to silt away overnight, to be firm with the captain, but we dove before breakfast and this meant, by Jack's hallowed tradition, a glass of red wine with breakfast (Vane does not permit us to eat before diving). And so, refortified in our resolve, we stipulate that *only* the sails will be used for our passage south to Mbalavu—from which Pat and I shall have to leave the party, to meet engagements in Australia more closely related in purpose to taking oil out of the North Sea than to cruising in Fiji.

Saturday. It was a fine sail, and I suggested to the first mate that we board the Zodiac and take photographs of the *Tau* under sail. The first part of the operation was accomplished, but at full power in the Zodiac in a choppy sea we found we could not keep up with the *Tau*, so bracing was the wind that morning and so lively the *Tau*'s performance, unleashed on a broad reach, even with the mainsail reefed. It was an awful exercise in frustration, attempting to communicate to the people on the boat that they must slow down in order that we might photograph them. All boats should have walkie-talkies, perfect for contact between dinghy and the mother vessel. Pat has mastered the exploitation of these,

The overweight counter at Mbalavu Airport, Fijis.

and reaches me at remote grocery stores in native villages with such importunities as *"Don't forget the guava jelly,* OVER!" The photograph reproduced in these pages is the forlorn result of attempting, on a cloudy day, to capture the *Tau,* headed adamantly across the same sound Captain Bligh passed through on his determined, legendary voyage. That night, another fine dive having been consummated, a sadness overtook the departing members, and the thought of going anywhere without Vane to guide me and Bindy to console me, and of leaving Jack and Drue, was a cruel capitulation to the world of getting and spending. The lot of them boarded an ancient open bus to see us off at what is called the airport. Our fourteen pieces of luggage were segregated and weighed outside a thatched hut where lukewarm orange soda was available. The terminal's scales were brought out. The device was what you get from Sears, Roebuck for the guest bathroom, and one by one the bags were weighed (and a careful calculation made of the overweight) and lugged into the belly of one of those airplanes Clark Gable used to fly over the Hump; and we headed downwind, because into the wind would have required taking off uphill, and we were, miraculously, airborne. Suddenly it was sunny, and all the blue, and the coral reefs that have decimated the merchant marines of the world, spread out ahead, carpeting us the 150 miles to Suva, where the maw of convention was waiting, impatient to swallow us up.

3

Six weeks after Fiji came Christmas-cruise time. Dick Clurman advised me, over the phone, in clipped accents, that he and Shirley would meet us at JFK rather than attempt the trip to the airport in a single motor vehicle with twenty-six pieces of luggage. This detail is not entirely extraneous to ocean sailing. The summer before, I had sailed the Aegean and one of the company, whom I had known since college though he is a few years my junior, arrived with a single moderate-sized duffel bag plus a wafer-slim briefcase good for one issue of the Paris *Tribune* and maybe three paperbacks. Every day of the week he was with us he turned up in serviceable but modish costume, and at night there would be a fresh shirt and colored pants or white ducks. Dick (Coulson) had sailed competitively since he was a boy, and twice he raced the Atlantic aboard a boat whose skipper is notoriously demanding. His disposition is quiet, he is organically unexcitable, and when he goes cruising he sees no need for chestloads of gear. If he finishes the books he brings, there are always others on board. If his laundry gets scarce, he washes it and it is dry the next morning. He has his

FOLLOWING PAGES:

_____

The cruising ketch Sealestial.

own foul-weather gear and one extra pair of Topsiders, and doesn't go to sea other than to go to sea.

Clurman and I are gadget-minded. He, for instance, even brings along his own voltmeter. He has, usually, three radios, and the paraphernalia that go with them. Then there is the fishing equipment. If he could catch a single fish per snare or hook he brings aboard, he would empty the Caribbean of underwater life. And now that we are onto scuba diving, there is that inventory. He reads at the rate of a book a day (I saw him begin Herman Wouk's *Winds of War* one morning and finish it at noon the next day). And mind you he does not do all of this in Carthusian circumstances. He talks at least three times as much as the rest of the crew combined, though he is always available to undertake any chore; he receives, transcribes and analyzes the news for us, explores the lives and problems of the crew, expresses his preferences on a) where we should sail to, b) when we should eat, and c) what we should eat. Then of course there are the magazines to catch up on—about forty, and they range from *Playboy* to *American Scholar*. He is perhaps happiest on the radiotelephone, calling his endless list of friends, discharging his responsibilities as a counselor to them all. No doubt he came to the habit of being constantly in touch with all points of the globe during his long tenure as chief of correspondents for Time Inc. The world is dotted with former employees, associates, and acquaintances whom Dick has helped. On one of our trips he had with him David Halberstam's new manuscript. The next trip out he brought along a copy of the published book for me to read. It was inscribed "Dick: I wanted you to have the earliest copy of your book which I took the liberty of writing."

I go in for navigational gear. Nowadays I regularly bring aboard the tables, the almanac, my own set of dividers and parallel rules, paper clips and rubber bands, plotting sheets, notebooks and logbooks, three computers, and two, sometimes three, sextants, plus books and unrequited correspondence. I leave the packing of my clothes to my wife, and she regularly sends me off with three sets of foul-weather gear and approximately four times as many shirts, pants, undershorts, sports shirts, sweaters, blazers, and shoes as I will need. Then, of course, I must have my peanut butter and my Swiss cyclamate. My happiest superstition is that if I take saccharine in my coffee, I can have hot-fudge sundaes for dessert.

(*WFB and Danny*) *After the fear of man overboard, fire, or dismasting, there is the fear of running out of peanut butter.*

WFB at the navigator's table.

Some women associate cruising with fashion, and aboard at night, for them, every day is Easter Sunday. On one jaunt, in May a year before the crossing, we had on board Jeff Hammond, the yachting editor, whose dress was generally ascetic, his interest being in photographs (add one aluminum bag for photographic equipment). But also we had Aileen Mehle, best known to a vast public as "Suzy," the name under which she reports, in her distinctive style, the affairs of society. I had that spring written a novel and was depressed, on going over it, that my women were inevitably dressed in "a white pleated skirt," or in "a blue cotton shirt," or in "a long, strapless red velvet gown." To my dismay I discovered that my vocabulary, in describing clothes, is positively primitive. Since Aileen is required by her profession to describe in detail the dress of the ladies she mingles with night after night, I thought I would take some instruction. I required her to describe what Pat and Shirley and she wore every night, and sought ambitiously to expand my sartorial vocabulary.

At the end of the eight-day sail I resolved to impose on myself a written examination. I set out to write a newspaper column after the fashion of the famous syndicated "Suzy" in order to exhibit my newfound knowledge. So at cocktail time I typed out and handed around a piece which the beautiful and amusing Aileen has never seen fit to publish as a guest column. Accordingly, I immodestly present it here:

SUZY says . . .

St. Martin. You know the famous line about the greatest concentration of brains that ever sat in the White House since Jefferson ate there alone? That was the charming toast by Jackie O's First, when he gave that unforgettable dinner for all the Nobel Prize winners. Well, I thought of that the other day. Where have the beautiful people gone, in the great May diaspora? The heaviest concentration of them is on a boat. A big boat? No, dear, a little eensy-weensy boat, which is what makes it all so, well you know—unique?

It's a dear little boat, though. It would have to be, to attract the people on it. You're getting impatient? Wait, just wait. It's worth waiting for. The boat is the kind of thing you put in little Johnny's bathtub and blow, and he giggles and giggles. Anyway, take that boat and magnify it twenty or thirty

times, and what you have is—the yacht *Sea-lestial.* Clever?
There's no stopping American ingenuity, and I hope some Russians are listening (I know there are. Don't ask me how I found
out. Do you think they would send me to jail? I know my
friends would let me pick out the jail, and Françoise de la Renta
said she and Mica Ertegun would stop everything and decorate
it for me. I think it would be fun to have pictures of all the famous killers, don't you? Caligula, Genghis Khan, Jack the
Ripper, Three Mile Island . . .).

You thought I had forgotten about *Sealestial?* I'm just increasing the suspense. All aboard one boat. It has, for the nautical buffs out there who are interested in particulars, two sails
and an engine, and the most *divine* steering wheel, with four
sterling silver spokes, positively fit for framing.

Who do you suppose is on board this unobtrusive, inconspicuous, anonymous little sailboat? To begin with, *Aileen
Mehle.* I know, I know, all you Mehle-experts will write to me
(sorry, darlings, I just can't answer my mail; not even presidents get acknowledgments) that Aileen—known to a few
dozen million people, plus the few hundred who really count, as
"Suzy"—doesn't travel on eensy-weensy sailboats. What you
don't know is that Aileen comes from pioneer stock. Her great-grandfather discovered El Paso. His great-grandfather discovered Mexico City (she speaks Spanish like a native: Aileen, *¿Tu
sabes cómo te quiero?*—that's a private message, and you
naughty voyeurs—wonderful word, but be sure, darlings, to
pronounce it correctly—it's *vwa*-yers—are invited to glide right
by that little—shall I throw you off the track by calling it a
graffito?). And *his* great-grandfather discovered the Inquisition. *His* great-grandfather (no slouch) converted the Khazar
Jews; *his* great-grandfather—but you have the idea, anyway; so
are you surprised now that Aileen Mehle was spending a week
in an eensy-weensy boat with sails?

Every night she would appear at dinner in something—special.
Even the blasé guests on board (just wait, just wait) couldn't
suppress that little gasp of true astonishment. I can't begin to
give you an inventory. But let me tell you about last night,
when the *Sealestial* was moored at a remote little harbor in St.
Kitts, known for the savagery of its native population, surrounded by a stretch of brown-white sand, well over a hundred

yards from David Rockefeller's little beach house. Well, she wore tulle dungarees, with a voile blouse, positively streaming with scarlet ribands that rustled with the wind in the cockpit, over dyed Chinese characters that everybody on board spent hours trying to decipher, everybody agreeing that the key to the Chinese puzzle (Aileen just smiled and smiled when asked directly what it was) lay somewhere south of her nose (I'm using navigational language, darlings, but so would you if you had been where I have been this last week), north of her feet, southwest of her chin, and northwest of her navel. She looked ravishing with her swishy blond hair held down by a babushka, but complaining (it was her only complaint, all week long) that her hair wouldn't stand up under the typhoon for more than one hour. (The captain didn't think it was a typhoon, he thought it was a *hurricane*, but then he doesn't come from adventurist stock. All *his* great-grandfather discovered was his great-grandmother.)

Now: What would bring Aileen out to such a boat, in the remote Caribbean? Well, for one thing, Jeff Hammond. Jeff, although he wears one of those beards, is a real softie. But that isn't how they think of him at the Hearst Situation Room, where they track him as one of the jogging juggernauts (I like that, and I hope *you* do, my darlings; because *I* like *you*, as *you know*) who are headed for the big time. Jeff is the editor-in-chief of *Motor Boating & Sailing*, and it was *he* who told me that the *Sealestial* was a boat! You can't put anything over on Jeff, he's too smart, so don't try. He wore khaki shorts and a T-shirt with *Charisma* written over the vest pocket. But he didn't have to do that, because we *all* know that Jeff was *born* with charisma!

Next? Would you believe, Dick and Shirley Clurman? They decided—they are so wonderfully sentimental—to celebrate the third week following the 22nd anniversary of their marriage, and *they* were the people who put together this whole marvelous experience. Dick was chief of foreign correspondents for Time-Life. But, as we all know, he was just warming up. He's been all kinds of things since, and if you wake up one day and find out he's President of the *United States*—just don't forget, you had a vaticinator (????—see below, and you won't be surprised) aboard the *Sealestial*. And Shirley—her best friends call her Shirleykins, and she roars with laughter every time—is as smart as her husband, and as accomplished. Beautiful Shirley was dressed last night in tapered white suede pants with a mauve shirt with pouch pockets studded with mother-of-pearl. Why? Because—*only Shirley Clurman would think of this!* Today was Mother's Day. No wonder she has served as adviser to the high and mighty. If Dick goes All The Way, Shirley will be the very best FL since JO, though of course we've had some darlings in between, haven't we, darlings?

Then to cap it off, Pat and Bill Buckley. Pat is as much at home on the water as she is on her beautiful estate in Connecticut, and apartment in New York. She is famous as one of the best cooks in the world—but, darlings, you should see her shinny up the mast to turn the boat around, or whatever it is they do up there. You're sitting there, talking to her about *The World According to Garp*—a trashy little novel we all decided to read, just to keep in touch with the people we all love—and suddenly she's gone—right to the top of the mast. You will ask, what is she wearing? You are right to ask: The last time she went up, she was wearing a hoopskirt (only Pat, who has an incomparable sense of humor, would do that, you know) of green chiffon, laced with a gold trim that would have knocked out the Incas themselves—but Pat Buckley didn't even seem to notice, though she wasn't in a position to talk about it, what with that nasty old big black wrench in her mouth.

And dear Bill. Yes, you guessed, *he* was the one who came in with "vaticinator," which is someone who predicts who will be President: the roots of the word are Persian, like the Shah. Well, Bill was busy with Jeff, all day long, doing celestial navigation. I'm telling you, Bill can do *anything*. Yesterday, while we were at St. Bart's harbor, he proved to us—I mean, he is so *persuasive*, you wouldn't begin to *dare* to disagree with him—that we were really in Antigua. As he put it, a computer *cannot* lie. Dick Clurman, who is so clever, said something about, What do you do when liars program a computer? But Big Bill disdained that comment, because, you know, he rises above everything. Well, tra-là. We'll be back soon, and if you feel New York is jumping again, you'll know that *Sealestial*'s loss was the Big Apple's gain!

For *l'homme moyen sensuel*, there is a sensible inventory (for a transatlantic sail), and in response to requests from the uninitiated I asked Danny Merritt to list what he intended to take, and I sent out notice of it in a memo to the crew:

Danny has made a list of the articles he plans to bring on board. I duplicate it, in that it might be useful to you. You may ignore the item that reads, 'radio-time tic.' You need not each bring a radio-time tic. A radio-time tic is an arcane device which Danny, Reggie, and I are aware of, and we feel no necessity to share our knowledge.

Dan's suggestions of individual equipment for a transatlantic trip:

SHOES
2 Topsider-type shoes
1 Topsider boots
10 white socks
2 dark socks

PANTS AND SHIRTS
12 shorts
2 pr Levi's/2 pr shorts
1 corduroy
1 dress pants
12 LaCoste shirts
2 dress shirts
1 flannel shirt

MISCELLANEOUS
1 heavy sweater
1 light sweater
1 hat with brim
2 pr sunglasses
sun lotion
foul-weather gear
rigger's knife
flashlight
safety belt with strobe with horn
1 sports jacket
2 belts
sewing kit

extra laces (shoe)

complete dock kit incl: toothpaste/toothbrush, soap, deodorant, hair rinse, shampoo, razors, lotion, comb/brush

camera/film

radio-time tic

spare reading glasses

duffel bags required—large plastic garbage bags for dirty laundry

address book

Arriving in Antigua ten days before Christmas, we were introduced to *Sealestial*. Notwithstanding my misgivings about large charter vessels and their capacity to sail, as voiced in my journal from Fiji, I had a feeling, on approaching her in the crowded dock at English Harbor, that this was a boat designed to sail. And, indeed, we discovered that the beautiful white ketch had been designed as that—a racing boat, built in 1973 at the South Ocean Shipyard in England, designed by E. G. Van de Stadt. The prototype was *Stormvogel*, against which we had once raced to Bermuda aboard *Suzy Wong*. *Sealestial*, its mast cut down by eight feet, was now a cruising–charter version of *Stormvogel*, 41 net tons, 47 gross, with 71 feet of length overall, 18.6 feet of beam, drawing 8.5 feet (disqualifying it for Bahamian waters, significant areas of which accommodate a maximum of 5.5 feet—*Cyrano*'s draw).

A boat is easier to visualize than to describe, and accordingly herewith a few shots of *Sealestial*, including its huge saloon and the owner's splendid cabin.

The owner of *Sealestial* is a Yugoslav-American physician who practices in Detroit, Dr. Papo, with whom I will deal later. The dominant figure in *Sealestial* was its captain, Allen Jouning.

We stowed rapidly, eager to test the boat. I took the helm, with no objection from Captain Jouning, eased the vessel back, and headed out for a short afternoon sail to the northwest, anchoring off a small, secluded beach. I felt an instant bounciness to the vessel, which responded joyfully to wheel and wind. I could see that she pointed (came up close to the wind) well, without losing speed. She had on a less than full-cut genoa, but we did 8.5 knots in moderate airs, and that's not only good but very nearly unheard of in heavy, large, charter sailboats. We were all very happy, and vaguely resolved that *Sealestial* would figure in our future.

Provided it is always safest to add, that Allen Jouning was aboard. I noticed first that he was quiet, emitting as few instructions to the paid crew as necessary, in comfortable contrast to the raucous types who make a drill out of every maneuver. I noticed next that he raised no objection not only to my acting as master of the vessel, but even to my maneuvering the boat into and out of

tight corners. He knew, of course, that I had sailed. But it is nevertheless the practice of most captains gently to edge themselves back to the wheel at just those critical moments when you wish to exercise your own skills. On most charter boats you are made to feel like the new copilot who is welcome to take the wheel after cruising altitude is reached, always on the understanding that he will give it back to the old pro for landing and takeoffs. Elsewhere I have commented that since age thirteen I have owned the boats I have sailed with fewer than a half-dozen exceptions. I find it easy to play a purely passive role on a boat, and easy to act as the boat's master; anything in between, I fidget.

Allen Jouning sensed this, as he seemed, with uncanny intuition, to sense other human idiosyncrasies, all of which he handled with humor, thoughtfulness, and dignity. He had been in command of *Sealestial* since November 1978. He was born in Auckland in 1946, and was schooled there. In 1969, having sailed eight years, he went to Fiji and did charter work for two years. From there he delivered a boat to Los Angeles in a harrowing forty-two-day passage, nonstop, beating all the way, running out of everything save the barest supplies.

He was determined to race, and found himself as first mate in the Onion Patch series aboard Bermuda's *Peanut Brittle*, and then on an Erickson 46, *Alita*, on which he did the Annapolis–Bermuda race. Just before coming to *Sealestial* he was master of *Venceremos*, a Swan 65—a "gold-plater," as they denominate boats on which no expense is spared, that they may bring home the silver. Captain Jouning wears a red walrus mustache, is balding, and his humor comes in brief, nonabrasive flashes. In the four passages I have had with him, I have heard him complain only once—about the defective workmanship of Detroit sailmakers who failed to secure with strong enough material the genoa clew,

FOLLOWING PAGES:

A fish-eye view of the main saloon. At 6 (o'clock), the passageway to two extra staterooms and crew's quarters. At 7, Tony, books, cassettes, radios. At 10, navigator's desk, occupied by Reg, who is facing instrument panels. At 12, companionway to main cockpit. At 3, WFB opposite a coffee table that lifts and unfolds for duty as dining table.

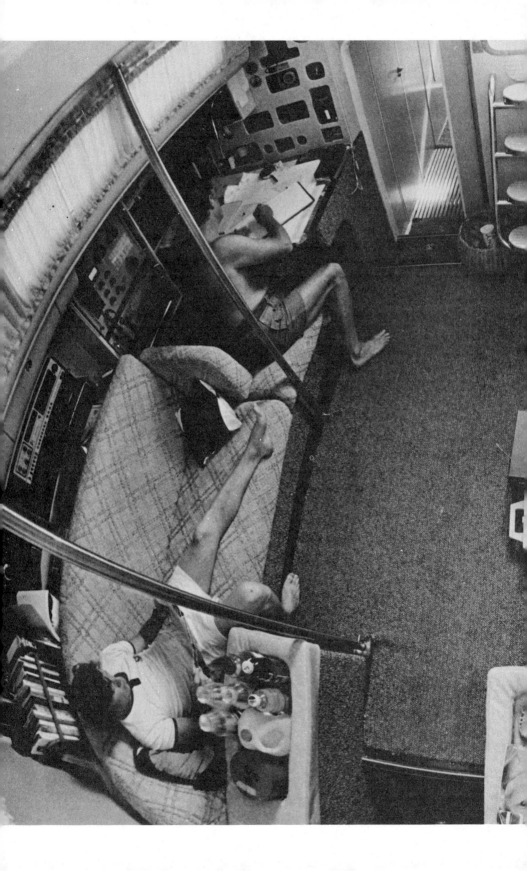

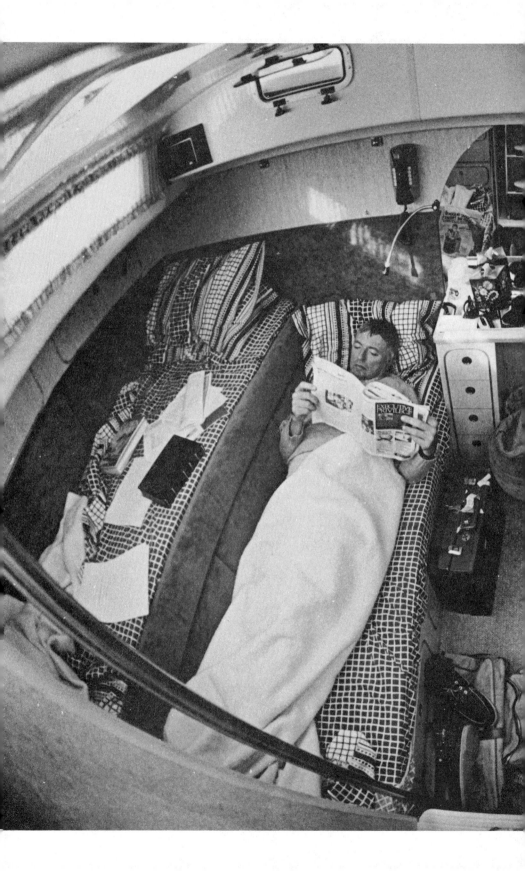

The disorder is man-made. There are compartments in the owner's cabin sufficient to stock wardrobe and books for a journey around the world. The vertical bar has structural responsibilities but is also useful for keeping one's balance when sitting in the great owner's chair (here occupied by Van) when the wind is starboard. The passageway leads past the owner's bathroom to the main saloon.

resulting in one of those noisily (and dangerous) chaotic sequences at night in uproarious seas when suddenly the sail lets go, the entire vessel vibrates with the whipping canvas, and one man starts letting down the fugitive sail halyard while two other men try, without being knocked out by the flying steel clew, to get hold of the sail and drag it down. "That's bad work," Allen said, examining the sail with a flashlight at the post-mortem. Such words, from that mouth, have the sound of fire and brimstone.

It was on our second outing on the *Sealestial* that we learned that in the summer of the following year, 1980, the owner desired to have the boat in the Mediterranean, for his own use and to pick up Mediterranean charters. I looked up suddenly at Dick—we were seated in the cockpit, during the cocktail hour. Allen was standing, leaning against the doghouse. I moved my head up, down, in a slow-motion gesture. Dick understood instantly. I put my index finger to my lips (meaning don't say anything to the ladies; my wife is always certain that any ocean trip by me will be my last, and is mildly resentful when her apocalyptic predictions don't eventuate). That night, taking a nightcap at the beach bar on Bitter End in the Virgins, Dick and I plotted. . . . The doc wants the boat in the Mediterranean—so, somebody has to get it there, right? . . . A nice route, one that would accommodate to prevailing winds, would be to head . . . north from St. Thomas (that is where the *Sealestial* would end its chartering season, Allen had said) to Bermuda; then across to the Azores, and then—Gibraltar—Marbella. We could arrange to fly in the wives for a joyous week's cruise in the Azores, breaking up the passage.

The day after returning to New York I called Dr. Papo.

The negotiations lasted over a period of several months. And then:

November 7, 1979:
Memo To: Dick Clurman, Van Galbraith, Tony Leggett, Chris Little, Danny Merritt, Reggie Stoops
From: WFB
The purpose of this note is primarily to say that I will be writing at much greater length in the very near future. Our splendid venture is definitely, unmistakably on—departure date is May 30 (by coincidence five years to the day after the beginning of the BO*). We will definitely get a book out of it, with Christopher Little's photography and probably a documentary. This last depends on a number of factors including financing, the answers to which I should have the next time I address you. In due course we'll organize a couple of those areas of responsibility that worked so well on the BO—e.g., an assignment to individuals of primary responsibility for our safety schedules, provisioning, that kind of thing. Reggie may have in his files some of the work we did in connection with the BO. Whether Reggie can find that which is in his files is of course another question, concerning which I shall be diplomatic. . . . I shall, after discussing a number of matters with the captain in December and looking at the weather charts, make estimates as accurately as possible of when we can expect landfalls along the way so as to make it possible to coordinate our other arrangements—e.g., the Azores leg. So, as I say the primary purpose of this memorandum is to advise you that the captain is alive, well, exacting, and solicitous.

The arrangements with Dr. Papo were, on the larger matters, entirely amicable. We approached a little snag or two over minor questions which we both had the good sense eventually to circumnavigate. On the matter of who would be in charge of the vessel, I devised a formula satisfactory to Dr. Papo which in due course we reduced to writing. I would be in charge of *Sealestial* during the passage, save that in any circumstance in which it could reason-

* *We had informally designated our transatlantic crossing in 1975 as the "BO"— i.e., the Big One.*

ably be held that the safety of the vessel was hostage, and Captain Jouning disagreed with WFB, Captain Jouning's word would prevail. (After all, it was Dr. Papo's boat.) A hypothetical situation would be a bad storm in which I elected to heave to, but the captain believed the wind so strong as to require running. Or a less melodramatic occasion: I might reason that I could wend my way between two shoals approaching, say, Bermuda; Jouning, if he disagreed, would have the authority to dictate the roundabout course. The contingency never in fact arose.

I was greatly amused when, forty-eight hours before our departure, I had an agitated telephone call from Dr. Papo informing me that his insurance broker had revealed that the understanding we had arrived at could have the effect of annulling *Sealestial*'s insurance policy, which was written around the presumptive mastership of Captain Jouning. There was no time to apply for a binder transferring authority to me. Dr. Papo suggested a solution, which was altogether agreeable. We would sign a fresh contract in which I remitted authority entirely to Captain Jouning. A single copy of this document would be typed out. No one but Dr. Papo and I would be aware of its existence. It would go from the signing ceremony, sealed, straight to Dr. Papo's bank vault. There it would die a natural death—unless the *Sealestial*, having set out to sea, was never again heard from, the vessel and all the crew disappearing from the face of the earth. In that event—to be sure, only after the requisite exhibitions of grief—Dr. Papo would put his claim in to the insurance company. If the company confronted him with the contract granting me command, Dr. Papo would triumphantly come back at the company with my subsequent reversion. It pays to think ahead.

The only crisis was personal, though that is to overfreight what happened. As I got on with the planning, Dick had begun to reconsider. As is his mode, he ended by giving his straightforward reasons for electing to undertake only the first leg. As already noted, the 1975 crossing five years earlier Reggie had nicknamed the Big One, and we found ourselves very quickly, and ever after without self-consciousness, referring to it routinely as the "BO." Dick felt we needed a theme for the forthcoming passage, one that

---

Allen Jouning with cap.

Allen forward. Visible, the extra fuel tanks for the Bermuda–Azores leg.

would stress less the adventure inherent in a virginal experience, no longer possible, than the exploitation of all the passage's possibilities. He came up with the idea of "The Ultimate Charter." After returning from the trip, revisiting the subject, he wrote in his journal:

> *The Ultimate Charter:* Let's (I had said to Bill) make it ultimate in every way, preparations, people, amenities, equipment, music, books, first-run movies, food—whatever. And so we agreed—but never did it.
>
> Why not?
>
> Two reasons: First, we were both too busy and running around too much doing other things to really carry through on that intention. Games are games but work is work. So while the

The schooner Cyrano, *powering past Cuba, 1976.*

The starters, May 29, 1980, St. Thomas: Dick Clurman, Dan Merritt, Van Galbraith, Reg Stoops, WFB, Tony Leggett. Missing: the photographer, Christopher Little.

planning, as can be read in the memos that preceded the trip, was good and careful, it was not "ultimate," just "good." Secondly and more important, my friend Buckley, among his lesser-known (to the outside world) qualities, is a real lover of his friends, not just his sailing friends, but his writing, painting, piano-playing, economizing, computerizing, lawyering, banking —all his real friends. Not that he's profligate with friendship nor does he debase the coinage. He's just intense about it.

For that reason he picked, along with me, four of his sailing friends—in fact three of the four had been on his only other transatlantic crossing. Splendid companions all, but hardly ultimate in the sense that I had originally intended. My thought was that six of us, from completely different and accomplished walks of life on land—who also like to sail—would make the trip and bring to our happy confinement not old friendships but different and preeminent perspectives. That we would get acquainted at sea and commingle our interests and experiences. To be sure that is a producer's way to proceed. And while part of Bill is always a producer, all of him is always a friend. So it was Bill and I, Reg and Van, Tony and Danny plus Chris, our very appealing and equally talented still photographer—unfailingly fine fellows but not a cast for a unique and memorable floating seminar.

. . . and [so] I concluded that as much as I thought a month at sea would delight me, I couldn't imagine spending that month, on the eve of the two political conventions, cut off from the world, the New York *Times* and in some ways the quadrennial apocalypse of my lifelong professional preoccupations. Also, in truth the abandonment of the month-long seminar (which apparently only I imagined) made me wonder, first point aside, whether I could spend a month dropped-out at sea happily with my companions. So, over Bill's reproving but understanding protests, I signed on for only the first leg, merely an appetizer passage to a much heartier full, salted meal.

And of course Dick was quite right. Someday I might just attempt a floating seminar aboard a sailboat crossing the Atlantic Ocean. As ever, one might learn from Plato. . . .

Richard M. Clurman (Dick) is a private consultant on public policy. He was Commissioner of Parks, Recreation and Cultural Affairs during the last years of the Lindsay administration in New York City, and before that, the longtime chief of correspondents for Time and Life publications. He was born in New York, and graduated from the University of Chicago (1946).

(Scene, the cockpit, midday.)

RICHARD: You see, my friend, when I asked you before what piety was, you didn't tell me enough; you said that what you are doing now—prosecuting your father for manslaughter—was a pious action.

WILLIAM: Yes, and what I said was true, Richard.

DANIEL: *Pass the ketchup.*

RICHARD: No doubt; but surely you admit that there are many other actions that are pious.

WILLIAM: So there are.

CHRISTOPHER: *Hold it where you are, Richard. The light's perfect.*

RICHARD: Well, then, do you recollect that what I urged you to do

Evan Galbraith (Van) is U.S. Ambassador to France. By profession he is a banker, though he began as a lawyer. He was born in Ohio, graduated from Yale (1950) and the Harvard Law School. He spent twelve years in France and England and sailed with WFB across the Atlantic in 1975.

was not to tell me about one or two of those many pious actions, but to describe the actual feature that makes all pious actions pious? —Because you said, I believe, that impious actions are impious, and similarly pious ones pious, in virtue of a single characteristic. How can you distinguish between the pious and the impious?

EVAN: *Impious sucks—how's that, Richard?*

WILLIAM: If that's how you want your answer, Richard, that's how I will give it.

RICHARD: That *is* how I want it.

TONY: *Aren't you going to eat your sausage?*

WILLIAM: Very well, then; what is agreeable to the gods is pious,

Anthony Leggett (Tony) is now a banker in New York. He graduated from Harvard (1976) and spent two years sailing and racing. He crewed twice with WFB before undertaking this passage.

and what is disagreeable to them, impious.

RICHARD: An excellent answer, William, and in just the form that I wanted. Whether it is true I don't know yet; but no doubt you will go on to make it clear to me that your statement is correct.

REGINALD: *If it turns out William's statement is not correct, Richard, I'll see you on the four A.M. watch.*

WILLIAM: (*ignoring Reginald*) Certainly.

Daniel Merritt (Danny) grew up with Christopher Buckley (son of WFB), and has sailed with the family since he was thirteen, skippering the yacht Suzy Wong *during several summers. He also crossed the Atlantic on* Cyrano *in 1975. He graduated from Regis College (1975) and is in the insurance business in Connecticut.*

RICHARD: Come along, then; let's consider what we are saying. The action or person that is god-beloved is pious, and the action or person that is god-hated is impious, piety being not the same as impiety but its direct opposite. Isn't that our position?
DANIEL: *No. Our position is Latitude 38 degrees 42 minutes north, Longitude 27 degrees 11 minutes west.*
WILLIAM: Yes, it is.

Reginald Stoops (Reg) is the son of a naval doctor, and went to school wherever his father was stationed. He graduated from M.I.T. (1948) and became a plastics engineer. He has sailed with WFB for twenty-five years, including the 1975 crossing.

RICHARD: And the definition seems satisfactory?

WILLIAM: I think so, Richard.

EVAN: *Count your silver when he says that, Richard.*

RICHARD: Haven't we also said that the gods are divided, William, and disagree with one another, and feel enmity toward one another?

WILLIAM: Yes, we have.

Christopher Little is a professional photographer. He is a graduate of Hotchkiss and Yale (1972). He has sailed off and on for many years, never before with WFB.

RICHARD: What sort of disagreement is it, my good friend, that causes enmity and anger? Let us look at it in this way. If you and I disagreed about the question which of two numbers was the greater, would this disagreement make us hostile and angry with each other? Shouldn't we quickly settle a dispute of this kind by having recourse to arithmetic?

REGINALD: *Maybe I can help? I went to M.I.T.*

WILLIAM: Certainly.

RICHARD: Then what would be the subject of dispute about which we should be unable to reach agreement, so that we became hostile to one another and lost our tempers? Very likely you can't say offhand; but consider, as I suggest them, whether the required subjects are questions of right and wrong, honor and dishonor, good and bad. Isn't it when we disagree about these, and can't reach a satisfactory decision about them, that we become hostile to one another (when we do become hostile)—both you and I and all the rest of mankind?

REGINALD: *Stand by to come about. Toss Anthony the winch handle, Richard, and grab the sheet winch.*

WILLIAM: Yes, that is the sort of disagreement, Richard, about the subjects that you mention.

RICHARD: (*panting as he tails the sheet*) And what about the gods, William?

WILLIAM: The what? I can't hear with the mainsail luffing.

RICHARD: (*shouting*) *The gods! the* G-O-D-S. If they do disagree at all, won't it be for just these reasons?

WILLIAM: Quite inevitably.

RICHARD: Then on your view, my worthy William, it follows that the gods too hold different opinions about what is right, and similarly about what is honorable and dishonorable, good and bad; because surely they would not be divided if they didn't disagree on these subjects. Isn't that so?

WILLIAM: You are quite right.

DANIEL: *I don't see why. They might be divided because they don't like each other.*

RICHARD: Then does each faction love what it considers to be honorable and good and right, and hate the opposite?

WILLIAM: Certainly.

EVAN: *Assuming they're Republicans.*

RICHARD: But according to you the same things are regarded by some of the gods as right and by others as wrong; I mean the things about which they dispute, and so are divided and fight one another. Isn't that so?

WILLIAM: Yes.

RICHARD: So apparently the same things are both loved and hated by the gods—that is, the same things will be both god-beloved and god-hated.

WILLIAM: Apparently.

RICHARD: Then by this argument, William, the same things will also be both pious and impious.

WILLIAM: Perhaps so.

RICHARD: (*smiling*) Then you didn't answer my question, my talented friend . . .

70

EVAN: *Let's go over that one again, Richard? Don't you agree, team?*
(CHORUS) *Yes! Yes! Again! Again!*

And then Van gave me *his* disappointing news. He had been living in London with his wife and three children (John is only four) for ten years, and was repatriating to the United States. He had to undertake a mission to Tokyo before the whole family got into the QE2 for the return voyage. So he would have to leave the ship at the Azores. The thought was very nearly unbearable, as Van is the source of unparalleled gaiety. Already I had assimilated the disappointment of traveling without my sister-in-law "Bill" Finucane, the devoted den mother of our first voyage (her husband was ill, and I could not even ask her). In any event, on April 21, 1980, another memorandum goes out:

MEMO TO: Reggie Stoops, Danny Merritt, Tony Leggett, Christopher Little, Van Galbraith, Dick Clurman
FROM: WFB

Random notes re The Crossing. . . . I have listed you beginning with those who are going all the way, ending with those who leave us first. To demystify the above, Clurman leaves us on reaching Bermuda, Van on reaching the Azores.

The *Sealestial* (iron rule: pronounced Celestial by anybody who intends to board and stay aboard) will be docked at Yacht Haven, to which we should repair by cab.

We will set out for Bermuda at 10 A.M. on Friday, May 30. It is not known whether we shall have to sail for an hour or two for the benefit of helicopter photography. If so, we shall be returning to St. Thomas to pick up Christopher Little, the cinematographer, and the sound man. The latter two will be sailing with us as far as Bermuda, disembarking there. We plan a documentary one-hour television program based on the first leg of the trip, supplemented if necessary by home-movie shots of especially exciting events from legs two, three and four.

Leg one: St. Thomas to Bermuda
Leg two: Bermuda to Horta

Leg three: Horta to São Miguel
Leg four: São Miguel to Marbella
I calculate arrival in Bermuda late Tuesday evening, June 3. We will tie up at St. George's, and bring *Sealestial* into Hamilton Harbor Wednesday A.M. I have reserved the dockside at the Princess Hotel where I have also reserved a suite, two bedrooms, one living room. The beds will be for Stoops, Clurman, Galbraith, and me, lest the younger members get out of training. We will depart Bermuda Saturday morning, June 7.

We should arrive in Horta on Tuesday, June 17.

We will leave Horta on Wednesday, the 18th, and cruise to São Miguel, with intermediate stops, arriving Friday the 20th.

We will leave São Miguel on Monday, the 23rd, arriving late Saturday, June 28th, in Puerto Banús, Marbella.

For the benefit of those of you inclined as I am to the natural sciences, some figures:

St. Thomas is at 18–22 N., 64–56 W. St. George, 32–24 N., 64–42 W.

—Distance, 842 miles (nautical) at initial heading of 000 deg. Horta is at 38–32 N., 28–40 W.

—Distance (from St. George), 1,785 miles at heading of 67 deg. São Miguel is at 37–33 N., 25–27 W.

—Distance (from Horta), 163 miles heading of 110 deg. Gibraltar is at 36–09 N., 5–21 W.

—Distance (from São Miguel), 966 miles at heading of 88 degrees.

I have an extensive memo on safety from Reggie. But I shall wait to remit an edited version of it until I speak with Dr. Papo on his return from Antigua early in May. At that time I will have the opportunity to question him about what gear he has and what he hasn't. You should bring your own foul-weather gear and boots. All luggage should be in duffels.

Watch captains will be Reggie, Danny, and Tony.

Assistants will be Van, Christopher, and Dick. I'll make up a duty roster with variable combinations. Four hours on, eight hours off, with standby duty by the watch that has been off duty the longest.

No one is to sleep in the saloon, which will be the decompression chamber for watches going off duty.

Everyone will infinitely oblige me (which is Very Important) by keeping a loquacious diary from which I will draw in putting together the book to finance this extravaganza. I will supply hard-cover diaries, but if you are addicted to a particular kind of notebook, please bring it.

Van Galbraith will serve as meteorological officer, and will acquaint himself with the vessel's Weathermax and keep a weather log.

When Van departs, Reggie will take over that responsibility.

More in due course.

4

It doesn't pay to arrive at your vessel too soon before a departure, because, as in so many other matters, the Parkinsonian principle will apply, namely that enough things to do will turn up to fill the time available to do them. The trick is tunnel vision: tell Danny that you need a size N spare battery for the Hewlett-Packard 41C, and if such a thing exists or can be flown over in time from Puerto Rico, he'll have it there. Try to find something specific for everyone to do. Make as few collective rendezvous as possible, but these should be firm. "We *all* meet at my suite at 7 P.M. At what time do we all meet at my suite, Tony? Very good, Tony. 7 P.M. is not 7:30 P.M., is it, Reggie?" Of course, when you say things in that tone of voice, it pays to make the schoolmasterliness hyperbolic, in which case it is all accepted in good humor. I mean, accepted in good humor by the kind of people I sail with, who are all splendid, having in common their recognition of my unique qualities.

And we made it worth their while to be there at 7 P.M. because Reggie, Dick, and I had undertaken to provision the wine cellar of the *Sealestial*. This is very serious business. On the one hand, money is very definitely a consideration. Anyone can provision a

75

The wine must not give out.

wine cellar successfully by averaging ten or fifteen dollars per bottle. My aim was to average $3.50 per bottle, and I can report that superb wines were drunk for twenty-nine days, at least by those who were not, at the relevant moments, emptying their stomachs rather than filling them. But as we all know, at three to four dollars you can with some effort get some of the best and with very little effort get some of the worst wines in the world, and at St. Thomas there is a most extraordinary profusion of the worst wines in the world. At any rate, at 7 P.M. we all gathered in front of twenty bottles of wine, half of them white, half red, for a grand tasting session, the results of which, on a point system of one to twenty, are faithfully recorded in my journal. My grading system was ostensibly democratic; and it was, in that everyone's vote was recorded. However—especially since no one else could see—I simply threw out the anomalies. At least, the negative anomalies. I tasted first, and secretly recorded my vote. If I gave wine a ten and someone then gave it a four, I'd throw out that four. But if I gave a wine a ten and someone gave it a seventeen, I'd taste it again, thinking that perhaps I was mistaken, that the wine had a delayed and highly positive reaction.

We were all sprawled about in the one-room suite, on chairs, beds, a couch, the floor, including Captain Jouning and the two girls, Judy Harman and Diane Bowlus, cook and stewardess, and David Murphy, the first mate, and two movie men. At the end of an hour not only the wine but the bonhomie flowed freely, and the tasters provided dithyrambic pronouncements on the virtues or vices of the wine freshly poured into a plastic glass, of which there were at this point about 300 in the room. Van gradually felt it necessary to contribute an appropriate facial expression to characterize the wine he had just tasted, and in one case merely smelled, reacting in such mephitic disgust that I thought he might take the next plane out to the offending vineyard in France to beat up the owner. I told him the story, which he much enjoyed, about the fury with which Toscanini read in the papers one morning in Milan, midway through rehearsing what he had understood would be the world premiere of *Der Rosenkavalier*, that the opera had been performed the evening before in Vienna. Without notifying a soul or picking up so much as a briefcase, he hailed a taxi to the station, traveled to Vienna, then took a taxi to the house of Richard Strauss, rang the bell and, finding himself face to face with Strauss, exclaimed in reverent tones, "As a musician, I take my hat off to you." Toscanini removed his hat. "As a human being," Toscanini's eyes spat out the fury, "I put it on ten times!" And ten times Toscanini removed and emphatically put on his hat; turning, then, back to the taxi, and to Milan to resume rehearsals. Van thought it was a funny story, but said he couldn't think of any reason to take his hat off as a gesture of respect to this particular vintner, and Dick said maybe the vintner should be respected for the sheer audacity of getting his grape juice all the way to the Virgin Islands without being arrested. Dick noted in his journal,

"Van refused to rate one Chablis, spurning it with the comment, 'This horse definitely had diabetes!' " We were in a fine mood, but agreed that of the twenty wines only four were suitable for mass purchase, and Dick and I agreed to do some more scouting about the next morning for a wider selection, which we would taste at 5 P.M. the next day aboard the *Sealestial* ("At what time will we meet aboard the *Sealestial* tomorrow to resume our wine tasting, Tony?"); and we adjourned, my companions and I going off to a fancy restaurant for dinner as guests of Dick, going (some of us) early to bed, waking in time to resume our chores.

The following day we set out. I had all along scheduled a 3 P.M. take-off and there were reasons for this beyond the obvious one that there are always things left over to do in the morning, so it is better to plan to leave after noon. Along the way, during the preceding months, I had decided to attempt a documentary. Ever since, years ago, I saw the surfing film *The Endless Summer*, I have wished that something of the sort might be done for ocean cruising. *The Endless Summer* had one irreplaceable quality, and another which could conceivably be imitated. The first was the advantage of showing the viewer what it is like to visit the surfing beaches of the world. Each is in its way different. The beaches in Oahu are visibly different from those in southwestern Australia. But the oceans of the world, after you have left land, although they are capable of greater volatility than anything in biology, greater even than the caterpillar-turned-butterfly, are indistinguishable as to location, so that a scene of a sailboat between the Azores and Gibraltar would, *ceteris paribus*, be identical with a scene of a sailboat in Block Island Sound or between Tasmania and New Zealand. Problem number one.

The second quality of *The Endless Summer* is the breathless excitement of the narrator, whose name, if I ever knew it, I have forgotten. He had a kind of husky, romantic, understated exuberance that made the viewer—in my case someone indifferent to surfing—suddenly care intensely about the sport, appreciate it hugely. But in surfing, the virtuosity is most obviously that. Virtuosity in a successful cruise comprises the interaction of a few dozen elements, none of which is in itself photogenic or discretely romantic.

Still, I thought it worth attempting. My first, naïve notion was that Christopher Little should also take movies. I learned, rather

Next stop, Bermuda.

abruptly, that I might as well have suggested to Isaac Stern that he also play the French horn. Photographers do one thing, cinematographers do something else, and the generic statement that both after all use film is as helpful as observing that ballet dancers and joggers both use their legs. That wasn't all. Apparently no cinematographer worth hiring will travel to the bathroom without a sound engineer. This is not, I learned quickly, an affectation. You cannot do first-rate cinematography while also worrying about the infinitely complicated business of getting first-rate sound. And without that, no exhibitor will show anything not shot by Zapruder.

So Christopher Little brought to my house in Stamford for lunch a youngish cinematographer of vast experience who had won all kinds of prizes and had a chestful of credits, and we talked —or, more properly, I listened—for three hours. It was heady stuff. He talked blithely of spending one hundred and fifty to two hundred thousand dollars. He would certainly need one assistant but would prefer two. He had visions of midnight filming during which I and someone else—"maybe Gore Vidal, somebody really interesting, somebody you disagree with"—would discuss Immanuel Kant, or Joe McCarthy. It would be absolutely smashing, but *absolutely* the best documentary ever. Eventually he left, and I called Christopher into my quiet little music room so that we could decompress for a little while, and I thought long and deep on the subject and said that we should indeed attempt a documentary, but that it must be restricted to the first of the four legs of the passage. No point in ruining the entire trip for the sake of a documentary, even a great one. The man who came to lunch was not interested in the proffered terms, so I wrote out (to whom it may concern) a memo and, at his urging, sent it to Walter Cronkite, with whom I share a friendship focused to a considerable extent on our common thralldom to the sea:

MEMORANDUM re a proposed one-hour documentary
FROM: William F. Buckley, Jr.

I propose to produce a one-hour documentary, most of which will be filmed aboard a 71-foot racing-cruising ketch bound from the West Indies to Spain. I say most of which, because the closing few minutes will be still photographs of the last two legs of a three-leg journey, with voice-over bringing the narrative to a conclusion.

The legs of the journey will take us, aboard the *Sealestial*, from St. Thomas to Bermuda (1,000 miles), from Bermuda to the Azores (1,900 miles), and from the Azores to Spain (900 miles).

Aboard the boat will be six members of my party (hereinafter "owner's party") and four crew. The owner's party will be responsible for all the sailing, all the navigation and piloting and, I hope, all of the revelry. The crew will look after the maintenance of the vessel, cook and serve and, in case of emergency, help as required.

I shall be the captain of the vessel, the producer and director of the film (except that I shall rely heavily on an expert cinematographer-director for guidance), the scriptwriter, and the narrator.

The owner's party consists of three men approximately my own age (54), and three young men age 25–30. All of us have sailed extensively. I am a personal friend of every member of the owner's party, including Christopher Little, a professional still photographer who will collaborate with me in the production of a trade book on the crossing, which Doubleday will publish in 1982.

I have sailed all my life, and have skippered ocean racing boats for twenty years, and served as captain and navigator of a transatlantic sail in June 1975. That voyage produced a book, *Airborne*, which sold 100,000 copies hard-cover. Excerpts from the reviews of the book are attached.

I have in mind an hour devoted only in part to the mechanics of sailing. These would be touched upon only insofar as they enliven the narrative. The documentary will be the story of six friends sharing an experience about which many people dream. The inevitable themes will be touched upon—the perils of the sea, the nature of the sea's emergencies, the precautions one takes, the mysteries of knowing where you are by celestial navigation, the telltale signs of wind changes and hazardous weather, some of the electronic and other gear that are fashioned to maximize safety, the design of the sail and the basic rigging, the transmogrification of the canvas and cable into the motive force that propels 60 tons of boat at twelve knots; and so forth. But I have in mind something extremely personal: my own reactions to the experience, my relationship with my friends, what we talk about during the hours we share together, whether at meals at midday or sunset, or at night during the long watches. Every member of the owner's party will keep a diary, and selected portions of it will be integrated into the final script, as deemed advisable. This technique was extremely successful in *Airborne*.

The cinematographer and his sound man will have been (so to speak) invited to share the first leg of the voyage with us. It will require about five days to traverse the first leg. The winds, in that part of the world, are stiff, and from east by north. This will pitch the boat in a close reach, giving speed and action. It is estimated that the cinematographer will shoot approximately twenty hours of film, from which the hour will be edited. I envision a closing film of the *Sealestial* and its crew departing on the long eastward leg to the Azores, at which point I hope the viewer would feel thoroughly experienced in the vicissitudes of ocean sailing, envious of its pleasures, well acquainted with the crew and the mix of personalities, wistful at not remaining aboard to complete the passage, but respectful of the privacy of the enterprise, which is a venture in companionship at sea.

And so it was that when we did leave St. Thomas, we left St. Thomas not once, but three times. Mark Dichter, as sound engineer, headed the team of which the other member was cinematographer David Watts. Both in their late thirties, tall, patient, experienced, models of tact throughout the six days we spent together, two of them turbulent. But however resolute their deference to our own preferences and requirements, they had a job to do; and that job required a comprehensive, cinematographic documentary of our leave-taking. This meant that the camera would be on board the first time we pulled out and ashore the second time, shooting us from a distance of about fifty feet. Tony, in his journal, described the technique: ". . . a wheelchair from the hotel and David perched crosswise in the chair with the camera on his knees. Mark pushed him down the dock like a proud father with his first son. That was the 'dolly shot.'" The camera sees the boat pull out of the slip, make a left turn into the channel (and into the wind), head for the midship section of a huge passenger ship lying to along the main wharf, raise the mainsail and then turn right, heading out to sea.

The *third* time, Mark and David—and Christopher Little—were aboard what in the trade they call a "chase boat," by which is meant a vessel hired to pursue the photographed object, permitting this to be done from different angles and from varying distances. We had the genoa hoisted by the time we were headed to the

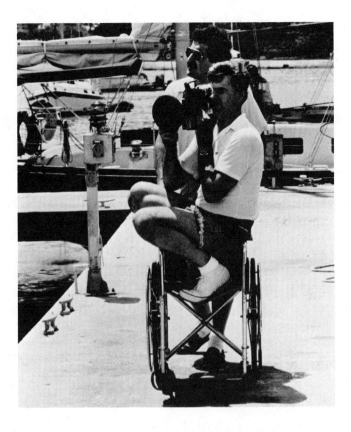

Mark Dichter and David Watts (with camera) filming the Sealestial's *departure at St. Thomas.*

mouth of the harbor, and then quickly the mizzen sail; and we jibed to head west. We had in any event an hour's westerly sail before we could round St. Thomas and head up toward Bermuda, on a course of 000° (due north). That was the hour of photographers needed, and to oblige them we did a little exhibitionistic ballet, raising and lowering the sails, coming about, jibing, raising the spinnaker. Curiously, we managed to do all this without feeling in the least foolish. This was in part because for the first time the home team was actually working this particular boat. Danny, the spryest young sailor afloat, tore forward and aft, helping to run the large genoa through the narrow section between the head-stay and the forestay, secured on deck for contingent use. There was the usual confusion—the crossed lines, the bad leads, the missing winch handles—but there was plenty of gusto, and at no moment were we ever made to feel, by Captain Jouning and his thoroughly professional first mate David, who knew the vessel as one knows one's old sports car, by word or deed that we were in any way maladroit. In due course the chase boat signaled that it had had enough, and I hove the *Sealestial* to (i.e., brought it into a state as motionless as possible, given a wind that is blowing and sails that are hoisted) while the photographers shakily boarded, with all their fancy equipment—an extensive operation, but satisfying because of the unquenchable enthusiasm of Christopher, Mark, and David, all of whom averred that *never in the history of photography!* had more beautiful pictures been taken of a more beautiful boat, more beautifully maneuvered, in more beautiful circumstances, human and natural. I thought their epithalamium on plighting their troth to *Sealestial* an auspicious moment to decree the beginning of the cocktail hour, the more so since I especially needed cheer, Captain Jouning having told me that he had not succeeded in making our brand-new Brookes and Gatehouse digital speedometer work, though he had been slaving over it for almost two hours now.

Some people like a functioning speedometer on a sailboat, some like one but are philosophical without it. I am a mad dog without one. Just as some people need tobacco, or sex, or alcohol, or *National Review*, I need a speedometer—so much so that at personal expense I ordered a fancy one to replace the plaything *Sealestial* had been getting along with. I ordered a beautiful machine that would record not only your exact speed to one one hundredth of a knot, but would also keep track of distance traveled, eliminating the necessity of the cumbersome taffrail log, that antique (but durable) device that measures distance traveled by trailing, at about 75 feet behind the stern, a propeller-like device that transmits its shimmy onto a mechanical register astern, via a line that twirls in exact synchronization with the blades. The residual problems being that the propeller device, while authoritative as regards the umbilical line, occasionally attracts sharks, which devour it (at fifty dollars per propeller, one hopes it is their last meal); and regularly attracts ocean dross—seaweed and like stuff—

*A thoughtful dialogue between WFB and Dick. Reg at wheel,
which he is operating with his big toe while talking to Danny.*

that binds the propeller, whose irregular movements then consti-
pate the register, causing great pain to the dead-reckoning navigator. That my beautiful new speedometer, after all this planning,
would not work was a blow that required deep reserves of manly
courage to absorb.

But always, before finally giving up, one invokes the inter-
cession of Reggie; and now he was fiddling with this and that, the
ends of a voltmeter in his mouth—when, suddenly, it began to
work! Captain Jouning, an immensely resourceful man, was both
pleased and chagrined at someone else's having figured it out, and
keenly read the instructions over Reggie's shoulder, to discover
that—mistakenly—Reggie had crossed two wires that the instruction booklet had said *on no account should be crossed!* (Beard-
McKie, under *Errata*—"On page 34, paragraph 2, in the sentence

that begins, 'The most important thing to remember . . .' substitute *never* for *always*.") Crossing them, however, caused the speedometer to work; and we there and then solemnly sealed the Sealestial Covenant: that no one would ever inform Brookes and Gatehouse that we had violated their operating instructions.

The wine was poured, we were on course. The wind was from the east at about twelve knots. The sun was sinking, over there to the left, in the general direction of Puerto Rico. Suddenly the babbling stopped, almost as if we had all been following the instructions of an orchestra leader; we heard only the lap-lap of the waves, patting firmly the headstrong hull of our ketch, white-gold in the falling light, the surrounding water turned now a viridian blue, oddly diaphanous, St. Thomas receding astern. No one spoke.

It is a period, I have found, that almost always comes, choosing its own rhythmic moment—the moment when, collectively, everyone on board recognizes that a journey has truly begun. Up there, toward which we are pointing, a thousand miles away, is a tiny little coral island. The object is to reach it, to arrive there without injury to ourselves or to our vessel. No one formally proposed a toast, but looking about—at Tony, with his floppy white hat so carefully tilted to shield his sun-sensitive face from those final ultraviolet shafts; at Dick with his jaunty captain's hat, reluctantly putting on his shirt as he yielded to the demands of lowering temperature; Van, hatless, with his light blue crew-necked sweater, squinting at that morning's New York *Times*, glass in hand; Reggie carefully screwing back the holding flange on the speedometer; Christopher, snapping away with an anfractuous photographic apparatus at the setting sun—I guessed that we were all thinking related thoughts.

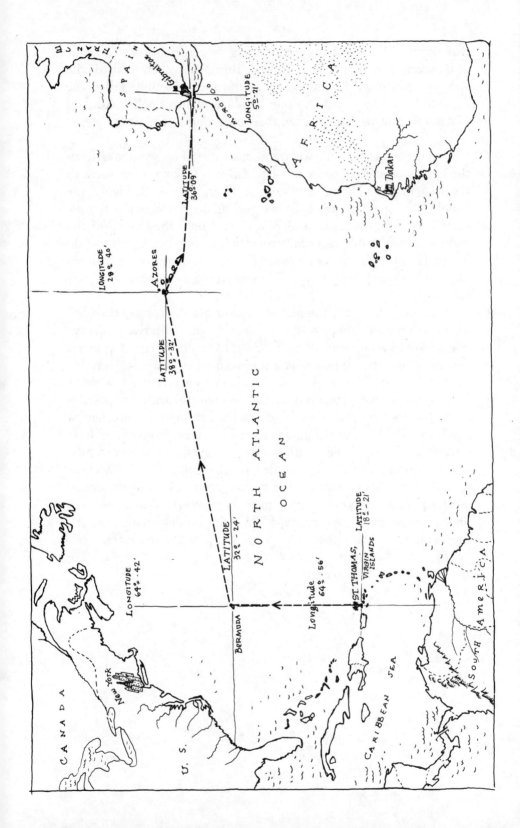

Book Two

5

~~~~~~~~~~~~~~~~~~~~~~

On the first Atlantic crossing I thought to ask everyone to keep a journal. The results, as to Danny and (my son) Christopher, were wildly successful. At twenty-three Danny's style was Huckleberry Finn; at twenty-one, Christopher's was Henry James. The counterpoint was striking, preeminently responsible, in my judgment, for the success of the book in which their journals are so extensively excerpted.

I found then what I now rediscovered, namely that when on a long cruise you ask your friends to keep a journal a) everyone will agree to do so; b) some will, some won't; c) some will keep them perfunctorily; ·d) others will attack them wholeheartedly. Tony's journal took me a full day merely to read over. It must be twenty thousand words long. Tony's father is a writer (the novelist John Leggett) and clearly Tony was being not only dutiful, but was giving way gladly to a hard case of *cacoëthes scribendi*. Even so the journal, from my point of view, is less than fully satisfying—because of what it does *not* say. It is very nearly drained of emotion. Clearly Tony had resolved to keep his private thoughts to himself, while conscientiously keeping a chronicle of events.

To be sure, as much can be said of Captain Joshua Slocum,

whose memorable journal can be read as a grocery list, but which somehow achieves, in the annals of writing on the sea: literature. No one, this time out, sought to write about the trip or about the sea in the manner of Joseph Conrad. Van, in his writing, has always managed with almost spooky success to denature his own ebullient personality. One would not know from Van's journal that he is among the half-dozen most consistently amusing and endearing men alive; only here and there a flash of this in the journal. I am reminded of a prodigious, heart-on-his-sleeve suitor of the mother of an old friend who, however, when he turned to correspondence could manage nothing—but nothing—that did not relate to the day's weather, and invariably he closed his ardently motivated, romantically obsessed missives, "Yrs., Chas."

Reggie resolves mightily to keep a journal—and doesn't. He gets hopelessly behind, and then the dread day comes (after reaching our destination) when he faces the task of reconstruction. It is on the order of having done none of the reading during the entire semester of Russian literature 10A or 10B and finding, the evening before the exam, that all you need to do before morning is read the works of Chekhov, Dostoyevsky, and Tolstoy. Since Reggie was born to be forgiven any transgression, he is promptly and unrecriminatingly forgiven when he turns up with a journal with a half-dozen technical sketches of sump pumps, speedometers, and chili con carne confections—and two or three notations. It pays, then, to force yourself to remember the number of lonely hours Reggie—the single companion who knows how to fix things—has spent poring over the technical literature of all the machines and devices that are out of order, while the dilettantes were attending merely their belletristic fancies.

Danny, who is conventionally restrained in his conversation about people, though not at all in his enthusiasm for events (the most beautiful sunset in the history of the world is whatever sunset Danny Merritt last saw), writes from the heart. The veil we all (or mostly all) wear during the day, drops: and Danny comes out with it, whether he is writing about the awfulness of a particular dish served at lunch or the uniqueness of his one true love. Dick Clurman, always the professional (though he is among the most sentimental of men, known by hosts on all seven continents as the most moving after-dinner panegyrist since Mark Antony), is characteristically methodical. He carries one of those little dictating machines and can be seen at odd hours of the afternoon talking into it. Eventually his secretary will transcribe it and it will be sent in. Trenchant, pointed, fluent, philosophical—and in this case a little vexed, because from the first moment on, having decided to participate only in the first leg of the journey, he felt a little bit the outsider, and so produced a journal psychologically encumbered by a sense of (self-effected) exclusion, like the hiker who signs up for the first third of the trip up Mount Everest.

My own journals are entirely hieroglyphic. Few people I know are as distressed as I by the physical labor of writing. I have on other occasions mentioned the wonderful gifts of the late William Snaith, who grabbed his logbook at the end of a day's sail and wrote his heart out in thoughts expressive and humorous, illuminating and philosophical, voluptuous in their fecundity. One has visions of Anthony Trollope writing page after page after page, sheer pleasure etched in his face—perhaps smiling, even, as he wrote. My own journal is intensely abbreviated, but I have found it serviceable. The notes I took during this trip filled only twenty double-spaced pages, one tenth the size of Tony's journal. They are, really, notes—unpublishable as such; useful only as *aides-mémoire*. But not for very long. (I have found that notes more than a few months old remind me of—nothing at all; and are in any event very nearly indecipherable.)

Tony, throughout, was much concerned about his health. His complexion reacts, or better overreacts, to the sun, and without his Total Eclipse sun-blocking lotion he suffers greatly. Moreover his stomach is weak, in proportion as his appetite is ravenous. "It was a great way to introduce the crew," he wrote about the wine-tasting session; "everyone cracked jokes about the voting system, but it was a poor way to continue my convalescence." The queasy stomach—to which he would allude time and time again.

Tony managed to permit, every now and again, a little flicker of professional concern over those practices aboard the vessel that were incompatible with the highest professional standards. Of us all, he was probably the most technically skilled sailor, having raced for so long in the company of professionals. I don't know that I would yield my own judgment to his at sea, having sailed thirty years longer; but as a precisionist he is impressive, and it is pleasant to see him making his points in the language of the technician. . . .

"The man overboard poles were in very bad shape. The fiberglass tubing just below the floats had gone rotten for some reason. I sawed them clear with the hacksaw, reamed out the Styrofoam, picked up a proper-sized dowel at the lumberyard, cut them to size to fit inside the tubing, taped them so they fitted tightly, and then glassed over the break. In theory it should be much stronger than the original, but the usual problem of glassing—bubbles at sharp bends—was quite grave here. Furthermore, one end of the glass was on the very soft plastic floats. We'll see if it holds."

It didn't, but the language is hard as sprung steel.

Tony too is grateful for the unobtrusiveness of the cinematographers: "Mark is very good at getting the action going without making it seem forced, and without the cameras and sound gear making much of an intrusion. It should get even easier to work in front of a camera as the trip progresses, because we will soon take the camera as part of the boat's gear. I was pretty pleased with what would have seemed a highly contrived setting, because the conversation about the wine went on whether or not the cameras were running. I think Clurman may be a bit of a ham, but maybe even he too will settle down a bit." (Clurman will *never* settle down, Tony will discover over the years.) As for his own self-consciousness before the cameras, it did not easily dissipate. . . .

"When it came my turn to undo the spring [line], for some reason the line was up tight with all the boat's pressure on it. I could hear the camera clicking away, focused right on my hands where I was supposed to perform, and I couldn't do a thing." In this respect there was something of a generation gap: "In a process that amazed me for the next week long, the active crew showed how easily it could become oblivious to the camera crew. Bill and Van and Dick started up their conversations and had to be interrupted abruptly and often to be reminded that the cameras required their attention. . . . I got in my two cents' worth [before the camera] about banking [Tony's new career] and Bill did a very creditable job on himself. I guess he's the authority on that, and also pretty good in front of a camera. Halfway through, Chris said, 'This is the most boring conversation I've conducted.' I don't care. All I want is to see my face and hear my voice on the silver screen." If I have any say in the matter, Tony Leggett will get his premiere!

There are few references in the journals to fellow crew members. Danny, as in other respects, is the exception, though his characterizations tend to be brief. "Van could perhaps be the funniest man alive, loves to enjoy self and crack you a smile. First to laugh at his own jokes, but knows they're good." . . . "Tony—less uptight, more self-assured. Easy to get along with, a good shipmate." . . . "Chris Little—I feel a warmth toward Chris—that unusual rapport one instantly has. Perhaps the energy, drive, good nature, is what dominates the feeling. I just don't know. Our crossing has been and is well-rounded." . . . "Reg?—is Reg!"

The first day's grace was abruptly interrupted. I wrote in the log, late the next night, "Log 382. Heavy winds (approx. 30 knots SSE), plus 7-foot seas, suggested course change to 350 degrees at 2130, to mitigate turmoil. On new course, averaged 9.5 knots. Van and Danny came on at 2300, moderately cheerful. Skipper (Allen) and David worked on brake shaft. Broken. Applied vise—so that engine *cannot* be started without first releasing vises. Only Allen and David can do this. So: anyone planning to fall overboard should pre-notify skipper or David, so that one of them can prepare use of engine to rescue man overboard."

Hard rain and heavy winds cause acute discomfort, and Tony let it all hang out in his journal:

"Conditions were still pretty bad, at least for my tender stomach. I could either stay on deck, or flat out in my bunk. I found that even reading made my stomach act up. So without interruption, except for lunch, I lay on my bunk trying out various positions and dozing. A major problem is that it is impossible not to be at least a little damp. When it is salt water that is in your hair it is very uncomfortable. Areas of dampness appear and grow: at the back of the knees, the small of the back, and the neck in particular. It makes sleep very difficult, and makes it a chore to stay in bed, but I had no alternative."

[And even the Forbidden Thought:] "I thought a great deal about Diana, but asked also what my motivation had been to get me on a boat going across the Atlantic in the first place."

Tony touched, too, on some of the practical difficulties of life in an active sea, like eating: ". . . we clustered around the saloon table below. The table opens up but its surface is polished stainless steel and it has no fiddles (or 'faddles' as Dick calls them).* Using gaffer tape and a roll of charts, one of our many on-board technicians put together a fiddle on the lee side. Bill, Van and I were directly adjacent to it. Since everyone had his bowl in his lap, its only function was to keep the wineglasses from spilling. But every few minutes, over one went, sending red wine all over the three of us, loosening up the gaffer tape and destroying the structural rigidity of the roll of charts. Eventually Van and I had to sit with our toes up against the charts, holding them in."

But what the hell, there is also the (acknowledged) excitement. The rain notwithstanding, one is, if awake, usually better off in the cockpit, eye-to-eye with the elements. "Van and Dan"—Dan wrote in the log—"chilled to the bone, will wake Chris and Tony shortly. Log 401.5 wind 25 seas 7–12 feet at least, but very comfortable, exciting. . . ."

Storms eventually abate. But there are always all those other dislocations. We were made conscious by our wives and publishers that we were sailing in the Bermuda Triangle, but Dick Clurman, in his journal, had a better explanation for the mechanical breakdowns:

"I've become fully convinced that Bill Buckley, who radiates such cheer and optimism, has his life blighted by one extraordinary downer. Above his head, invisibly circling, there must surely be

* *Until reading Tony's journal I don't remember having come across "fiddle." Webster: "Naut. A frame or railing on a ship's table to keep dishes, etc. from sliding off in rough weather—vt -dled, -dling." I'd have used the word "lip," but find no authority for it in the dictionary.*

"Log 382. Heavy winds (approx. 30 knots SSE), plus 7-foot seas . . ."

The "fiddle" is designed to keep the dinner from sliding off.
From left, Christopher, Danny, Tony, WFB, Reg.

Tony, safety harness snapped to the handrail forward of the bin-
nacle, keeps course.

the rarest bird of all: an albatross, loaded with electronic sensors, which jams, malfunctions, destroys and wipes out every battery-operated piece of his equipment on the boat surrounding him (on his own beloved *Cyrano*, it was characteristic that the following equipment was *not* working *at the same time:* the autopilot, air conditioning, high-seas radio, radar, generator, not to say the galley refrigerator and toaster).

"Well, Buckley's electronic albatross arrived the second day aboard the perfectly functioning *Sealestial*. First the radio—and hence all two-way communication—went out. Then, in order, the weather-mapping printer wouldn't work, along with, worst of all, Buckley's navigational Plath computer marvel, his Olympic electric stopwatch, and the newly installed digital log. And a warning from Diane [our stewardess]—we would run out of ice before we got to Bermuda. That, the worst news of all, since both Buckley and I are ice junkies and just assume that any boat we travel on carries enough ice for a Dartmouth Carnival at sea."

In a single entry in his log, Van was systematic on the matters at hand:

"Marinefax [also, Weathermax]—Captain tried for one hour. We read the manual jointly, and finally concluded that the printout mechanism was kaput. [Beard-McKie, under *Errata*—"On page 103, the steps for lighting an alcohol stove were printed out of order. The correct order is 4-2-1-8-3-5-6-7."]

"Portable Radio—Works to a degree, after a lot of listening, but doesn't pick up the designated weather reports as found in *Radio Signals* Volume 3.

"Panasonic—Worked for a while and to a degree but finally could get no voice on any frequency. Captain tried, Dick tried and I read the manual and tried. I think something is wrong with the antenna."

Clurman: "In the middle of the night the engine bell goes off. Allen and our mate, David, established that the engine brake is gone and the heavy seas are turning over the flywheel. . . . Allen awakens me again to tell me the stuffing box is leaking. I say to him, 'How come? We've been aboard the *Sealestial* three times and nothing ever went wrong?' 'I was saving it,' he replied. Someone remarked to Captain Allen that there must be an easier way to travel. 'Try American Airlines,' he cheerfully shot back."

"I've become fully convinced that Bill Buckley, who radiates such cheer and optimism, has his life blighted by one extraordinary downer. . . ."

A pleasure very nearly unique to life at sea is the transformation when the weather finally does settle down. It is as though the universe had grudgingly agreed to compose itself, the coy mistress to shed her coyness. Dan's entry in the log read: "Moon fully out at 0340, clear skies, perfect sail. I'm rested and as relaxed as could be. Perfect morning."

There is time now for routine preoccupations, concerns, crotchets. Dick wrote, "We have all brought our shore-bound interests to the boat and certainly, starting out, they prevail. We have our electronic toys, our timekeeping gadgets, our esoteric radios for various interests (time, news, weather, etc.), our books, our political disagreements and our land-based eccentricities."

Among the eccentricities was epicureanism. Poor Judy tried very hard, but we had exacting eaters on board. It is necessary to keep one's eye on discontents that have any likelihood of festering.

Dick wrote, "Even more at sea than on land, Bill refuses to allow around him, not only by noncontribution, but by his very attitude, unpleasantness among his friends. Monday night, we had an inedible dinner of pork chops and mashed potatoes and went soggily to bed." I suggested, via the captain, a less hearty approach in the galley. . . . It's getting back to normal. From Van: "I had a good late watch with Reg, straightened out a few macro problems; discussed his future work about which he seems more tranquil

WFB tending the circuit breaker. (Beard-McKie—"Circuit Breaker: An electromechanical switching unit intended to prevent the flow of electricity under normal operating conditions and, in the case of a short circuit, to permit the electrification of all conductive metal fittings throughout the boat. Available at most novelty shops.")

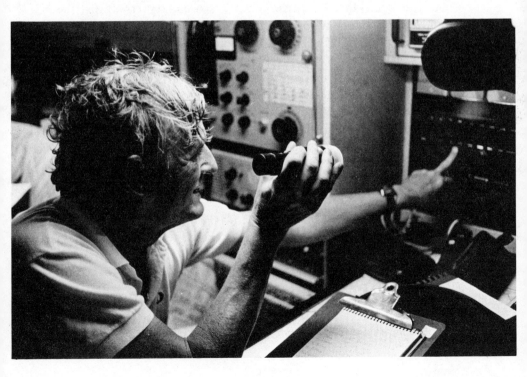

than I would be; and looked dumbly at the trillion stars." Van at this point ventured a generalization about the crew: "It is really a pretty good mixture of types and ages with each individual having some charm. Bill must consciously have anticipated the integration of the four old friends with the two new mates. It has worked out well and our social hour sparkles."

Danny, characterized by Dick as a man of action, not words, is intuitively shrewd as men of action need to be. I, for instance, had not at that point descried his own private drama, but he sensed that I had a private sorrow. He wrote in his journal:

"Aside, 14th afternoon thought:

"Bill, I've written a Sunday prayer and dated it with our latitude and longitude in my private journal, which, if you like—you may have.

"I wonder if I've been distant these last few days, sheltered in thought. Probably so; I'll explain later. Concern is what I feel—for you. Have you ever failed yourself? You seem to question the ability to prove daily."

At the end Dick Clurman—we *all* sensed—regretted that he would not be sailing with us. He took explicit pride, even, in the navigation that had brought us to Bermuda:

"Not remarkable, you say? Well, consider this. All day before, Bill had been doing running sun-shots. Contrary to our compass, contrary to our radar readings, our RDF and every other navigational aid, Buckley asserted we were way off course by his handheld sextant reckoning.* He was right. Had we continued on that course we would have missed Bermuda entirely."

* *This gallant navigational gallimaufry I discuss later, in a commentary on navigation at sea.*

6

~~~~~~~~~~~~~~~~~~~~~~~~~~~~

The documentary is, as I write, unconsummated, and it may all come to naught, though that disappointment I don't expect. I dreaded the interference I knew would be caused by the presence, on a boat every bunk of which was already spoken for, of an additional set of people; but my curiosity in the matter was terminally engaged, and from the beginning I got on well both with the producer, Bob Halmi, and his splendid cinematographers Mark and David, described above. Bob Halmi's name was given to me by Walter Cronkite after CBS turned down the documentary. Whether CBS did so out of sheer ennui at the very notion of a documentary on an Atlantic sail, or whether it was actually for the reasons Cronkite gave me isn't absolutely ascertainable, because although Walter can be very direct, he will not hurt anyone's feelings wantonly; and besides, he thought enough of the proposal to suggest on his own initiative that he turn it over to his documentary people for examination.

In any event, the verdict was No—based on the rather surprising datum that CBS only does a half-dozen special documentaries per year. And since they do only six, Cronkite said, "they want them to be more socially oriented." I found this reasoning perfectly ac-

ceptable on purely rational grounds. There aren't many slums aboard the *Sealestial*, no bilingual education (though David the mate is studying French, and we go through the motions of speaking to each other in French until we exhaust one another's vocabulary, which happens after about fifteen minutes). Reggie and Tony were going through an Italian phrase book. I could, citing Dick Clurman's skills as a sail handler, have argued that manifestly we practice affirmative action on board, but that, on reconsideration, was an oblique way to make a tenuous point. "No problem," said Walter; "it's a buyer's market—you'll get another network, or a syndicate, or cable." He then gave me the telephone number of an old friend, Bob Halmi.

Halmi was a Hungarian freedom fighter, and has become a successful television producer, juggling a dozen balls at any given time (when he met us in Bermuda he was greatly distracted because that morning he had fired Joan Fontaine, and could any of us think of a suitable replacement?). Halmi is direct, but courteous; a nice sense of humor; probably a tough hombre in the business, though I greatly like his informal, nonprehensile approach—probably the documents we have exchanged would not fill a printed page. He is also very sure of himself, and was nice enough to read my then current novel (*Who's On First*) and tell me he liked it. I told him I was especially glad to learn this because Professor John Lukacs, himself a Hungarian, and a brilliant historian, had teased me for giving the name of Frieda to the principal Hungarian dame in the book, on the grounds that Frieda is an unknown name in Hungarian, to which Halmi remarked that Professor Lukacs was clearly too innocent to have known of, let alone patronized, the most famous prerevolutionary whorehouse in Budapest, which was called Frieda's.

I don't know where it was—not likely at Frieda's—that Bob Halmi acquired his big-think habits, but he was not only excited about the documentary I had in mind but about a second documentary, his own idea. He did a real L. B. Mayer "I-can-see-it-now!" bit, right in my office.

Nothing to it. I would, on the final leg, bring on John Kenneth Galbraith and David Niven (combination ✻1), or (combination ✻2) Senator Barry Goldwater and Senator Daniel Patrick Moynihan. While we sailed across the irenic great circle route to Gibraltar, we would converse about the Important Public Questions facing the American people. "My idea," said Halmi as I stared at him dumbly, "would be to run the program as you sail into Gibraltar. I'll do the editing on board, *and the last ten minutes will be live*"—he was very nearly feverish with excitement. I told him it was a wonderfully provocative idea, but that I thought he should get the sponsorship before I approached Team A or Team B about the idea, and he said of course. Four weeks later he called me in Switzerland, utterly dejected. He had got the sponsorship—the money, everything. But he *couldn't buy* an hour of prime time. *It was all spoken for,* the hours being especially congested with political broadcasting on the eve of the two national conventions. I told him I was really sorry about this, and much later, as we plowed, for the most part underwater, from São Miguel to Gibraltar, I wondered what it would have been like to have had Galbraith and Niven on board talking about social security, SALT 2, and abortion. David is a splendid sailor and would have managed, if not to discuss the issues, to survive the passage. Ken hates boats, and by the time he reached Gibraltar would have insinuated into the Democratic platform a plank calling for the nationalization of all pleasure boats—though he'd have found it hard convincingly to designate *Sealestial* a pleasure boat after that particular passage.

In any event, Halmi wasn't himself present in St. Thomas for our departure, so I spent a little while with David and Mark talking about the documentary, and Mark confessed that it wasn't clear to him exactly how the documentary would succeed in reaching a climax. "If you see first-rate tragedy," he added helpfully, "you are looking at first-rate theater."

I told him we hoped most earnestly not to see first-rate tragedy and that in any event if we did, the probability of its being filmed was slight. Mark is a highly educated and experienced movie man and began talking about various techniques available, one of which is something called "pixillation." I didn't, of course, know what that was, and he said it was a technique first used by Charlie Chaplin, and requires jumping frames about to cause exotic effects, as in the illusion of hecticness in the assembly-line sequence in *Modern Times.* "It is a standard technique, but there might be a place for it in an ocean cruise." I told him my Chaplin story. It was two months after the assassination of President Kennedy, the hosts were my wife's old friend Vivi Crespi, and James Mason. We met the Chaplins in a private room at a little restaurant at Vevey and, beginning immediately, Chaplin was on stage, giving me a hard time on the assassination, doubting strenuously that JFK had been killed by Lee Harvey Oswald acting on his own: Probably it was the work of CIA types, or Texan Birchites.

"I don't trust the FBI. Do you, Mr. Buckley?"

"No," I said. "After all, they let you get out of the country without paying your income tax." (At this point my wife was kicking me under the table, which went on for quite a while until, in the ladies' room after dessert, Oona said to her, "Mrs. Buckley, you mustn't mind. Don't kick your husband. I've been kicking mine for thirty years, and it simply doesn't work.")

Chaplin was elated by the exchange and did splendid imitations of J. Edgar Hoover, General Eisenhower, Allen Dulles, and Hitler. To everyone's surprise he announced that he would join us at the *boîte* to which we were now headed—usually he went home before 11 P.M. Entering the little nightclub he was instantly spotted, and the orchestra switched directly to his theme song from *Limelight*. He felt the theatrical compulsion to requite the courtesy. He turned to me and said, "Have you ever seen a midget spotting a painting of a nude woman through the window of a gallery?" My answer was obvious: whereupon he turned, and diminished to one half his normal height.

His walking stick disappeared, and also his neck. His back to the audience, he began to weave, in time with the musical beat, as though straining before a store window, the better to see the pictures in the gallery. Suddenly he stopped. He had spotted the nubile lady! And, the better to see all of her, suddenly he began to grow. Beginning at about four feet tall, he grew to five, six, seven, eight feet. By dextrous use of the walking stick behind his cape, he seemed simply to elongate under the motive power of his lust. At no point, even at his tallest, was any flesh visible. The crowd went wild. He shrank back to normal size and, pleased with himself, said to me, "I learned that one doing vaudeville at age seventeen."

Mark and David liked that, and said it is a part of the cinematographical challenge to provide illusions pleasing to the eye and stimulating to the imagination. I threw a little cold water on it all, suggesting that a line had after all to be drawn—it was one thing to leave a dock three times, simulating a single departure; another to let someone fall overboard as though it had been accidental—and they both agreed. We reached no conclusions, other than that once under way, we would think about pixillation, Chaplinesque innovations, the whole bit. What happened after we got under way was that we were, for the most part, preoccupied with a) keeping the boat safe and on course, and b) relieving poor David of his awful seasickness.

One reason for my excitement, when celestial navigation time came around, was that this would be the debut of the Hewlett-Packard 41C computer. In due course I shall tell about Plath's marvelous Navicomp, which in its own way is preeminent. But one exciting feature of the new 41C, for which the designers had yet to issue a Navigational Package, was the alphanumeric feature of it. The word you have just read means that the computer will talk to you not only in digits, but in letters.

I am so fortunate as to have, for a very close friend, Hugh Kenner. He is a genius who lives now with his second wife, Mary Anne (Mary Jo, R.I.P. 1964); the author of a dozen books, probably best known of which is *The Pound Era*. He has actually published a book on tetrahedrons, if I have correctly designated whatever it is that Buckminster Fuller invented, or was it geodesic domes? And, unsatisfied merely to be perhaps the foremost literary critic in North America (he is Canadian), he is as much at home with computers as in Joyce's Dublin. I told him that Ken Newcomer, the scientific whiz kid at H-P, would not be doing a Nav-Pac in time for my crossing—and so Hugh, not quite knowing, I now imagine, what he was getting into, volunteered himself to program a Nav-Pac for me. I was stunned. This meant that he would need to program the geographical position of the sun, the moon, the stars, and as many planets as he had time for, for every second of every day during the month of June. Gallantly he went about it, and weeks later he confessed that he had devoted 120 hours to the project. But the great night came for the demonstration. I had lectured in Baltimore, the three of us had dined, and we were now in his house. He brought forth the 41C, smiling.

He handed it to me. "Let us take a problem involving the sun. Okay?" He brought out a copy of *Airborne*, in which, while illustrating the mechanics of celestial navigation, I give a hypothetical problem based on our crossing in 1975, but here I substitute from the *Sealestial*'s log.

He depressed a button in the hand-sized computer, in the top right-hand corner. Across the display section I saw:

"SUN"

This was by way of reminding you that you had summoned that program, not a different one. The "SUN" stayed lit for one second, whereupon it was replaced by:

"GMT?"

This may strike the layman as curt, even indecipherable. To anyone with any experience at all in celestial navigation its meaning is as self-evident as a red light to a motorist. It is saying to you:

"What time was it in Greenwich, England, at the time you took your sight?"

Greenwich Mean Time (GMT) is the anchor time with reference to which the positions of the sun and the planets are given. If, for instance, the sun is at 000°, it is directly over the meridian that runs through Greenwich. If it is at 180°, it is halfway across the globe while at Greenwich it's midnight. All navigational tables are based on GMT. Inasmuch as the sun moves 15 degrees in one hour (in navigation, the earth is visualized as static; everything else "moves"), if you live in New York (longitude 74 degrees) you live in Zone 5, and in order to calculate GMT, you must add five hours to your local watch hour (LWH).

The machine's question mark indicates its desire to know the time at which you recorded your sextant sight. That time was written down by a friendly member of the crew when you called out, "Mark!"

You punch in the time—16 58 37 (4:58 P.M., plus 37 seconds)—and depress the key marked R/S, which is the activating key. Whereupon you see:

"HS?"

That means, "What was the angle at which you caught the sun?"

("H" stands for "Height"; "S" for "Sextant.") You punch out 59 (degrees) 52 (minutes). Whereupon you see:

"UPP? YES = 1"

The machine is asking you whether you measured from the horizon to the *bottom* or to the *top* of the sun. Most navigators measure to the bottom of the sun but the tables allow for either—sometimes the bottom is clouded over, not so the top; in which case you will go for the latter. The machine assumes you went for the bottom, but if the answer to the question "Did you go for the UPPER?" is "YES," then you are directed to depress the numeral 1, advising the machine it must make the appropriate alterations. Since you did *not* go for the upper, you bypass by pushing, once again, R/S.

"LAT? S="

The machine wishes to know what is your assumed latitude. All celestial navigation is based, as elsewhere explained, on the process of exclusion: i.e., you figure out where you are by the process of figuring out where you are *not*.* You take as your assumed latitude the most convenient point from which to plot—a good round number. In this case, a flat 37 degrees. But wait—"s=": this is to remind you that if you are sailing in the southern hemisphere, you must record your latitude and then follow it by the minus sign for the computer, which is CHS (for "Change Sign"). But you are north, so you ignore this, entering merely 37 00. You activate the machine and now see:

"LONG? E="

The machine of course needs also your assumed longitude, in this case a round 43 degrees. The "E=" is to ask whether you are sailing in the eastern hemisphere, in which event once again you will need to follow your entry with the minus sign (CHS). You enter the longitude and activate, and see:

"YEAR?"

This needs very little translation. The answer is "1980."

"MONTH?"

Months are given numerically, and June is the sixth month of the year so you depress 6. . . . .

"DAY?"

It happened to be the thirteenth. 13. . . . .

"H. EYE?"

The angle of the observed body is obviously going to change, depending on whether you are one foot above the water when you take your sight or one thousand feet (the higher up, the larger the angle). You figure, standing alongside the cockpit, you are approximately ten feet up from the water: 10.

Now Hewlett-Packard provides what looks like a tiny seagull. It makes its way fitfully across the viewing screen. Its exclusive function is to tell you that the machine is hard at work for you, assimilating all the data you have given it. Most machines (the Almighty Plath—see below—included) merely give you a blank while you await the result of the calculation. Giving you the flying bird

* *Beard-McKie:* "Latitude and Longitude: *A series of imaginary lines on the earth's surface drawn at intervals parallel to the Equator (latitude) or the poles (longitude) as an aid to navigation. Since they are invisible, many mariners find them of limited usefulness.*"

Bringing down the moon.

is the equivalent of giving you recorded music when you call United Airlines and a voice says, "All the reservation lines are busy. Kindly stay on the line, and an operator will be with you shortly." Followed by music. You are reminded, as long as you hear the music, that you haven't been cut off. In seconds, the bird reaches its destination, and now the display reads:

"ZN 250.1"

That means that you must go to your assumed position, which was Latitude 37° North, Longitude 44° West, and strike out in the direction of 250°—child's play with a protractor or a parallel rule. By way of orientation, you will recall that 180 degrees is due south, 270 degrees is due west. But, you ask, head 250° for how long? Depress your trusty activator, R/S:

"15.8 AWAY"

"AWAY" means that your pencil must travel in *the opposite direction* of 250 degrees (i.e., 70 degrees. The "reciprocal" of any azimuth is that azimuth plus 180 degrees. If by adding 180 degrees you break the bank, defined as going past 360 degrees, then instead of adding 180 degrees, you subtract 180 degrees). You know now not only the exact direction you must travel, but how far: namely, 15.8 miles. Call it 16 miles. Measure (with a divider) sixteen miles and put a dot on the line extending from your assumed position northeast at 70 degrees. Then draw a line perpendicular to where that dot sits on the line you have drawn. That new line is your Line of Position (LOP).

All celestial navigation is based on the accumulation of Lines of Position. When they intersect, you know your position exactly. If, for instance, as often is the case, the moon is also discernible, depress the button that brings in the moon on your computer and repeat the procedure above. You have two lines of position intersecting.

Hugh Kenner's program includes all the navigational stars, and these are of course (assuming no overcast) simultaneously visible against the horizon for about ten minutes beginning forty minutes before dawn, and for about ten minutes beginning about thirty minutes after sunset. Set the LOPs for two stars, and you have your position.

It's difficult to convey the kind of excitement a celestial navigator experiences with such a machine in hand (later, as I say, a machine in some respects more advanced is described, the Plath

The miraculous Hewlett-Packard 41C programmable computer.

Navicomp). I attempted in an earlier book (*Airborne*) to use a metaphor to describe the pleasure of celestial navigation without almanac and tables, but even that recently the instrument (the HP-65) was preposterously primitive alongside the 41C, whose Nav-Pac by H-P's Ken Newcomer will be available when these words are printed. I can only say that if you are one of the millions who kiss your wife, open the front door in the country, walk out, take your car out of the garage, park it at the station, take the train to Grand Central, take the subway downtown, and walk into your office on lower Broadway one hour and twenty minutes later, you would need to conceive of kissing your wife, opening your front door, and finding yourself *in* your office on lower Broadway to conceive the liberation from tedium given to the navigator by the calculator. With such an instrument as the HP-41C I would undertake to teach celestial navigation to Laurel and Hardy in fifteen minutes.

The great moment came, my first use at sea of the 41C, and as I had coached Danny, serving as assistant navigator, on its use, I asked him to bring it up. Five minutes later (for Danny, five minutes is a geological age—in five minutes he can prepare a meal, eat it, and clean up the mess) he arrived at the cockpit, forlorn.

"What's the matter?" I knew it had to be grave.

"It doesn't work. It just plain won't turn on."

I had him fetch up Hugh's instructions, as unambiguous as a draft notice. I read them out loud. It was as simple as that when Danny pushed the "on" button, *nothing happened.* I knew that if we removed the memory module, the program would be lost forever. I called for Reggie, he took the machine in hand and started gently poking. His finger brushed the *"alpha"* key—and the display signal instantly blazoned out: "SUN." It worked perfectly ever after, but I came close to growing old during those moments.

Other problems did not yield to Reggie's numinous fingers, nor yet to the solid, patient, seductive ministrations of Allen Jouning who—the nearest anyone ever came to hearing Allen yield to exasperation—muttered to me, through the half-dozen nuts, bolts, screws, between his teeth, "Had more problems, pahst coupla days, than pahst six months!" Characteristically, Allen said this rather joyfully than complainingly, as though to be greeted at 6 A.M., as that same day he had been, with the news that *both* the central toilets were stuck with an evening's accumulated evacuations was a perfect (Oh man! A problem to solve!) way to begin the day.

It requires only one weighted sentence to communicate the gravity of a nonfunctioning radiotelephone. The radio is the means by which, *in extremis*, one electrifies the impalpable but omnipresent ocean grid to one's distress. Our phone worked once, two nights out. A call from me to my wife. As a collective social occasion the call, when it finally came through, caused me considerable personal amusement, recalling the high moment of personal mortification in my adult life. For reasons no one professionally engaged in the engineering of radiotelephones has ever given me, telephones aboard yachts are megaphones. I cannot understand why the signal from the telephone can't come in via earset, so that the conversation, to the extent it is overheard by the crew, mightn't at least give some privacy, as in:

"Hello, darling. OVER." (audible)

"Don't hello-darling me, you bastard. I know all about Flo. OVER." (inaudible)

"Oh, well what do you know! How *is* my goddaughter?" (audible)

"Who the hell do you think you're fooling? Goddaughter—sheeyit; I *suppose* you're having a good time. How many girls do you have aboard your 'men-only' cruise?" (inaudible)

"Ho ho ho! That's wonderful. Well, do give her *my* love also. Oh-oh, have to cut out—trouble with the . . . line . . . hello, hello? . . . This is Whiskey Oscar George 9842, Whiskey Oscar George 9842, signing off. Thank you operator."

Nothing, of course, went that way. But when the radiotelephone is situated at or near the center of the boat, as is usually the case, there is no such thing as a *private* conversation. No public conversation is, really, emotionally satisfactory. "Try to get me on Flight one-oh-one on the twenty-ninth, Iberia, Marbella–New York" is okay; nothing much tenderer than that. Still, you document that you are alive.

Finally I reached my wife. After the two-hour effort to make the connection on the deteriorating radio, I counted eleven sets of ears that could, and necessarily did, overhear our conversation, which accordingly took the form of Basic Social Exchange ("Christopher is fine. And how is Van?").

Eight years earlier I was at the South Pole. What was I doing at the South Pole? No answer to that question, really, satisfies any reasonable curiosity. The fact is, I was there, at the solitary Russian outpost. (In the treaty, "they" drew Magnetic South Pole, "we" drew True South Pole, 1,700 miles away.) And, fifteen minutes after festivities (caviar, vodka) had begun in the Russians' central igloo, Senator Barry Goldwater, premier virtuoso of the ham radio community, walked in, dressed in the swaddling clothes of the Antarctic. He was on the wagon, and so was not distracted by the general jollity in that tiny frozen little encampment of thirteen souls who hadn't had visitors for six months, visitors whose airplane's motors you could hear even in the ice cellar because the propellers continued to turn—one daren't turn the motors off, lest in the 50° below zero cold they should fail to start up again when the time came, ninety minutes later, to return to headquarters at McMurdo Base. Goldwater turned to me, all smiles.

"Just talked to Peggy."

"You don't mean it?"

"Want to talk to Pat?"

"You mean *I* can call Pat from *here?*"

"Follow me," said Barry, while the toasting proliferated, and beckoning to two other members of the party we slunk out, through the cold and the squeaky snow, to the private little igloo, fifty feet away, of a young American scientist whose avocation was also ham radio. He spent the day measuring the isotopes 29,000 feet below the earth, or whatever else it is one finds interesting at 29,000 feet below the earth, and the evenings patching in ham telephone calls to his wife and little daughter. Would he ring my wife?

"Sure try, Mr. Buckley."

An incredible six minutes later, in that padded little ice station, with the scientist, Senator Goldwater, one admiral, the Secretary of the Navy, and one warrant officer present, I heard the telephone ring.

"Hello . . ."

"Is this Mrs. William Buckley?"

"Yes. Who are you?"

"I'm patching a call from Orange Kalamazoo Igloo Zingping. Will you accept a collect call from Harrisburg, Pennsylvania, from Mr. Buckley?"

"Mr. Buckley isn't in Harrisburg, Pennsylvania. He is off somewhere in the Antarctic."

"I know, ma'am. I'm patching in the call. All you have to pay for is Harrisburg–Connecticut. Will you accept the call?"

"Yes."

"Go ahead, Orange Kalamazoo Igloo Zingping. Come in, Mr. Buckley."

"Hello darling!" I said trying to imagine how Bertie Wooster would try to sound under the circumstances.

"Do you realize what time it is?"

"I'm calling from the South Pole!"

"It is four o'clock in the morning. When you go to the South Pole, do you need to go at four o'clock in the morning?"

"Ho ho ho"—I looked around, and the senator, and the admiral, and the secretary, and the radio operator, and the warrant officer, were making valiant efforts to affect total ignorance of an exchange they could not have avoided hearing unless stone deaf. "Well, darling, just wanted to say hello. The connection is awful, so I'll have to sign off. *Thank you, Harrisburg, Pennsylvania.*"—I thrust the receiver into the hands of the scientist, who completed the formalities.

Grant, then, that conversations of an intimate nature are encumbered in small vessels crossing the seas. But there would be nothing intimate about such a message as: "MAYDAY MAYDAY MAYDAY. This is the yacht *Sealestial*. We are on fire and sinking. Request all assistance from ships at sea. Our estimated position is Latitude 32 degrees 30 minutes north, Longitude 64 degrees 10 minutes west" (you repeat this, over and over again, pausing every two minutes for thirty seconds, hoping desperately to hear an acknowledgment).

In any event, the radiotelephone, after that one conversation to my wife, simply didn't work, and the pooled talents of Reggie, Allen, Dick, and Tony were insufficient to put it back together again. There is a little curtain—gossamer-stuff, but a curtain nonetheless—that closes when your boat loses all radio contact. The flywheel within you that has gone along chirpily, well lubricated, works now with a sense of contingency that brings to every problem the slight edge of crisis. In the mind of every sailor there is an automatic table by which the escalation, or, more accurately, the graduation, of crisis is processed. When you are plowing through the seas and they are a menacing gray, fleeced with altarboy white lace, the knot meter registering 9.5, every twelfth wave ripping down the lee deck like the flick of a whip over a mule team, you know, without ratiocination, that Man Overboard is Man Lost. When the radiophone doesn't work, you know that certain kinds of emergencies at sea—a fire, most prominently; a capsize, of course—are more menacing in their terrifying reaches. We did have aboard—part of Reggie's mandatory safety equipment—a contraption designed for life rafts which is guaranteed to emit, for seventeen hours, signals that would reach the radios of passing aircraft over an area of 400 square miles. Such a device would easily work to permit triangulation on an object in distress; and, of course, the device could be activated not necessarily from a life raft, but from a disabled 71-foot ketch—one whose mast, let us say, had been toppled, and whose engine had been swamped. . . . So travels the imagination; and, at sea, one doesn't incline—far from it—to gallows-talk, though there was spirited discussion, this time, on the tortured experience of the yachts that had participated in the previous summer's Fastnet Race. Fifteen drownings, twenty-four yachts lost. Late at night, once or twice on this run, the waves roared by like express trains, leaving you (even after thirty years of sailing) with that surrealistic sensation of immunity. The juggernaut has failed to topple you. Like the nightmare, a pleasant nightmare, in which you traverse the speedway down which the racing cars are hurtling, and—somehow—you walk casually, without particular plan, right across the track, this one just failing to hit you from behind, the other just failing to knock you in the stomach as you make your way nonchalantly through. But in such situations, every now and then you find yourself rehearsing, either in your mind or in conversations with such as Van—he likes to know everything—Just What Would We Do If. . . . It is engrossing, the more so if the radiotelephone is withdrawn as a contingent resource.

In his journal, Dick made perfunctory note of our radiotelephone problem. This was sheer stoicism on his part, since he is given to spending significant parts of the day on the telephone. He weathered, even, the Weathermax crisis. This one was, primarily, a crisis of pride. Dr. Papo had said, at the beginning of our negotiations, that he would not think of dispatching his beautiful $650,000 ketch across the Atlantic without the advantages of a Weathermax, which after all was now available at something on the order of five thousand dollars.

A Weathermax is a most remarkable instrument, the only problem being that, in my experience, it seldom works. My sailing is usually done on the relatively indigent side of the track, and in my own boats I never dreamed of such luxuries as Weathermax, or Omega navigation. But in 1977, sailing from the Dominican Republic to New York on the Argentinian cadet ship *Libertad*, a magnificent 360-foot three-masted schooner, I was introduced for the first time to the Weathermax, which proudly puffed out a four-foot-square silver-paper isobar map of the entire Atlantic Ocean indicating exactly where the highs and lows were, and inviting attention to those little telltale signs of hurricanes abrewing —especially interesting at the end of August, which was both hurricane season and the period during which the *Libertad* sailed north on this leg of its six-month journey. The problem was that, after that first demonstration, the Weathermax didn't work again. Nor, as a matter of fact, did the Omega navigation system, although the admiral was wonderfully proud of having it on board, and enjoyed greatly telling you what it would do when it *did* work.

The *Sealestial*'s Weathermax didn't work at all, ever. Somewhere along the line I ceased asking after it, as one would, say, after a dozen years cease to ask Allen how was his arthritis this morning, if the first hundred exercises in solicitude drew the identical response. We Omitted Mention of Dr. Papo's Weathermax.

What else? It is, in an enumeration that began with the subject of survival, embarrassing to recall: but beyond any question this was the one serious crisis we *all* felt. We were matter-of-factly informed, three days out of the Virgin Islands, that for all intents and purposes the *Sealestial* was not merely short of ice, as Dick had written, but out of ice.

Dick and I were on watch when Diane gave us the news. I take longer than Dick to externalize True Shock. He was at least thirty seconds ahead of me when I heard him say, "What do you *mean* we're out of ice?" Diane has one of those matter-of-fact voices, as in, "Sorry, we're out of blood plasma."

"We can't make our own ice in the deep freeze," she explained, "because it's full, and the extra supply of ice we brought on board has melted."

Dick and I looked at each other. It wasn't necessary to say anything. We were wired to the same circuit, and the shock passed through us simultaneously.

I said—I was, remember, commander-in-chief—"We have to do something."

That meant we called Reggie. Hours later we had arranged a kind of commutation system. The meat, chicken, lobster, and other extraneous stowaways in the deep freeze were taken out for just so long. Just so long was defined as that interval that a) kept the meat, chicken, and lobster from deteriorating permanently; and b) permitted the energy of the deep freeze to devote itself to the fabricating of just enough ice to fill our evening's cups. Fine tuning, of the kind Walter Heller writes about, was called for; but it was not beyond Dick's and my resources, not when faced with such an awful alternative. I engaged my companions in a flashback, about which I had very nearly forgotten, though at the time it had totally absorbed me.

It was 1958, and the Spanish Ambassador to the United States, a close friend, called me at my office with the information that he needed most desperately to speak to me privately on a matter of august importance. Seeing me is relatively easy, even on matters of non-august importance, and an hour later José María de Areilza, Count of Motrico, Ambassador from Spain to Washington, now President of the Council of Europe, was in my tatterdemalion office at *National Review* explaining the nature of his crisis.

As I knew, he said (I had been at the reception the night before), the Count of Barcelona, a.k.a. Don Juan, King (uncrowned) of Spain, was in New York, having sailed (he is a great yachtsman) from Lisbon to Puerto Rico to Washington—where he was received by President Eisenhower, the okay having been given, via Areilza, from Franco—to New York, where he was currently being lionized.

The problem, the ambassador explained, looking at his watch, is that this is Tuesday, and at noon on Saturday Franco has scheduled a speech on the subject of succession. It is a speech deemed *so* important, we cannot expose the King to the dangers of impromptu reflections on it in response to questions by the press.

"Therefore," said José María, dramatically, "the King must be 'absent' from the United States when the speech is made."

"Well," I said, "where's he headed? Bermuda?"

"Yes. But the *Saltillo* is not fit to sail. It needs substantial reparations. You know the boatyard people in Connecticut. You must take his boat to the boatyard tomorrow, arrange for the necessary repairs, and hide out the King and his crew until after Saturday morning—he estimates repairs will take one week. They will wave goodbye to the press from the pier at Seventy-ninth Street [at the Hudson River] as though they were setting out for Bermuda, but you will pilot them around Manhattan, up the East River, to Stamford, and hide them out. Say you will, my dear Bill."

I found the invitation not only enticing, but positively Grau-starkian. The next morning, however, I was off to a very bad start, having misread the current charts in such a way as to ordain a cast-off time that had us in the East River not floating with the current, but fighting a foul current approximately equal to the engine power of the *Saltillo*. I tried to joke about how one should cruise slowly up the East River the better to enjoy Manhattan, and fortunately the King was well-disposed, and rather enjoyed my awful miscalculation: but it was only when the King offered me a gin and tonic that I saw my advantage.

"Sorry I can't offer you any ice," he said.

I made bold to say, "Why not, sir?"

"Because," Don Juan said resignedly, "the *Saltillo* carries one ice chest, and it lasts approximately four hours. We are out of ice."

I drew the King of Spain to me, and whispered in his ear. Five hours later we were docked at Stamford, the royal ensign carefully concealed, even against the unlikelihood of its being recognized by a reporter from the Stamford *Advocate*. My wife and my son Christopher (aged five) welcomed the royal party, and I think it fair to say that seven days later, the repairs to the *Saltillo* having been effected, Don Juan departed crying bitter tears at leaving Pat to whom—as also the British admiral-navigator, the first mate, the young Count of Alcazar, the sundry younger officers, including one bearded lieutenant who spent the whole of his time on the telephone to Jane Fonda mooning his eternal devotion to her—he had become totally attached. He invited us both to sail with him as far as Bermuda, but my schedule prevented it and, fortunately, Pat declined, because the *Saltillo* ran into a most fearful storm, very nearly foundering.

But the great excitement was the refrigerator. I had told the King, in the desolation of the East River, that conceivably I might arrange the installation of an ice-making refrigerator on the *Saltillo*, which would absolutely alter his way of life in the forthcoming 3,500-mile sail. He couldn't believe it was true, but I went ahead and had it done at City Island, notwithstanding that the installation required the dismembering of the entire companionway, a decision that was slightly less easy to make than merely through an indulgence of royal caprice, inasmuch as the *Saltillo* belonged not to Don Juan, but to a close friend of Don Juan, or at least I hope he was a close friend, because the configuration of his boat was substantially and permanently altered.

In any event, that was 1958, twenty-two years before we of the *Sealestial* ran out of ice. They talk of entropy, of exhausted planets, of closed frontiers; none of these satisfied Dick or me, and we resolved that come what might, we would not run out of ice. I realized then that no thought had been given to the major challenge, leg number two, Bermuda to the Azores, twice the distance of St. Thomas to Bermuda. If we were to run out of ice after five hundred miles on the first leg, how would we make do on a two-thousand-mile second leg? I summoned Danny and Reggie, and advised them that first priority must be given to that problem on reaching Bermuda. They understood. They always understand, when a situation is *truly grave.*

The heavy winds came, and went. It is good that this should happen, as one thereupon feels baptized. Speaking of which, on the Sunday morning before the winds I was at the helm, and Danny approached me and said did I want to do something "about its being Sunday." I said I did, that we could go to my stateroom, that I had brought a Bible on board, and also the text my colleague Bill Rusher had given me of the communion service at his Anglican church. That conversation had come about after my telling him on my return from South Bend, Indiana, that I had not in my lifetime been so moved as by the liturgy in the ordination of my old—in every sense of the word: I have known him for thirty years, and he is seventy-two—friend, Professor Gerhart Niemeyer of Notre Dame, as an Anglican priest. Perhaps it was the sight of a septuagenarian lying on the floor, the whole of his body covered by white cloth, pledging a lifetime's devotion to the work of God; but also the noble language, in such archaic relief over the Dick-Jane-Gypese with which the Roman Catholics have profaned their language, at least in America. The Bible I had brought along was the King James, and I told Danny I would scan it for a few suitable passages.

It pleased me hugely that Danny should bring the matter up, because in the interval since our last sail across the Atlantic he had been divorced, and now lives unabashedly with a sweet and intelligent girl. Danny and I—the best of friends, given the generation gap, since he evolved at age twelve as my son's closest companion even though Christopher was a mere ten—have talked everything over, including religion. He used to write me long letters, a practice that ended eight or nine years ago. But he remains one of the very few people I feel I could approach in the spirit with which then-Monsignor Fulton Sheen once approached Heywood Broun, a total stranger, on the telephone. ("I would like to talk to you, Mr. Broun." "What about?" the famous iconoclast asked gruffly. "Your immortal soul," Monsignor Sheen answered, a few months before receiving Broun back into the church.)

Looking about, it occurred to me that our little extemporaneous Sunday service would end up being rather exclusive. Dick is Jewish-agnostic; Tony's journal contains an agnostic inflection; Van manages to stay clear of the subject but, *pace* the exhibitionist iconoclasm of a Mark Twain or Henry Mencken, as is true of most men of great humor not grounded in cynicism, there is piety there somewhere. I could not invite the crew—there would be no way to make the gesture without intimidation. Only Reggie would react naturally and spontaneously. The last time he and I had bowed our heads in unison was at his wedding, when I served as best man, almost two years earlier, at which he and his beautiful, vivacious, imperious southern divorcée with four children plighted their troth, till death should tear them asunder. A year and a half later she had flown to the Dominican Republic, where troths can be unplighted in a single day. Reggie had told me a few days earlier, at St. Thomas, that he could not yet spend one entire day without thinking of her. I would, without singling him out, find a prayer of a quite comprehensive sort, importuning providence for the contentment of everyone aboard. But that afternoon the storm came in, and the service went clear out of our minds.

Two days before landing, the weather having settled down, I had a sudden and entirely unforeseen access of literary energy, and fished out of my briefcase a sorely neglected commission from *Esquire* magazine—to write about someplace I had never been, one thousand words. If I wrote it now, Dick could take it to New York! . . . It was five, and the wind semitropical on the flesh, but cool enough to ward off torpor, and the boat moved serenely, as if on ice skates, the angle of heel absolutely steady. I went below and zipped it off, bringing it up fresh from the typewriter to show Dick, who loves better than anything in life to see manuscripts, and for good reason, because he is a peerless editor and knows, in most cases (I have one exception in mind), what works and what doesn't. I wrote:

> . . . I have never been to Heaven. Please note the capital letter. Ten years ago Ralph de Toledano wrote a novel in which he capitalized the word and also the word Hell, wherever they appeared; and always the copy editor would return his manuscript with the initial letters in lower case. Painstakingly, Toledano would recapitalize them. And so it went until, exasperated, the copy editor scribbled a note: "Why do you insist on capitalizing heaven and hell?" "Because," Toledano replied, "they're places. You know, like Scarsdale."
>
> To describe the Heaven of my fantasy requires a series of negations, principal among them that Heaven is a place where you cannot be unhappy. When I was a schoolboy, we heard, during a three-day Lenten retreat, from an amiable old Jesuit who ruminated on a friend of his, a widowed lady of advanced years who had said to him, "Father, do dogs go to Heaven? Because if my Fido can't go to Heaven, I shan't be happy there."
>
> "I told her," the priest explained, "that if it were true that she would not be happy in Heaven save in the company of Fido, then she could absolutely be confident that Fido would go to Heaven."
>
> You will see that there is a sizable jesuitical banana peel there, lest the priest commit an enthymeme, which for a Jesuit is a cardinal sin. You begin a) with the proposition that you will be happy. If b) for this you need Fido, Fido will be there; on the other hand, c) perhaps it will prove that you can be happy *without* Fido, even though you do not now know this. The Jesuit was sophisticatedly, but not sophistically, stating that his friend should perhaps consider the possibility of happiness without Fido.
>
> Christianity tells us about the resurrection of the body. This is at once reassuring (one gets used to one's body), and distracting (bodies need a great deal of maintenance, particularly when

the time comes to die). One must assume that the only way to square that circle is to contrive a maintenance-free body, and that is the responsibility of the Lord, not of Elizabeth Arden health centers, or the Mayo Clinic. So, in my fantasy, I leave the problem to Him, with full confidence.

The editor inquires, "How does the architecture look, what does the food taste like, how does the place smell and what about the people?" Well, let's take that last question, which is the most delicate, first. Is Heaven crowded? Or is there a divine metabolism that prevents that overpopulation about which Margaret Sanger and Dr. Malthus were so concerned? I pen these words in a small craft with ten souls aboard, and there is a sense here of crowding, because you can walk only 71 feet from stem to stern, only 18 feet from beam to beam. In the intimate sense of the word, there *is* a little crowding. On the other hand, it is probably safe to say that there aren't ten more people within one hundred miles of us in any direction. (Oh, sure, there is the random freighter. But we are not in a shipping lane, and we haven't spotted a vessel in four days.) In that odd way, there is totally absent *any* sense of crowding. Here I think is something that touches on a divine dialectic: intimacy without crowding. Mustn't it be better yet in Heaven than here, midway between St. Thomas and Bermuda?

This begs, of course, the question, who the people are with whom you are intimate. But from this exercise I am saved by the injunction that I judge not, lest I be judged. To be sure, it is axiomatic to this fantasy that *I* have been judged and, after sitting it out in the cooler for a few millennia, admitted. What then happens, surely, is that the people there, while not losing their flavor, manage somehow to lose that about them which once made them—human. They are transfigured, by the central energy; and so you find sweetness that does not cloy, argument that does not vex, humor that does not lacerate, work that does not tire. The oxymoronization of life, the use of which word may jeopardize my chances of making it to Heaven.

But isn't that an appealing fantasy? And if this is possible, then doesn't it follow that the least likeliest people can make it there? Oh, not Giovanni—it would be a theatrical disaster to pass through the gates and stumble over Don Giovanni—but . . . well, we all know one or two people whose presence in Heaven would surprise us. But in the nature of things, that surprise would turn out to be a delight. Right? And anyway, this is my fantasy, over which I am sovereign.

As to the food, well: food is a sensual pleasure, so we may as well lump all the sensual pleasures together, and face *that* problem. Would we eat if we had no appetite? If we had no appetite, would this be because, as on earth, our organs are not functioning properly? No sir, it wouldn't be that, not at all. You will not be hungry because you are sated. Not sated in the Neronic sense; sated as St. Francis was sated merely by looking out at nature. Even here on earth there are moments when you are not hungry and would reject the pleasures of cuisine— because you are, simply, too content. Would you hail the Good Humor man while listening to Flagstad singing the Liebestod? But that brings perhaps a tougher question: will there be music? Music is my Fido. If ever I harbored a blasphemous thought it was that Heaven without J. S. Bach would leave the carper with something to say for earth. But, of course, it cannot be. The Jesuit, in disposing of the problem of Fido, disposed of the problem of Bach: either he will be there—or we won't want to hear him.

Architecture? Well, how about many (stately) mansions? Isn't there authority for that . . . metaphor? I shall conceive of Heaven as containing stately mansions. If you don't like stately mansions, the beauty of what I'm talking about is that you don't have to quit Heaven: I won't be there to say to you: "Love it or leave it." You just won't *see* any stately mansions. But I will. Did you ever see a dream walking? Well, I did.

We come then to the dynamo in my fantasy. Well, the major poets, with maybe one or two exceptions, have described Him, and I shan't try. But it is part of the rules that you cannot succeed in describing that fantasy: For it is written, Eye hath not seen, nor ear heard, neither have entered into the heart of man, the things which God hath prepared for them that love Him. I understand this to mean that a No Trespassing sign has gone up for the fantasist, and I for one intend to observe it.

We would come in, I calculated, sometime near dawn the following day. When you do a lot of navigation, particularly if you are incorrigibly sloppy concerning detail—a problem that has plagued me all my life (my father reached the point of terminal despair over my penmanship when I was fifteen and ordered a typewriter to be sent to me, along with instructions that I was never again to address him in longhand)—you are often rescued from grave error by needling instinct. I had set course for Bermuda, and my logbook gave the longitude of St. George's at 64 degrees 24 minutes. At this point we were about one hundred miles south of there, so that I put aside the plotting sheet and pulled out a large-scale chart that shows the actual island of Bermuda. I then extended the rhumb line as drawn on the plotting sheet and found it rising north merrily, passing Bermuda about thirty miles east of the island.

How in the name of *God* could that have happened? And so, in navigation, you start the process: the patient retracing of your steps, one after the other to see where you went wrong. It was a full ten minutes before it occurred to me to measure the longitude of St. George's right there on the chart. It wasn't 64–24. It was 64–42.

I thundered at Danny, who came loping down to the navigator's desk. We embarked on an act of total reconstruction.

The figure written down in the logbook had been taken from the memorandum I sent out to the crew, reproduced above.

The coordinates of all the destinations of the passage had been read out by me from the New York Times Atlas, in my study in Stamford last January, to Danny—who wrote down the figures in my notebook and then, for convenience, dictated them back to me when I composed the memorandum.

Either he had spoken "64–24," and I had correctly transcribed what he said—the illegitimate seed that now, six months later, had germinated as a real possibility that we would bypass Bermuda altogether—or Danny had read out the *correct* figures, and *I* had made the inversion.

Whose was the mistake?

There was one way to tell: Danny had written down the penciled coordinates, from my dictation, in the notebook that lay in a bundle of papers in my stateroom.

I looked up at Danny's grave face, and winked.

"Let's agree," I said, "that neither of us will ever open that notebook to that page."

At this moment the notebook lies three feet from me. It is still virginal, and will remain so.

The very first thing you learn from ocean cruising is that when you spot a major light at landfall time, you are still hours away from your destination. The second thing you learn from ocean cruising is that you have forgotten the first thing you learned (note, above, our arrival in Yucatan). Year after year, decade after decade, I find myself bounding like a child toward Santa Claus on first spotting a light, grabbing the helm. Characteristically it is about six hours later that I leave it. At midnight, I reaffirmed the likelihood of spotting Gibbs Hill Light "at about dawn—5 A.M." I asked Reggie, who was relieving me, to wake me when the light was in sight. At 4:12 he did so, and I took the helm as we approached Bermuda, its pink blue green pastels gradually reifying as first twilight came, then dawn. By the time we rounded north opposite St. George's, it was after seven. We plodded on into the north channel, destination Hamilton where, at the wharf of the Princess Hotel, in the early morning blue, we threw out the docking lines at 9:30. When one lands, never mind the hour, one drinks—champagne, if it is handy. We had champagne, and so we popped open two or three bottles, and drank, slouched about the cockpit, ten feet below the hotel guests who, leaning over the railing, peered down at us, occasionally clicking a camera. One of them—a slim, dark young man clutching as if for life to his girl— honeymooners, Bermuda's June specialty—waved at me.

"Where did you sail in from?"

"St. Thomas," I said.

"Where's that?"

I wondered how should I put it. "East of Florida?" . . . "Near Puerto Rico?" . . . "North of Venezuela?" . . . "West of Antigua?" . . .

I said, "A thousand miles"—pointing—"down the line." The girl giggled. The boy giggled. I giggled.

7

~~~~~~~~~~~~~~~~~~~

Bermuda is something of a blur, though we stayed three days, the last day mostly for the convenience of Bob Halmi, who was determined to film some extra talk sequences in *Sealestial* which he thought Mark and David had neglected. And then he wanted some aerial shots of *Sealestial*, to which end he set out busily to rent an airplane. He found one, available at the dizzying cost of eight dollars per hour, including gas and pilot. The antique amphibian had been built sometime in the mid-thirties, and a veteran flier in Bermuda keeps it in tenuous operation: one of those biplanes with struts all over, open cockpits fore and aft, not ideal for movie-making because of the struts, which are ubiquitous. In addition to the airplane shots, there was to be a second session with a chase boat.

We had some serious business to attend to, notably the repair of the radiotelephone. Whenever I have problems in Bermuda, and I can't remember when I haven't had them—I have entered Bermuda by sail seven times—I go to Teddy Tucker. He is the most intriguing of men, learned, jolly, omnicompetent. He is made to order for *What's My Line?* because *his* line is discovering buried treasure, from which pursuit he has done nicely, thank you. He is available as an expert on any subject that touches the sea (Peter

Benchley dedicated *The Deep* to Teddy and his wife, Edna): one is always trying to think up ways of repaying his acute kindnesses. I knew Teddy because of Reggie. Reggie lived in Bermuda for a period and went to school with Teddy Tucker forty years ago. We had already asked Teddy, by mail, to get a carpenter to build some cradles for tanks of extra fuel.

Allen didn't think we really needed the extra fuel (the *Sealestial* burns only two gallons an hour, and carries 350 gallons, or enough for 175 hours of cruising; at seven knots, makes (175 × 7) 1,225 miles, or about 60 percent of the distance to Faial, our landfall in the Azores. Ah, I say, Yes, yes; but the answer to the suggestion that we proceed without the tanks is No, no. You see, once on *Cyrano* I ran out of wind and fuel thirty miles from Bermuda, and there is no exasperation to equal that exasperation; so Teddy and the carpenters arrived with the wooden cradles, and on the third day we loaded on four fifty-gallon drums. Good thing, as it happened, though without them we would actually have limped in— with about four gallons to spare. What would have been hell was the preceding three days, the fingernail-chewing period during which we'd have treated our diminishing fuel supply with exaggerated parsimony.

Then we had, of course, to solve the ice problem. The assignment was given to Reggie, and his report at the end of the afternoon, when we convened at our hotel suite to exchange information, was classic. You must understand that it is Reggie's style to speak very slowly, hesitantly, tentatively: in sixty seconds he can turn Dick Clurman into a churning mess. His report, faithfully transcribed, read something like this:

"There's no dry ice in Bermuda. . . . But they make dry ice in Canada. . . . They fly dry ice from Canada into Bermuda every third day. . . . The dry ice in Bermuda is used by the chorus girls. . . . Where? In the Cabaret. Here at the Princess. . . . You can't order dry ice from Canada unless it comes in to protect something—I mean, you can't just order 'dry ice.' . . . No, Bill, you can't order three hundred pounds of dry ice with an ice-cream cone inside. . . . What do the chorus girls use the dry ice for? . . . I couldn't figure it out, but it has something to do with the last act, when one of the girls goes up in smoke. . . . Dry ice releases a gas that can be made to look like smoke, if you shine the lights just right. . . . What does the dry ice from Canada for the show girls come in covering? I don't really know; I'll make a note to ask. I guess it comes in covering something, or maybe they've worked out some sort of exemption with Eastern Airlines. . . . How do we get the dry ice away from the chorus girls? . . . Well, I spoke to the manager about that. A very nice guy—we were in school together, we figured, though I don't actually remember him. He says that if we leave on Saturday after the last show, he can give us what's left of *Saturday's* ice because the next show isn't until *Monday*. . . . How much is left after a show? Well, they use the three hundred pounds for three shows, Thursday's, Friday's, Saturday's. They figure there's about half left, about a hundred and fifty pounds. . . . Will that last us till the Azores? . . . I figure yes, if we pack it just right . . . Danny and I will figure out just how to pack it—"

"Reggie! Danny! Stop! *Don't say another word!*" Once every year or so, I simply *assert myself:* "Will you both personally guarantee me that even if it takes fourteen days to get to the Azores, we'll have all the ice we need? I mean *guarantee?*"

Reggie's face was solemn as he raised his right hand. Danny was a little slower, but entering, as usual, into the spirit of the occasion, he raised his hand.

"I solemnly swear you will have ice," said Reggie.

"I solemnly swear you will have ice," said Danny.

"I solemnly swear I won't raise the question of ice again. All in favor?" Van, Christopher, and Tony solemnly raised their hands. We had a compact.

That night at dinner Teddy told us endless fascinating stories, eventually disconcerting his patient wife Edna, because his appetite to tell his stories got in the way of his appetite to eat the food that sat, getting old, on his plate. My absolute favorite involved a Russian freighter, though I suppose my delight should be mitigated by the near certainty that, as I write, the navigator of the freighter in question is off in Gulag. But the episode couldn't have happened to a nicer country. Teddy's story recalled my own memory . . .

I had a friend called Carl, who used to sail with us regularly. He was a shipmate of exact, entirely unfocused, intelligence. If you gave him a line and told him *on no account* to release it, he would hold on to it even if his old aunt fell overboard and he alone—at the cost of temporarily releasing the line—could toss her a life preserver: boy-stood-on-the-burning-deck stuff. Once, coming down Buzzards Bay after an entire night on the helm, I gave him a course of 260 degrees and asked him to hold it while I snatched a couple of hours' sleep. It was midafternoon, bright as Holly-wood Bowl, when I was awakened by the unmistakable shock of yacht-running-smack-into-rocks. I bounded up to the cockpit and found us aground. The rocks we had hit were not submerged. They rose six feet above the water. I had made a terrible mistake. My instructions to Carl should have been: "Follow a course of 260 degrees until you see a rock. When you see that rock, go 240 degrees until you have passed the rock. *Then* go back to 260 degrees."

Well (Teddy with great amusement reminisced), this here Russian navigator was using plotting sheets, sailing from the Baltic to the Gulf of Mexico. Plotting sheets are squares of paper marked with horizontal lines, each one representing one degree of latitude. You draw in the vertical lines, representing the meridians of longi-tude, spacing them apart to correspond to the distance between meridians at those particular latitudes—as simple as applying your divider to the little graph printed at the bottom right-hand corner of every plotting sheet. What this does is save you thousands of charts of empty stretches of ocean, which after all you don't need.

Provided there isn't an obstruction in the area.

Bermuda is an obstruction. It is, in fact, one enormity of an ob-struction—as thousands of vessels, beginning in 1515 when Juan de Bermúdez first ran into the magic island and its surrounding coral bed, have discovered: incidentally providing, centuries down the line, for the financial security of Teddy Tucker. But the Russian navigator, laying out his plotting sheets from the British Channel to the Straits of Florida, clean forgot about Bermuda, so that one night in March this great big boat was coasting on down toward Florida, with a couple of million dollars' worth of cargo—I forget just what: gold, copper, spies—when suddenly the boat hit—Ber-muda. Well, not exactly; but they hit the reefs off Bermuda, and were most thoroughly grounded. (As I live and breathe, the sen-tence I just finished typing was interrupted by a shudder, fol-lowed by a thud. I ran out of my cabin, to learn that we had been rammed. I am writing this book while cruising around South America, Rio to Valparaiso. A freighter, Panamanian registry, at the last minute decided to pass us port to port, cutting across our bow. I deduce from the shudder that our boat, the Delta Line's *Santa María*, either veered to starboard to expedite clearance and ran aground, or went into reverse. Something caused the shudder preceding the moment of impact. Both vessels are under the command of pilots. We are eight miles from Buenos Aires, in that long channel opposite Montevideo. More precisely, directly opposite where Hitler's beloved *Graf Spee* was hunted down and scuttled in 1939. We are proceeding on our way. The tort-feasor appears dim on the horizon. Perhaps it can't turn around due to a falling tide. (Beard-McKie: "*Collision:* Unexpected contact between one boat and another. As a rule, collisions that result in the creation of two smaller and less seaworthy vessels from the hull of one are thought to be the most serious.")

Teddy said his team had had to blast a ditch along an entire mile astern of the freighter, to make it possible to drag it back to flotation level. One tug was brought in from Germany, another from Georgia, at a cost of $35,000 per tug per day, and God knows how much for Teddy and the underground blasters. It was a high old time—but worth it, apparently, given the value of the cargo. The moral is not to use a plotting sheet for an area in which there are objects shallower than your draft, unless you take the time to plot in those objects, so that you can maneuver around them. I thought it a great story, and remember wondering whether Reagan could make a joke out of it during the campaign. Decision: Negative. At this point Dick Clurman left us. His journal read:

" 'I'll miss you, Richard, when you get off in Bermuda,' Bill said when we are about to get some sleep. And I'll miss him too, along with the rest, and the whole experience which grows day by day into something unlike cruising, or day sailing or, for that matter, doing anything else. Crossing the Atlantic with a destination 3,000 miles away, knowing you're going all the way, is different from getting off at Bermuda."

The day we paraded out through the channel (a two-hour trip) to hit the deep water opposite St. George's was Bermuda at its best. Bermuda has a nasty habit of attracting a kind of haze that obscures the vernal splendor and color of the island, causing a bleary etiolation. We had reckoned with such a possibility, and Halmi and Mark and David and Christopher were fatalistic about it: if the weather conditions proved inauspicious for photography, somehow we'd have to manage without the airplane scenes. What was excluded was that we could simply lie over another day, hoping for better weather. A trip like ours requires too much planning (I concede the point) insouciantly to take delays of one or two days, let alone three. But the sun shone magnificently, and again we went through our paces, returning to St. George's in the late afternoon. We took taxis back to Hamilton, since I had already paid for the suite for the third night, intending to set sail at noon the next morning after fueling, watering, and icing. We agreed to meet for dinner at the dining room of the hotel.

But Danny didn't show up. Reggie went to telephone him, but the line to his room was busy.

When we had finished, an hour and a half later, we went up—and Danny was still on the telephone and, as deferentially as he could, motioned us please to congregate in the other room, which we did. I began to worry. I think within thirty seconds I had figured it out. Gloria was pregnant.

Danny was on the phone a total of two and one-half hours. I had gone to bed before he finished talking. I dreaded the next morning, fearing the worst: Danny would announce, whether giving the reason or not, that he would have to pull out of the cruise. If a great deal of thought is given to the composition of a cruise, a single absence is totally dislocative. It is as if you approached a painting, turned to the artist, and said, "Try it again, this time without using any blue."

But Danny was silent, engaging himself totally in the last-minute details of the journey.

I had to write one final column and telephone it to New York, so Van agreed to pick me up at noon. He, Reggie, and I would taxi to St. George's, board the *Sealestial*, and head for Europe. What shall I write about? I asked Dick, as he closed his bags for the final time—he was headed for the airport to New York. "Write about the trip, what the hell." So I did.

SEE YOU LATER

Bermuda. Syndicated columnists are given two weeks off every year. And this, I note in passing, is by no means a venerable convention (in my case, the vacation came only after my fifth year in the trade). Moreover, there have been columnists who as a matter of principle never took a vacation, lest their public discover that life was possible, nay even keener and more joyous, without the columnist's lucubrations. The late George Sokolsky wrote six columns a week for King Features, and then a seventh for the local Sunday paper. When he learned that he had to have his appendix out, he carefully composed columns ahead based on all the variables in the art of prognosis: two columns in the event everything went smoothly; four columns in the event of complications; six columns in the event of major complications. I asked him, on hearing the story, whether he wrote a seventh column in the event of terminal complications, but he replied that his interest in his worldly constituency was only co-extensive with his life on earth.

Mine isn't. When I go, I intend to hector the Almighty even as, episodically, I do from here, to look after my friends, and (most of) my enemies. But I confess to being uncomfortable at taking my two weeks together, instead of separating them as is my practice (one week in the winter, one in the summer). But I am setting sail on a splendid racing vessel, from here to the Azores and on to Spain. The next leg of my journey will keep me incommunicado at sea for eleven days, in the unusual posture of being only on the receiving end of the world's events. During that period President Carter, Senator Kennedy, the airlines, the people who spend their days profaning the English of King James, may perform their abominations safe in the knowledge that there will be no reproach from me. It is horrifying to meditate what enormity the White House will execute, I having advertised my isolation. On the other hand, if President Carter is determined to make me a boat people, I am splendidly well ahead of the game: I need only to sail on.

But sail on to where? Ah, there's the rub, as the poet intuited four hundred years ago. Where can we go, if distress should come to America? There is only Switzerland, and this would not be the season to rely on U.S. Naval helicopters to pick up my boat and ferry it into Lake Geneva. [I wrote a few weeks after the abortive attempt to rescue our hostages in Iran.] Accordingly, I adjure my lords, secular and spiritual, not to be too licentious while I am gone.

What shall I concern myself with? Well, the exact time of day. I really must know—no kidding—exactly what time it is. I wear a chronometer which for several years lost exactly one

The Sealestial *pulls away from dockside, Princess Hotel, Hamilton, Bermuda, bound for the Azores, distance 1,900 miles.*

second per week. Even folks as disorganized as I can cope with such retrogressions, and I happily set it right every Christmas and every Fourth of July, and I always knew what time it was. But in an idiotic fit of hubris I returned it to the clockmaker, reminding him that my watch was guaranteed not to gain or lose more than twelve seconds per year. It has never been quite right since. So . . . well, I have a computer I navigate with, and it has an inbuilt chronometer. It keeps—excellent time. But you see, excellent time will not do; you need the *exact* time. So I also have a little radio ($36 at Radio Shack) which is supposed to bring in wwv from Fort Collins, Colorado, which vouchsafes to all the ships at sea the exact time. Mostly, the little radio brings in that signal. Every now and then it does not. In which case I ask Danny for the time, and his watch is pretty reliable. Dick's cheap little Casio keeps disgustingly good time. And I can tell from Reggie's sly smile that he believes, in a pinch, he can come up with the time.

I need sun. Not to darken my skin, because in fact the doctor says that sun is the enemy of fair skin and I must use something called Total Eclipse ✳15. I need the sun, and the time, to discover which way to point in order to effect a rendezvous at the Azores. If in this matter I should fail, the reader may deduce, two weeks hence, that I am absent without leave. The moon is getting lean right now, but will flower again; and when it is half-bright, it gives you a horizon, and on some magical moments you can combine that horizon with the north star, and before you know it, you have your latitude, even as Columbus had that, and only that, having little idea of the time, and yet managed to discover our wonderful country.

The chances, then, are overwhelming that, like MacArthur, I shall return. In the meantime, the Republic is on probation.

8

The following leg was uneventful, if you take into account only the weather. The most drastic literary compression of external conditions and social circumstances was Van's formal entry, "3 days perfect sailing, 7 days winds 0–10, powering 75 percent of the time. No casualties. Many dolphins. Much swimming. Radio-telephone, no work. Occupations, varied."

I lean, for a little while, on Tony Leggett's journal.

Tony's posture toward his journal is at all times dutiful. Clearly he considers it a matter of personal honor to confess to his journal when he is feeling less than . . . whole. ("For the next three or four days I was a little unsteady.")

During the first few days, when we had the fine sailing wind, Tony took leisurely thought to compare the experience of the helmsman, on duty and off, in a boat the size of *Sealestial* by contrast with the racing boat, only a little more than half *Sealestial's* length, Tony had previously sailed across that Atlantic:

On board *Imp* at night during a solo watch, I always got a feeling of tremendous vulnerability. *Imp's* deck was absolutely flush. There was a well, about two feet deep, for your feet. The

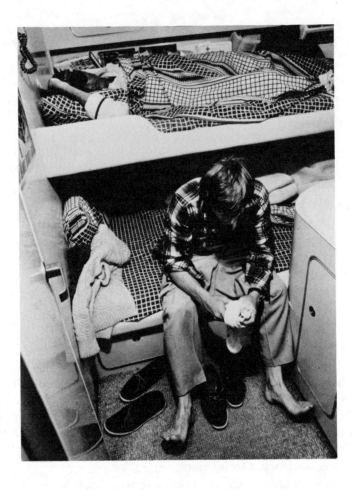

Reggie off watch. Tony, coming on watch.

dodger over the main hatch had only one purpose, to keep spray out of the hatch when it was open in rough conditions. It was not considered a means of sheltering anyone on deck. Therefore going on watch at night was something I always had to prepare for, mentally and physically: the wind came right at you off the water, unobstructed; and the flat, open deck made one feel very exposed. The opposite—going off watch—was a tremendous joy.

To see a light below through the companionway as Robert got ready to relieve me was very heartening. The passage from deck to cabin was marked. Down below, the air was still and warm. The light was usually weak, but it illuminated just enough so that the cabin felt like a cocoon. Finally to crawl into the sleeping bag and wedge myself between the bunk and the hull was bliss. The bag soon warmed up, and the water rushing past only inches away was both soothing and an indication of how fast and far we were going. I remember thinking one night how crazy it was to imagine this little cocoon of warmth and light, out there bobbing around a thousand miles from the nearest land, in an environment totally inhospitable to man.

On *Sealestial* I get very little of those sorts of emotions. For one thing *Sealestial* is too big to seem vulnerable in the open ocean, and the cockpit and deck layout provide lots of protection from the elements. Going on watch, therefore, involves none of the trepidation of a much smaller boat. For some reason, I find the most disturbing activity at night is taking a leak. The leeward rail aft of the cockpit has sheets, backstay tails, and vang lines crisscrossing it, making secure footing very difficult. There is also the need at the end to lean far outboard to miss the wide gunwale. To do this at night with an irregular swell, pitch black, no moon, and especially the fear of going overboard with the autopilot on and no one on deck is more disconcerting to me than it logically should be.

Going below, then, has less of the sharp contrast than it did on *Imp*. The cabin is warm, and well lighted, and inviting, to be sure, but it misses out on that siege mentality so evident on *Imp*. It is even difficult to hear the boat's passage through the water when down in the saloon.

All this is true. A fortiori, the passage across the Atlantic on the 16-foot *Tinkerbelle* was a closer-to-nature-experience than on *Imp*. Sailing aboard the *Sealestial* is different from sailing aboard a kayak. But it requires dormant imagination to forget that the *Sealestial*, for all its apparent mass, stem to stern, is only as long as eleven Tony Leggetts stretched end to end.

What hit us, after the third day, was something very nearly like the doldrums. I think I remember that we always had the mainsail up, but that is easy to do if you sheet it down tight so that there is

Christopher Little, Reggie Stoops, night watch.

no lateral movement whatever in the boom, and vang it down to discourage floppiness in the sail itself. But it was only every now and again that there was wind enough to justify hoisting the genoa. The days crawled by. Van deduced that the chances now were very nearly gone that we would reach the Azores in time to make his connection to Switzerland for the conference he had contingently agreed to attend.

So what?

"We haven't made the expected time, and the conference in Switzerland looks doubtful. *Tant pis* and as Agnew said, if you've seen one conference you've seen 'em all." Van is by temperament impatient, by philosophical discipline, stoical. How to pass the time on watch? "I had the 2400 to 0400 watch with Danny last night and we played double-ended Ghost which allows for adding a letter before as well as after the word. The four hours were absorbed very quickly and I recommend it to all semiliterate mariners in search of a time killer when reading is impossible."

When the sea was calm sometimes we would swim three times a day.

Van permitted his thoughts to roam. He got around to describing a typical day in the doldrums. "The Muses rarely lyricize over the empty bowel, but they should. My diet of roughage has paid off, crapwise. Our routine has become routine. Everyone flops around, above or below, in the morning after breakfast reading or writing. Not too much chatter. Then Swim Time. Gregarious lunch in the after cockpit, naps in the afternoon. More reading. Swim. Read. And cocktails at 1900, dinner at 1930, talk escalates and then fades. Night night." He acknowledged the special problems that disadvantaged us during those languorous hours: "In the Problems-of-the-Idle-Rich-Department: Reg and I keep bumping into each other while swimming which leads to comments like, 'This ocean is just not *big* enough for the two of us,' or, 'The water is refreshing but there are just *too* many people.'"

What were the aggravations, excitements, irritations, fantasies? Tony addressed himself to these. For instance, there was the aesthetically distressing matter of Danny's indescribably unattractive cap, his teddy bear:

Danny has a horrid, dirty, once-white plastic and acetate visor baseball cap which says Something White Water on the front. Bill was desperate to get Danny to stop wearing it. The first solution obviously was to give him another hat to wear, but Bill was shocked for two days when he realized he couldn't *find* the five hats which Pat had so carefully packed for him: a) because they were such useful hats, and b) because he could not therefore give Danny a substitute. [Yesterday] Bill came on deck in the late afternoon, triumphantly bearing his five hats: a blue Greek sailor hat, a brown Greek sailor hat, a Black Diamond Sou'Wester, and two strange Australian sun hats. Danny got the brown Greek sailor hat and I hope we don't see his white baseball cap again. Bill's first attempt had been a plaintive [Tony meant, "seductive"] innocent 'Danny, let me look at what size your hat is,' but I guess he (Danny) had heard that tone of voice before and all Bill got was a 'Oh-no-you-don't-Bill.'"

Tony is too young to have taken in the street wisdom of the soldier, and knew not the dangers of volunteering:

As well as ship spotter I have another shipboard task. I found the tapes in tremendous disarray, and decided to rectify the situation. Since there are at least sixty tapes and they were all confused, it took me a goodly long time to straighten things out. I arranged them chronologically with Bach getting a big drawer

all to himself. In gratitude for my meritorious service, the Master appointed me the keeper of the tapes. Now this position involves some selection also. Problems arose immediately. I put on some Strauss waltzes which I thought were perfectly appropriate for a coolish midafternoon listening session down below. While I was on deck for just a moment Bill switched it hastily to something a little more baroque [Tony meant, "a little less awful"]. Come on, everybody knows that Bach is O.K. for the evening, but *not* for midafternoon."

But then I am not everybody, as from time to time I was required, by example, to remind Tony and such other philistines as didn't know it already.

Probably a single volume—the novel *The Shipkiller*—was most immediately responsible for such surrounding sense of spookdom

Reggie's single theatrical act: An imitation of a German World War I submarine.

as there was weighing on us—that and the shark sighted a few minutes after (or was it before?) one of our daily swims. The novel went the rounds and I think everyone (myself excepted) read it. It is an apparently engrossing story in which a huge freighter runs over a little sloop innocently cruising across the Atlantic, killing the wife but leaving the husband alive to plan—Grrrr!—a galvanizing and satisfying revenge. The story gripped the imagination. . . .

With all this talk of supertankers [Tony later wrote about a ship's party] running down sailboats, it seemed funny for us all to be sitting down below in the late afternoon, with the hatches closed, and no one keeping watch but the autopilot. How would that have sounded at the admiral's inquest? "Well, Mr. Buckley, where were you and your entire crew at the time of the collision?" [Tony had the admiral leading with his chin, because the inescapable response would have been, "Where were *you*, admiral, and your entire bloody navy that's supposed to maintain the freedom of the seas?"]

Halfway to Faial, yielding to the entreaties of Christopher, we took immense pains to empty the Zodiac, fill it with air, lower it into the water, winch down the outboard motor onto it: all this in order to photograph the *Sealestial* at sea. It happened that during the operation a range of clouds descended to the south, occluding our view. The creaky motor was energetically primed, and in a few moments Christopher, David and I (I had in hand the idiot-proof moving picture camera, entrusted to me by Mark with solemn instructions to film our vessel from a remote distance) were ready to cast off—when the evanescent mist suddenly became dimly transparent, so that we could descry through it, five miles off, a freighter traveling roughly in the opposite direction. Van quickly improvised a scenario: David and Christopher should proceed at full speed with the Zodiac, through the cloud, toward the freighter. I would follow in bathing trunks, towed on water skis, sextant in hand, held tightly to the eye. We would zoom past the stern of the freighter, I would momentarily drop my arm, look up pointing in the direction we were traveling, and shout out, "Azores?" If memory serves, Christopher took a picture of us reacting to Van's proposed safari . . .

Inevitably the end came, and analytical wits, unused for so long, devoted themselves to contriving the means of deciding which was the likeliest moment of landfall. A day or so earlier I had meditated that to pull in at Faial at four or five in the morning would be thoughtlessly—aggressively—antisocial; and so made appropriate adjustments, duly recorded by Tony.

The ship's photographer executes a self-portrait 81 feet above the water. We had all become very fond of him.

Another brilliant, cloudless, airless day. After lunch, with the noon position in mind, and wanting to arrive in Horta at a nice reasonable hour, Bill decided to goose the engine a bit. From the usual 1,750, we put it up to 2,000. After hardly a minute, Allen appeared in the hatchway and casually looked at the knot meter, the sails, and the engine rev counter. "Skipper ask for an increase?" We nodded yes. He smiled and went back below. Three minutes later David came up and repeated the procedure. What a conscientious and careful crew *Sealestial* has.

And then, the final suspense on this leg, the details faithfully recorded by Tony:

> Everything focused a bit at lunchtime because we all put in our figures for the pool. The central group of the Azores is an interesting landfall because you can see the island of Pico for

such a long time. With its height of 7,600 feet it can be seen theoretically for 103 miles. How long did it take us, and how many computers and inputs from Reg to figure that one out! So, sitting there at lunch about 80 miles out, we should have been able to see it. This process gets pretty interesting now. Bill will give an approximate position (I mean a fix, I guess) and everyone does their figuring. I thought it was a pretty useless exercise, because our sighting of Pico depended entirely on the humidity in the atmosphere since there weren't any clouds to speak of. So, I just advanced the ETL (estimate time of landfall) a few hours from the time right then. I felt pretty outclassed by some of the problem-solving I learned [about] later. Bill was counting on the fact that the mountain would not be observed until sunset, and then we would only see it at the extreme range of the lights listed on the chart, say fifteen to nineteen miles. Pretty smart! But talk about sophistication. Reg asked the Navicomp what sunset would be at our position and then got an ETL by taking the time when the sun would provide the maximum horizontal illumination which would reflect back from the mountain at us. I can dig it. After that, I wouldn't trust anybody else's calculations.

So, we scribbled down our ETL on bits of paper napkins and on the clothes clips which had been holding the tablecloth. Our official pool tip sheet was a bunch of bits of napkin with four laundry clips holding them together.

Mine was 1600, which meant that it extended to 1730, because Chris's time was 1900. After my watch was over, I slapped on some Total Eclipse and treaded up to my perch on the spreaders. I tried lots of different positions, and kept myself aimed by looking around. There was a surprising amount of plastic containers and floating polypro line and other stuff, but goddam, there wasn't any sign of Pico. People were egging me on and asking questions like, "Have you seen anything yet, Tony?" Did they think I'd just sit and keep a sighting of Pico all to myself?

I came down a little disgruntled with the whole deal, and enjoyed watching Chris pace the deck while his appointed hour flew by. The ranting and raving seems so futile, even ludicrous, to everyone but the person who knows that the sighting will show up then.

Chris resigned himself to defeat and *exactly* two minutes later, Allen came running back from the bow to the cockpit, *"There it is! There it is!"* And sure enough, in one of the breaks in the clouds, something that could only be a mountain peak stood right up. I'm sure that I had been looking right at it many times while I was up the mast; it's just that I had been concentrating on the horizon, rather than 10 degrees off it.

Chris was pissed off. To lose the pool wasn't bad, since five people had to lose it, but to lose it by *two minutes,* and knowing that it must have been in view before that, but worst of all, to lose by two minutes *to Reggie!* Reg laughed, commiserated, and acted as if he had known exactly when it was coming up. Horizontal beams from the sun lighting it up? My ass. It was just sitting there, right up above the clouds.

Danny's demeanor, during the first days out from Bermuda, was unchanged. His log entries continued to specify, and to vibrate. *"Missed moon sight today—was in bunk reading* Shipkiller, *just now getting interesting. Feel very clumsy, off balance kind of thing."* Or, *"Log 1614.0 Course 096 degrees. Speed 7.2. Wind 10 knots from 150 degrees. So much perfect conditions it makes you sick."* Again Danny, *au naturel:* *"Since 2400 I've eaten three apples, two candy bars, three glasses of water and one juice; two cereals and one beer. And I still have one hour 45 minutes left."* The next entry read, *"Add one cup coffee to above. Do not eat soggy steaks. Reg, if the moon shows itself, sight it please. Also the sun."*

The party was today. The day before, Diane had asked me when might one safely say that we had come *halfway* from our point of departure in the Virgins to our destination in Spain, and I said, Tomorrow: June 13, Friday. The preparations were extensive. They included the decoration of the entire saloon, party hats, fake noses, whiskers, noisemakers—the whole bit. A picture of the animated grotesquerie not only survives, it was published in *People* magazine about a month later. That was the reticulated excitement: the third act, entirely unprogrammed, would be produced by Danny, who had announced exuberantly that to reciprocate the crew's party, he was giving Judy, the chef, a night off. He

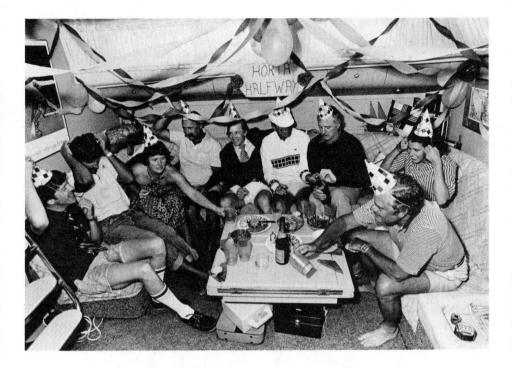

The halfway party. Dan, David Murphy, Judy Harman, Allen, Tony (note costume: after all, in a month he would be a banker), Van, WFB, Diane Bowlus, Reg.

would himself cook steak for us all on a broiler slung over the sea astern, dangling from lines attached to a dinghy davit.

Danny is a born gourmet. I know no one who, with so little formal training, reacts more exultantly to choice food and wine; and on this night, midway from America to Europe, he was resolved to make the meal truly memorable, the more so since (gently in conversation, ardently in his journal) he had registered misgivings about the quotidian fare. After finally succeeding in lighting the waterlogged coals, which achievement came an hour or so after virtually the whole ship's company had been well lit at the party, Danny approached me—I was below in my stateroom, snatching a

Van, practicing ambassadorial toasts.

few minutes of Henry James's *The American* (which I gave up on at about page 150—could ever the social pace have been so slow as to countenance the attractions, so excruciatingly recalcitrant, of the American?). Danny said he wanted to talk to me "about something." Danny is chronically reluctant to *impose*. "If you have time, I mean." Manifestly, time was what I had most of that day,

Danny's barbecue. The grill, hanging from the dinghy davit, will stay level no matter what. Danny remained level for approximately two hours after this picture was taken.

and the succeeding fourteen days. I said, to my son Christopher's oldest friend and to my own dear friend, of course; and he replied that perhaps right after dinner would be ideal, because right now he would be needing to tend his steaks *continuously*.

As is his way, he leaped up the companionway (when Danny saunters, it is in the manner of Travolta in *Saturday Night Fever*, a kind of coiled, springy saunter: the racehorse bridled on his emphatic way to the starting gate). Van had elected to help Danny with the cooking and was there, arm around the running backstay, stirring and testing the sauce as Danny now gave it a little more of this or that. The bottle of wine between them rapidly emptied— and of what use, pray, is an empty bottle of wine? It was nonchalantly offered to Neptune, and instantly (a round trip by Danny, after cockpit to refrigerator and back, is measured in microseconds) replaced. By the time we sat down in the main cockpit to eat (superb steaks, with sautéed potatoes, nicely seasoned vegetables, brandied cake and parfait au liqueurs), the wine had had a

Danny, cleaning up after himself.

decisive effect on Danny and on Van; so that when after dinner I made myself geographically approachable by moving to the after cockpit where Danny could discreetly join me, he had no sooner begun the conversation when Van hove in, instantly volunteering his own philosophy on—marriage, abortion, British bonds, Taiwan, Danny's future, and disarmament.

What Dan had only just managed to blurt out to me was that he had made Gloria pregnant, that he wished ardently to marry her, that he harbored no reservations at all about marrying her, that neither she nor he desired an abortion, indeed that he disapproved of abortion ("personally and philosophically"), that his worries were exclusively over the question: how would his little four-year-old girl, living with her mother in Colorado but regularly and delightedly visiting Danny in Connecticut, absorb the news?

And how would his former wife take it—might she interfere with future visits by his daughter? And what did I think about the wedding, and might it be a good idea for Gloria to go to Spain and be married there, or might *that* appear to be furtive; Danny didn't want furtiveness—he was very proud of Gloria and wanted all the world to know it, and he loved her deeply; and, well, he guessed he wanted me to know, and maybe to have my reaction. Van instantly volunteered to give my reaction on my behalf, and his own on my behalf; or something of the sort—Van had trespassed his private little threshold (the only time on that journey) and I kept an eye on him until, finally, he went to bed, though only after he concluded that this was an ideal time for me to initiate him in the felicities of celestial navigation, and assured me that if President Reagan designated him as president of the World Bank (Van is, simply stated, one of the brightest bankers in the Western world), that would not prevent him from joining me on *any* future transatlantic cruise; to which I replied that no ocean cruise would be the same without him, which is certainly true.

Van approached our stateroom and with exaggerated precision achieved the passage to the upper bunk, having meditated that 4 A.M., when he would next be on duty, was not all that far down the line. I agreed, turned off the light, and went softly back up to the main cockpit. Christopher Little and Danny were talking animatedly. The moon was radiant. The only wind we felt was of our own making: 7.5 knots of it, bearing down on us from our easterly course. I mentioned to Danny merely that I understood everything he had told me, and that perhaps tomorrow we might talk more about it. He poured me a glass of wine and said, Sure!

The next morning he was pale. A few weeks later, on receiving his journals, I took note of the relevant entry: "*Last night proved to me, once again, that I can't drink and hold my booze. They say I (1) did not eat dinner which I so laboriously cooked off the fantail and (2) stayed up to within 1½ hours of my watch drinking every wine in sight. Ah, but I awoke for the 4–8 shift and stayed awake for most of it. I found my glasses on the deck, why unbroken I don't know. I figure I'll atone today for last night. I hate myself. . . .*"

And later, "*I'll atone for my sins by dying after a slow painful agonizing afternoon of gas. How does one get so paralyzed by just a few bottles of Mateus—one white and one red? Wine is medici-*

nal—at what point does gluttony reverse the good effect?" Answer: At a point several miles behind the point Danny had
reached.

But (it transpired) Danny had kept not just a single journal, but
a second. And what he told me, the afternoon of his distress, was
that he wanted me to have not only the first, but the second. "The
second is personal." I said that was okay, and I appreciated his
willingness to let me read it, but that after all I was committed to
composing a book. He paused and said he didn't care how many
people knew how he felt about Gloria.

Danny and I flew back to New York two weeks later, the day
after landing in Marbella (the others would dribble back over the
next days and months). The day after arriving in Connecticut, Pat
and I ceremoniously congratulated Gloria (they lived four houses
down from us, in a garage apartment). After the Bermuda telephone call Gloria had proudly announced, to Pat and two house-
guests already known to her, a) that she would soon be married,
and b) that she was expecting a baby. On both counts she was
congratulated. When, on my arrival, my son Christopher telephoned me, asking routinely about the passage, I gave him a quick
briefing. Quickly we talked about Danny, who had already called
Christopher to invite him down from Nantucket (where he was
holed up writing a book) for the wedding, which would be held
on the Fourth of July, and to invite him to serve as best man.
Christopher was glad to do this, enthusiastic as he is about Gloria,
in sharp contrast to his dark forebodings about her predecessor at
the altar, side-by-side with a love-struck Danny; at which ceremony he had also served as best man.

The Fourth of July was a very beautiful day in Connecticut,
and in the morning, dressed in the customary Levi's and sports
shirt, Danny cruised around to my garage office, two documents
in hand.

"Here are my journals."

I thanked him, laying them aside, and we talked about his plans.
He would honeymoon aboard my yawl, *Suzy Wong*, taking only
the weekend off. The marriage-making justice of the peace was
due exactly at one, and Danny's landlord Peter Starr (an old

friend and sailing companion) and his wife Sandy had volunteered their huge lawn, extravagantly decorated, a large awning set up for the lunch. A hundred people had convened, Danny's parents and grandparents having driven all the way from Florida in a camper.

I forgot about Danny's journals until the next morning. It was fitting that I should have seen the second journal during Danny's honeymoon. What it comprised was spurts of objurgative passion, done stylistically as only Danny could: total candor, totally unselfconscious. *"Gloria, how I love you and miss you. Oh what presents you'll enjoy, especially—me." "I want your body against my own . . . I want this child and you." "Gloria, it's Wednesday, the 11th. I physically hurt from missing you so. I wish never to leave you for such a period again lest I die, which I prefer not. I've never wanted anyone so much. I feel that we're truly one person. I know how you feel now and I want to be with you to cry and hold you and love you. I'll see you in just over 2½ weeks. Can't wait."*

The very night of the mid-ocean party he had managed an entry in his journal, *"I love you Casale [Gloria's surname]. I'll always love you, you will be my cutie now and God willing for the rest of my life. Glor, we've had such an evening. We're half way, a party of sorts, God knows how much champagne, wine and booze but I lie in my small and lonesome bunk, wanting one being, you. I close my eyes and feel you, touch you and smell you and for one moment know you are in me and we are together. But that fleeting moment lingers in my mind more than my body can stand. I'm 912 miles away from the nearest point of land. I love you. I look forward to your being 'Mrs. Gloria Merritt' . . . Yes! . . . . She is my wife."*

The following entry he wrote in the morning, entitling it "Dan's Prayer."

"I pray Lord I live a full life with the woman I choose, the being I love so; who is with me now and always, and I pray to the Lord for the blessing you might favor us.

"I wish to openly make amends for my sinfulness and open my heart to thee and my brothers around me. Please protect that which I love and care for and those who enter my life, help me Lord to be more like thyself. Let me grow as those around me have taught.

"I believe."

It is difficult to conceive of a marriage in which the bridegroom, formal theological difficulties to one side, more closely approached a state of grace.

At 1:15 the justice of the peace hadn't even arrived. Danny and Christopher (Buckley), dressed in white ducks, blazers, and gray silk ties, and looking like college freshmen at a fraternity induction, came into Danny's living room where the Christopher Littles, Pat, and I were having a glass of wine, waiting for the ceremony to begin. What to do? How to get a justice of the peace at one in the afternoon of the Fourth of July! I called the home number of an old friend, member of a large law firm. He wasn't there, but his wife was, and she gave me the names of two of her husband's partners who were, she thought, also justices of the peace. The first one was indeed at home, mowing the lawn. Twenty minutes later he was with us, in full regalia. While the guests were being assembled he chatted. "I've been an AA for thirty-three years. But I keep up my license as J/P, want to know why? Under Connecticut law a J/P can lock up a drunk for thirty-six hours, no questions asked. I'm telling you, I use that power every now and again —maybe once a year—and I sometimes prevent real damage, wife beatings, suicide, maybe even murders. Yup." We were advised that the guests were ready. It was 2 P.M.—at which moment the original justice of the peace drove in, utterly indignant at a substitute's having been retained; and completely soused. I turned to Number Two and told him he had a splendid opportunity to use his powers on Number One; but, in the event, they just exchanged a fraternal wave. The latecomer slunk away. Christopher B. had, protectively, sheltered Danny from the hugger-mugger. Danny was by this time properly nervous. He and Gloria exchanged their vows in the midday sun demurely, perfunctorily, rendering quite conventional their passion—as if Romeo and Juliet had grunted out their consent to live as man and wife. After a toast to the bride and groom, the Littles walked back with Pat and me to our house. I felt that our presence, as survivors of that crossing on the *Sealestial*, was somehow obtrusive. Danny's party lasted until after midnight.

9

~~~~~~~~~~~~~~~~~~~~~

Before recounting my great discovery in respect of star sights, I owe an explanation of the Plath celestial computer. In *Airborne*, when I got around to explaining celestial navigation, or rather to explaining how to navigate celestially (a very different enterprise), I warned that the reader might wish to skip the chapter I was embarking on. What follows here is less technical, and I should think it likely to hold the interest even of someone who never intends to come closer to navigation than to call the ship's bridge and ask where we are. However, this particular chapter does indeed end—on page 169.

As owner of a Hewlett-Packard 97 I concluded that progress had ended in putting computer technology at the service of the celestial navigator. I was wrong. Along came Plath, and one is dizzy with the wonder of it all. Before I forget, I should add that the HP-97 (a generation back from the HP-41C described above) has two features, one of which Plath doesn't even try to imitate, the second of which it does, with minimal success. The HP-97 gives you a printout of your calculations. This is marvelous to have for three reasons. The first is that people like me make mistakes in actually punching in the numbers, and the result can be—and this is fortunate—chaotic. You may forget, for instance, to push the minus sign (indicating which hemisphere you are in) and the computer will humorlessly advise you that you are 10,803 miles away from your Assumed Position, on an azimuth of 272 degrees. What on earth did you do wrong? Clearly it was egregious. Did you poke the wrong year? Wrong month? You scan the little piece of paper, and in instants the mistake screams out at you; and you do it again, right. The second advantage of the printout is that you can detach it from the roll, and Scotch-tape or clip it to the log, a vivid *aide-mémoire*. One of HP-97's programs permits you to request a fresh azimuth to your destination at any longitudinal increment. I felt especially importunate one spring evening in 1979, pulling out of Madeira (Latitude 32–45N, Longitude 17–00W) aboard the Royal Viking *Sky*, and so I commanded my HP to give me a great circle course to our destination in Miami (Latitude 25–45N, Longitude 80–15W, distance 3,289.9 miles), indicating the distance traveled between every degree of longitude, and the new heading on reaching that longitude. I sat back in a pharaonic trance as the HP chugged out my pyramid—seventy-two inches of detailed instructions and data. I arrived at the captain's dinner looking like a ticker-tape parade, and presented the captain with it. He told me laconically that the *Sky* was not taking the great circle route to Miami, it would be "warmer zee ozzer way." The third reason for the printout is that it's fun.

The Navicomp, as I say, attempts no printout, and is therefore one third the size of the large HP (the HP-67 has no printout but is otherwise identical to the 97). It does give you battery life, but here Plath isn't even in a league with Hewlett-Packard. HPs can run for three hours from a rechargeable battery pack. If you set out on a long journey without shipboard current for recharging, you can take along, for a few dollars, a half-dozen precharged battery packs.

By contrast the Navicomp is wedded to what is most usefully called an "iron lung." This is a desk case which must *always* be connected to your power supply. It is designed to accept 220V, 110V, or 12V; it can be adapted to other voltages. The drain is

about half an amp—not much, and it is surprising under the circumstances how hot it gets. Now you can remove the computer from the lung, and indeed you are expected to do so when you take it up on deck. But if you do not return it to its iron lung within about fifty minutes, it asphyxiates. Everything you have stored in it is wiped out. To be sure, every time you turn off the HP-97 you also wipe out its memory (not so the HP-41C). But the memory of the Navicomp—brace yourself—includes:

A chronometer. Yes, and the day, the month, and the year. Keep it in its iron lung, or return it after not more than a forty-five-minute absence, and it will tick away the seconds, the hours, the days, the months, the years (even allowing for leap years) until New Year's Eve, 2050. However, you will in fact want to

reset it—the work of a half minute—in order to correct the chronometer from time to time. (Plath guarantees the accuracy up to a quarter of a second per day, which means a possible error of eight seconds per month.) Moreover, if you move about a lot or change sextants, you will want to adjust for height of eye or for index error, both of which adjustments are also easy. But the wonders have merely begun.

Let us assume that you are going to take sights with a sextant whose index error is —1.5. And that you will take sights from ten feet above the water. You enter these givens. Then, with the aid of a radio or a chronometer or a telephone number (in New York, 936-1616), you get the exact time. You program this into the Navicomp. Then you enter the month, the day, and the year.

You have made four entries—and you have done two thirds of your work. That two thirds you never have to do again, if you are on the same vessel, using the same sextant, unless you are adjusting your chronometer.

All you now need is: your Assumed Position, and then your Sextant Altitude. The Navicomp gurgles a few seconds and gives you an Intercept (indicating Toward or Away) and an Azimuth. You have your Line of Position (LOP).

Moreover, there is a rubber connector, about four feet long, which plugs into the Navicomp. At the other end is a rubber-encased button. When you have the heavenly body just where you want it, you push the button with the same hand that is calibrating the sextant mirror, and the exact time of the sight is recorded in the computer. You have then only the sextant angle to punch in.

That isn't all. You have just shot, let us say, the sun, an hour before sunset. The new moon is clearly visible, so you punch in the key for "Moon (lower limb)" which is 102. You look up at the moon and when it is nicely situated on the horizon you depress the button again, and you have recorded the second, minute, hour, day, month, year. You punch in your altitude. You receive the Intercept and the Azimuth for the Moon. Do you go now and plot the two LOPs for a fix? That's for the proles. *You* merely push "D" and in a few seconds the Navicomp flashes out at you your latitude and your longitude.

Suppose that you are shooting stars. The above also applies. If you shoot a third star, the Navicomp will give you a latitude and longitude based on the last two stars you entered. You like the third star and the first star? Repeat the time of the first star and its sextant angle, and you will get latitude and longitude based on the third and first star—*ad infinitum.*

You have fifty-eight stars to choose from, two planets (Mars and Venus), lower and upper limbs for the sun and for the moon. I asked Plath (via its genial general manager Donald Gilluley of the North American Division in College Park, Maryland) why they didn't give us Jupiter and Saturn, to which the answer is that when the computer was developed, the relatively eccentric elliptical patterns of those two planets hadn't been programmed beyond the year 2030, and the Germans wanted to produce a machine that would take us uniformly right up to the year 2050, would you believe it! I would settle for a foreign policy that would take us to the year 2000. Anyway it's a pity, since they are very bright planets, always in the way. The moon's pattern is by far the most idiosyncratic, but of course you cannot have a navigational computer without cracking the moon, so the software for it was developed. You have to make do without Jupiter and Saturn (Mercury is too dim to make the effort worthwhile).

In addition to LOPs and fixes, the Navicomp will give you Latitude by Polaris, Geographical Positions of the Celestial Bodies, Great Circle Distances and Directions, Local Time, and Greenwich Mean Time. As you would expect, Navicomp will act as a conventional calculator, providing the usual services—mathematical, geometrical, and trigonometric.

Worth a paragraph's discussion is the last of its listed services, namely Sunrise/Sunset, Meridian Passage. The promise is obvious, namely that you can ascertain the exact time of sunrise and sunset anywhere in the world anytime before the mid-twenty-first century by merely vouchsafing the time, date, and estimated position. Now, this is a convenience that goes potentially beyond the point of telling you when, roughly, you will be needing to put on your running lights. If you can clock the exact moment when the sun disappears below the horizon you can deduce your longitude, even as clocking the exact moment when the sun passes over the meridian gives you your latitude.

At this point I interrupt to describe a glorious feature of the Navicomp, namely its functional simplicity. In order to work with the star Vega, for example, it isn't necessary to find, from an inventory of capsules (Texas Instruments) or 1½-inch-long shavings of flexible plastic (HP-97), the item containing Vega, and insert it into the computer. You merely look at a little plastic wallet-size index card under "Vega" and note its code number (49). You depress P, which signals the computer that you are about to orient it toward a particular system, then you depress 49, then you depress D, which is the activator.

The Navicomp, at the left-hand corner of the display bar, will give you a number in response to any rational activity on the keyboard. Depress P, for instance, and the numeral 1 appears. Whenever you see 1, the computer is saying: *"What program do you desire?"*

You depress 207, which is your Sunrise/Sunset, Meridian Passage, and push D to activate it.

The number 2 is displayed. Whenever you see 2, there is only one datum the Navicomp is asking for, namely: "*What is your Assumed Latitude?*"

If you are at Stamford, Connecticut, you depress 4103 (the little index card also informs you of the relevant protocols in the use of decimal points. None between degrees and minutes. But if you wish finer calculations, you may have them—e.g., 4103.2).

Depress D to enter the datum, and the number 3 flashes. That means: "*Give me your Assumed Longitude.*" You comply (again, from Stamford): —7332. That minus, by the way, is a chauvinistic giveaway. In fact, an American firm (Litton Industries) owns Plath. But it remains a thoroughly German enterprise, and the scientists who designed the Navicomp believe that normal people reside in the eastern hemisphere (Hamburg: Latitude 53°00′N. Longitude 10°00′E). So that whereas U.S. navigational computers require you to put a minus sign before introducing east longitude, the reverse is the case with the Plath.

Depress D. The number 4 appears. It means: "*Tell me what time it is in Greenwich.*" The theoretical reflexes balk. We are working with a chronometer. Let us imagine that we are making our calculations on May 1, 1979, at 0700 Eastern Daylight Time. When the Number 4 is displayed, the operator has two alternatives. Either he can write in a time which is hypothetical (let us say you desire the time of sunset at Stamford on Christmas Day) or he can log the time at the moment he is doing his reckonings—in this example, as I say, 0700, May 1. He need not bother, in the latter case, to punch out the time—it is always ticking away in the chronometer. So he merely depresses D. The chronometer registers GMT 11-00-00 (add four hours for zone time). The numeral 5 now appears, always the same thing: "*Give me the month, the day and the year.*" That too is ticking away, prerecorded, so you merely depress D again.

The Navicomp then sets out to calculate. In about ten seconds it displays on the left the numeral 7, which is a so-called Display Numeral. It isn't asking for anything now, it is telling *you* something. You get alternative displays (at intervals of two seconds) of 452.7 and 1849.8. That means that sunrise will occur (add one hour for daylight time, $1/10$ of a minute is six seconds) at 5:52:42. And sunset at 7:49:48. (If you then depress D again, you will be given the time when the sun will pass over your meridian—namely, 11:51:18 or, EDT, 12:51:18.)

You are entitled to wonder: Why am I being asked to give the machine the time at the moment I happen to be inquisitive about the time of sunset? Haven't I already given the machine the Assumed Position? And the date? Why is it relevant to ask me for the time?

I inquired rather deeply into the question, and ended with a cable from Hamburg (and eighteen conversations with Plath). I should interrupt to say that if you know the exact time when the sun disappears at an assumed position, and you clock the time when it actually disappears, the difference will give you your longitude. Hamburg cabled, "As the only time-dependent variable in the formula for sunrise and sunset is the declination of sun, which varies only very slowly throughout the day, it is formally sufficient to key in an approximate GMT. For higher accuracy, it is recommended to repeat the calculations for both sunrise and sunset, now using the times achieved during the first calculations (converted from zone time to GMT)."

We all know that, on May 1, the sun's declination is gradually increasing. The rate is about nine minutes (nine miles) per twelve hours. So that if you ask the computer for sunset information at seven in the morning, but sunset is at approximately seven in the evening, will your calculations be approximately nine miles off?

We can check by running the program with 7 P.M. input, as opposed to 7 A.M.

The answer: Sunrise at 5:52:06. Sunset at 6:50:24. (Compare with sunrise 5:52:42 and sunset 6:49:48.)

The difference in seconds for sunrise is 36. Four seconds of time equals one nautical mile of distance. If you take chronometer time at 7 A.M., you will miscalculate your longitude by eight miles.

Let us therefore try out Hamburg's instructions, and instead of using 7 A.M. time, use instead the sunset estimate yielded by the 7 P.M. time, namely 1849.8. This translates (add four hours) into GMT 22:49:48. What do we come out with?

The results are identical to the hypothetical 7 P.M. sunset: i.e., 6:50:24.

Let us now go through the agony of calculating the time of sunset for May 1 at the latitude and longitude of Stamford, Connect-

The sail trim is caught by photographer Little, sitting on bosun's chair. (Beard-McKie—"Bosun's Chair: Nineteenth-century nautical execution device consisting of an iron chain to which a lightning rod was attached. The condemned sailor was strapped into the bosun's chair where he remained until a fortuitous bolt of lightning or a lethal dose of St. Elmo's fire resulted in his execution. The necessity of sailing into dangerous storms to attract the required voltages and the typically long delays between sentencing and execution were considered major liabilities of this technique, and it was consequently never widely adopted.")

Below, clockwise from winch, Reg, Danny, WFB, Tony.

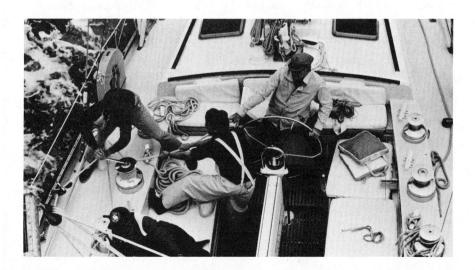

icut, through the nautical almanac. I get 18:48:08. For an error of 1 minute 40 seconds. An error the equivalent of 25 miles. Unless I missed something, longitudinal navigation by sunset is not possible with the Navicomp. The time of sunset is close enough only to alert you to the approximate time when to begin your star sights. The question, on which others will wish to meditate, is rendered more mysterious by the testimony of Mr. Leroy Dogett of the National Observatory. He advises that the variable effects of barometric pressure on refraction are such that the almanac rounds off sunsets to the nearest minute. Curses! Anyway, you try it.

This sunset-sunrise business is the single failing in the Navicomp (other than the unfortunate neglect of Jupiter and Saturn). Correction—there is a second, intensely annoying feature, which is that notwithstanding the highly touted Polaroid case, which protects the instrument and is designed to permit you to read the red figures simultaneously, in fact, you can't do it. The sun's brightness completely obscures them, and so you need to duck into the shade to see the numbers. The engineers should have used L.C.D. (black numbers on gray background), which in any event is a terrific power saver, rather than L.E.D. (red numbers on black background). The next model, one can safely assume, will incorporate this reform (and include the missing planets). Conceivably it will do away entirely with the iron lung, and perhaps even give us the means of translating Loran sights into latitude and longitude. The Navicomp is by any standard the most comprehensively useful electronic navigational calculator made, although I have described the glorious features of the HP-41C. But as noted, the HP does not have an inbuilt chronometer—that stroke of genius is Plath's. And, at $1,482, it certainly should be unique. A British writer estimates that its use saves one and one-half hours of paperwork per day for the navigator. Here is a suggestion for boat owners. Buy an extra iron lung ($210), keep it in your study, and take the computer home when you leave the boat. The advantages are threefold: 1) you reduce the risk of the computer's being stolen from the boat; 2) you eliminate having to readjust the voltage from 110 to whatever you have on board the boat; and 3) for a modest investment, you have a chronometer and a calculator for home use.

Plath is renowned for its fine service. Although Plath-North America will make no explicit promise, the chances are reasonable that if your computer should break down, or the chronometer need adjustment, or whatever, and it would sorely inconvenience you (let us say you are setting out for Bermuda) to be without it for the two weeks required to get it to Germany, through the factory, and back; and if the computer arrives at College Park and somebody hasn't spilled a chocolate malted milk into it—they'll send you a spare until your own is returned. That's the kind of people they are. I should add that although it doesn't give you visibility in direct sunlight, the cover is a beautifully designed tinted vinyl that fits snugly over the instrument, onto the iron lung. You can keep the vinyl cover over the instrument when you remove it from the lung. The Germans are really amazing, if you don't count world wars.

10

〰〰〰〰〰〰〰〰〰〰

The mortal enemy of continuously accurate celestial navigation is the plain, dumb, silly mistake. Some great pedagogue of yesteryear divined this, and so he came up with—a Form. There are different forms available, depending on which navigational system you use (different systems use different sets of tables, though they are identical in conception). You are supposed to buy and use these forms (there is a nice man at *Time* magazine who sends out his special form to all skippers preparing to race to Bermuda). The forms are designed to protect you from making silly mistakes.

Let me give an example. As we know, there are sixty seconds in one minute, and sixty minutes in one hour. What I have just said applies equally in measuring angles, except that one "hour" becomes one "degree" of arc, of which there are 360 in a circle, or a globe. Chicago to Chicago is 360 degrees.

Now let us suppose that you have reached the point where you are ready to extract the difference between a line of position (LOP) on which your ship would indeed lie if the assumed position you asserted, as a necessary step in the process of discarding falsities, were accidentally accurate, and the line of position on which you in fact lie, as witness the angle you measured with your sextant.

Here would be a typical example. Your (corrected) sextant angle (Ho)—for Height observed—was, let's say, 35 degrees 52 minutes. Your observed (i.e., hypothetical, or "calculated") angle (Hc) was 36 degrees and 12 minutes. What is the difference? Well, I would merely close my eyes (as you might do) for one quick second and mentally calculate that the difference between 52 and 60 is eight, and eight plus 12 is 20. There you have it. Right?

Right; and it is, I swear to you, at this vulgar level that mistake after mistake after mistake is made. I am not saying that there aren't among us a legion of practitioners who will go the whole of their lives without making an error in so preposterously simple a situation. I am saying that there are a few of us who *will* make such errors, and a generation's experience with navigation establishes that I am one of them.

The purpose of The Form (which, I confess at the outset, I do not use, but highly recommend) is to make it impossible to make such an error. Well, not quite impossible, but The Form does reintroduce every methodological seam, in order to discourage gulping down two steps in place of one. Accordingly, such a form would require you to proceed:

Ho: *35°52 minutes*
Hc: *36°12 minutes*
Are the Ho and the Hc the same as to degrees? Check one:
(*yes*)
(*no*)
If no, then rewrite, reducing the degrees of the higher number by one (1) and adding sixty (60) to the minutes. Your larger figure then becomes:
Hc *35°72 minutes*   *Now repeat your other sight:*
Ho *35°52 minutes*
What is the difference between them?

Too much of that kind of thing and you feel like getting up and strangling the teacher. Ah, but teacher knows best. Do it that way and the likelihood that you will write down something other than twenty minutes is greatly diminished. Almost certainly you will spend less time at the navigation table. Because doing it *my* way you whiz through, and come up with your answer in no time flat, especially with the computers there to do most of the work, including calculating the difference between Hc and Ho—but there are a dozen other silly mistakes, examples of which would serve to make the same point (a common one is reading your watch time plus or minus one minute, or the vernier scale on your sextant off by ten minutes). Then you may end by spending an entire hour triangulating in on the error you made.

But let me show you how thoroughly vexing the whole business is. I give a striking example—an episode the very first day out from Bermuda.

I thought it would amuse my companions, after lunch, to play for them one of the cadenzas of the HP-97: plotting a great-circle course from one point to another, as described above in the example from Madeira to Miami—i.e., giving the course changes after every five meridians of longitude.

I brought up my HP-97 and the printed instruction booklet, which gives sample problems, flipping it open to the indicated page, under "Great Circle Course and Rhumb Line Navigation."

I turned to page 02–04 and read:

"EXAMPLE: A well-known amateur naviagator [*sic*] sailed from St. George's Harbor, Bermuda (32° 23′ N, 64° 41′ W) to Horta, Fayal Island (38° 32′ N, 28° 38′ W). Plot the great-circle track at 5-degree intervals.
Keystrokes:
32.23 ENTER 64.41 f A
38.32 ENTER 23.38 AB"   [The outputs are then given.]

I let out a shriek of delight. I had completely forgotten that Ken Newcomer, in making out the instruction booklet, had taken as a sample problem the route I had described in *Airborne*. Indeed, on June 19, 1975, we had set out from St. George's for Faial. "Now get a load of this," I exclaimed to my friends. . . .

And I keyed in the position of St. George's as given in the key-stroke instructions: 32.23, 64.41. And the position of Faial, 38.32, 23.38.

I punched the key that would yield me the Initial Heading, and the Number of Miles.

To my great distress, I found a significant disparity between the HP's mileage, St. George's to Faial, and Plath's mileage, St. George's to Faial. One said 2,022 miles at 067.7°; the other (Plath) 1,787 miles at 067.8°.

There is nothing more distressing psychologically than to prepare an elaborate demonstration only to have it fail. I had had a memorable experience of this a year or so earlier—fortunately, only as a voyeur. I was to be on the Johnny Carson show, merchandising one of my books, and the guest host that night was Orson Welles. He arrived with a gleam in his eye because, sealed in an envelope from a Dutch soothsayer, he had a magic number; and he was going to demonstrate to the studio audience, and to forty million or whatever others who watch the Johnny Carson show, how that soothsayer's secret number could be divined by a series of random mathematical operations based on data taken from the audience, as per the soothsayer's instructions.

There ensued the most confusing and chaotic twenty minutes since the Lord ordained that there should be light; including blackboards, Ping-Pong balls, social security numbers, drivers' license numbers—a mix positively defiant in its complexity, but through it all Orson Welles was sustained by his vision. Finally the numbers written out on the blackboard were added together by a guest (who made an error, which was promptly corrected). It came to something like 3,482,999.

"Now!" said Welles triumphantly to Ed McMahon, his assistant, "hand over the envelope to this member of the studio audience. Come right over here, sir, don't be afraid! Now—" Orson Welles leaned back for his moment of triumph.

In the Green Room, where I sat with Vincent Price and the program's producer, I saw the producer clutching his throat.

"Open the envelope and read the number!" said Welles.

The man did so, with some gravity, lifting the notepaper to the light.

"It says 212."

"It says what!" Welles screamed.

"Two hundred and twelve."

Never was the forthcoming advertisement for Halo shampoo more universally welcomed, by advertiser, star, and producer. When the show resumed, Vincent Price (there to promote his Oscar Wilde one-man show) was sitting opposite Welles. "Orson, how long have we been friends?"

"Oh," said Welles, "I'd say forty years?"

"Then dear Orson, you *won't* mind if I tell you you have laid the biggest egg in the history of television?"

I hadn't done quite that, but I was miserably disconcerted, and excused myself to rework the problem on the Plath—which gave me back cockily the identical readings it had done earlier, and on the basis of which we had set our course.

So back I went to the cockpit, seeking to recapture the attention of my friends. It is wise, when you wish to move with great precision, to have someone else depress the buttons while you dictate instructions.

"All right, Danny, St. George's, 32.23, 64.41; Horta, 38.32, 23.38—"

Danny looked up. "That's not what the manual gives."

I looked up. Surely we had had enough problems with the coordinates of our itinerary to last one voyage.

But there it was: a simple error. The HP people had printed the *wrong* longitude for Horta. They had it right (see above) under "Example," wrong under "Keystrokes," from which we were reading.

I have come to know Ken Newcomer well, mostly over the telephone. And I chided him, in another book, for the mistakes in the printed literature of Hewlett-Packard, and for the opacity of the explanations Hewlett-Packard gives (although by contrast with Texas Instruments, H-P is like following a fairway). Even Plath, with its expensive machine, sends along a printed list of errors in its instruction manual, which *you* are given the burden of correcting, for reasons not entirely plain, since *you* aren't the person who made the mistakes—you are the person who paid fourteen hundred dollars.

And then, one day you will present identical figures to two machines—only to get different results.

I note the log for June 10, with my lapidary exasperation written out on the left-hand page in capitals.

DATA: GMT 18-23-28
HO 51-06
TABLES: Zn 263°, 31 Towards
PLATH: Zn 263°, 68 Towards
H/P: Zn 263°, 31.5 Towards

I find a notation: "*The Plath is inconsistent with previous sun sight (at* 11:22*). Question: was that sight done on Plath? If we* *saved data, we could check with H/P. Tell Danny.*" And, still fretting about it an hour later:

"*1330 FLASH! Trouble with the Plath. It is giving false and ir-regular conclusions. Its GMT is correct.* [I should have noted that its chronometer was correctly set.] *Not to be used until further notice.*"

The next day I ran it through a series of tests—and it worked perfectly.

I suppose, then, that one can conclude only that a) the experts also make mistakes, and do so in the coolness of their air-conditioned offices, surrounded by professional copy editors; so that navigators at sea, a fortiori, are going to make mistakes, though some of them make more mistakes than others.

And then there are glitches which no layman can hope to anticipate. In describing difficulties with the HP-65 in my last book I provoked a number of correspondents who proffered possible explanations. Only a month ago I received one wholly arresting and satisfying commentary on the endeavor, to account for the anomalies I had plotted.

"In Step 1," writes Mr. John F. Hartray, Jr., an architect in Chicago, "the calculator rounds off the date, 19 June 1975, to the nearest hundredth of a year, 75.47 or 47% through 1975. This is too crude an approximation for your purpose. In a hundredth of a year 3.65 days pass, during each of which the earth must rotate about one degree beyond a full circle to compensate for its orbital motion (see enclosed sketch). This results in an increase in the Greenwich Hour Angle (GHA) of Aries of about 3.6 degrees. Step 2 converts the program from solar to stellar or sidereal time (366 days per year). This transfers the high rate of change in GHA from the fixed stars to the sun which is undoubtedly why it takes two chips of almanac data [Mr. Hartray was referring to the obsolete HP-65] to load the sun into the program while stars require only one chip. The 3.65 day rounding-off probably had little effect on star calculations. The only variation which must be accounted for grows out of the change in the earth's orbital velocity at various points on its elliptical path (faster when closer to the sun). This doesn't change much in 3.66 sidereal days. On sun sights, however, the rounding off can result in an error of up to plus or minus 108 nautical miles (3.6 degrees × 60 miles divided by 2) for sights taken east or west at the equator. This error

ANNUAL ORBIT OF EARTH AROUND SUN

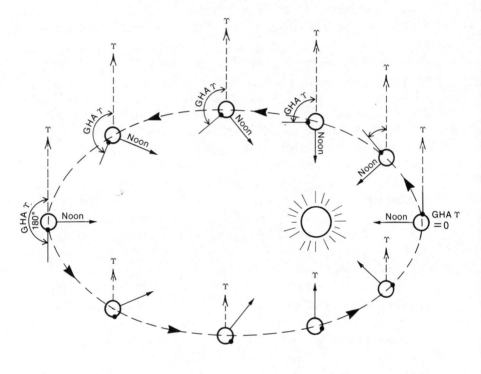

Annual Orbit of Earth Around Sun
Viewed from above North Pole.
Black dot represents Greenwich.
GHA is Greenwich Hour Angle.
Noon sun sight at 270° long.
In 6 months GHA ♈ increases 180°.
In 1/100 of a year GHA ♈ increases 3.6° ±.

decreases as: a) the time on which you take your sight approaches the center of the 3.65-day period, b) the azimuth of the sun at the time of the sight approaches north or south, c) your position moves away from the equator.

"Perhaps," the author meditatively concludes, "the program writer felt that enough of these conditions would usually apply to enable him to escape detection. Besides, if the calculation doesn't work out, most yachtsmen would be more likely to place the blame on their sextant, eyes, or arithmetic rather than on such an expensive new gadget. Actually it shouldn't be too difficult for Hewlett-Packard to develop a program for solar navigation based on the initial rounded-off date which remains on solar time and uses the same GHA data that appears in the printed almanac. Within the solar time frame, the relative movements of the sun are negligible over a 3.65-day period."

Sounds plausible to me, though there was a faintly huffy put-down by Ken Newcomer. He would—given the advances in the navigational programs—in any event consider the question posed as of purely antiquarian interest. The point is nevertheless etched in concrete: the experts slip up. Their machines, though marvelous, bear watching. Don't—ever—forget how to use the tables.

For all that you are constantly reading about navigators bringing down the stars at night, what you most generally get, on small sailing boats, is navigators *trying* to bring down stars at night. The conditions are simply not propitious. David, the first mate, had taken a job during the preceding winter that required him to spend much of the night out on deck in a cargo vessel that slowly, ever so slowly, traversed the Pacific. Being of active mind, David decided there and then to master star identification, which he did; which I have never done, consulting instead on every occasion the star-finder and groping my way through individual star recognition, rather than star recognition by constellation, which is how the experts do it.

In any event, faced now, traveling from Bermuda to the Azores, with a two-thousand-mile eastern passage, I could know that pretty much the same stars and planets would make an early appearance off the starboard bow at dusk. In shooting your stars, you should begin with the easternmost stars, because they are the first to become visible, the residual light from the sun setting in the west giving you too bright a horizon to bring down the western stars until the sun is well down—by which time the eastern horizon may be too amorphous.

So: decide which stars you are going to shoot, and keep the list short—not more than four became my rule. These you can select by reference to their location and intensity on the star-finder, or by consulting the tables in HO 249 (one of three generally used systems) which gives you "selected stars" for every situation (measured by the Greenwich Hour Angle of Aries at the time you propose to shoot).

Now the textbooks teach you to locate the star, and to approximate the anticipated angle on your sextant. Let us say that you are looking for Arcturus and you know that at 7 P.M. it is scheduled to show up at 42 degrees and 15 minutes at an azimuth of 210 degrees. You note that where you are there is a variation of 16 degrees west longitude, so you turn 226 degrees by the compass with your sextant pre-set at 42 degrees 15 minutes. You spot a star that may very well be Arcturus. You are using a fine sextant, let us say a Plath or a Tamaya, both with telescopic lenses, powered at about 4 × 1, so that when you find Arcturus it is much brighter than it would be if you were merely making it out with the naked eye.

You begin, then, to adjust the vernier scale to fine-tune the star on the horizon. What regularly happens is that you will either a) lose the star; or b) lose the horizon. If the latter, it is because the horizon has become too indefinite and you cannot with any sense of assurance conclude what is horizon, and what is sky. If the former, it is because you have been so pitched about by the movement of the boat that what you had carefully trained on as Arcturus turns out now to be another star nearby.

Remember, with the telescopic apparatus, even as the star is magnified four times, so the field of vision through the sextant eye is reduced by a factor of four. This means that, thanks to the telescope, you have one-sixteenth as large an area of the sky to look at. To hang on to a star when the deck is pitching requires something on the order of an in-built gyroscope. In a way, that exactly is what our complicated musculature provides us, else it would be impossible to take even a midday sun sight in a sea, let alone walk across Niagara Falls on a tightrope. But the difficulty at night advances geometrically as the tiny star surrounds itself with other tiny stars, leaving you uncertain as to identification; and meanwhile the horizon is becoming progressively elusive, very/ soon achieving indistinguishability.

Most celestial navigators know the old trick of turning the sextant upside down when they have trouble aiming at the desired celestial body. The idea is to sight, say, Arcturus by looking straight at it through the eyepiece. The arc of your sextant is then, roughly speaking, concentric to the curvature of the earth, rather than the opposite. You need therefore to keep your eye on Arcturus and, with your right hand, work the sextant knob and vernier to lift the horizon up to Arcturus, rather than do the conventional thing of bringing Arcturus down to the horizon.

Now, old salts will not be surprised if you start out that way—if you are having trouble finding Arcturus. Bring the horizon, they'll tell you, to where it is close to Arcturus. Then resume the normal sextant position, both ends of the arc curving once again heavenward: *now* do your fine tuning.

I say nuts. Do your fine tuning with your sextant inverted.

As I advanced on these insights, I left my Rolls-Royce Tamaya in its case and brought out my little fifty-dollar emergency sextant (I cannot give its brand name because I never remarked it, and it was stolen on the way back from Spain). I could divest it, with a twist of my fingers, of its little telescope, and aim through the naked eyepiece. I inverted the sextant, on the night of June 12. For the first time in my life I achieved an absolutely perfect little triangle, bringing down, or rather taking the horizon up to, Spica, Vega, and Arcturus. And here is an important dividend. Since you are pointing now at Arcturus, having brought the horizon up to it, you have substantially eliminated what one might call the pendulum factor. When you bring a star down to the sea, you cannot know that it sits truly on top of the sea unless you simulate with your sextant the movement of a pendulum, to establish that you are holding it perfectly perpendicular. If your hands are slanted, you will find, when you arc the sextant, that you are sinking the star into the ocean or floating it up into the sky.

But when you lift the horizon, you all but eliminate the pendulum. If the horizon is now tangential to the heavenly body, it makes little difference if the sextant is at an angle—the distance measured doesn't change. You can swing your sextant fifteen degrees clockwise or fifteen degrees counterclockwise, and if Arcturus was touching the horizon in the first instance, it will be touching the horizon in the second.

To eliminate the pendulum factor is a huge blessing particularly in heavy weather. The sensation is really breathtaking. There it was, my fix. Moreover, it revealed a considerable southerly drift since taking the noon sight, and so I altered the course instantly. Every night thereafter I succeeded in getting three stars, or at least two, and one planet. With the Navicomp, as noted, even the inconvenience of plotting is eliminated—by asking the machine for a fix based on the two most recent sights. I am, as I write, experimenting with a Plath model sextant that comes without magnification. I have not repeated my successes of the summer, but on the two occasions I tried misty clouds stood between me and the stars I had my beady eyes on. But I shall have them, I warrant; and so will you, if you do exactly as I say—always a good idea.

11

~~~~~~~~~~~~~~~~~~

Van, having for the second time in our joint experiences traversing the Atlantic Ocean accepted the commission of meteorologist, undertook—as is his way—to make some systematic inquiries. He was very penitent, after the first trip, about his failure to apprise himself of the radio frequencies through which vital weather data are given relevant to the particular region in which you are traveling. The same day we landed in Marbella in 1975, a trim and seaworthy yacht sailing from Bermuda to Newport capsized. We read deeply in the matter, and it transpired that just a little *essential* information would have given the boat's skipper (he and his crew were all rescued by a Russian freighter) time to anticipate the movements of the oncoming hurricane, by rushing back to the sanctuary of Bermuda.

Blame ⚓1): Bermuda Radio was an unconscionable one-day late in relaying information issued by the National Hurricane Center in Miami (telephone 305-666-0413). Blame ⚓2): The skipper, proceeding insouciantly, under the dispensation of the Bermuda weather report, sallied on down the rhumb line ignoring savage empirical data until it was simply too late. Blame ⚓3): Observing that things were obviously getting worse than anything anticipated by Bermuda Radio, the skipper should have more ingeniously improvised a strategic retreat from the firestorm.

All this Van knew; and, to be sure, he proceeded on my assurance that we would have a functioning Weathermax on board. To find oneself without such an instrument, if you began by assuming its presence, is a little like being dispatched as navigator on the assumption of a functioning chronometer on board, only to find that it doesn't work. If you have no chronometer, you are sorely handicapped; but Columbus made significant headway without one, as did Cortés, Magellan, Drake. If you don't have the Weathermax, you assume that you will get, from the radio, essentially the same information it yields, only by different, more complicated means.

I have a more or less permanent impression of Van crouched over the most imposing radio on board. To speak of the most imposing radio on board the *Sealestial* is on the order of speaking of the most imposing automobile in the Paris Automobile Show. It was a Panasonic Kandy-Kolored Tangerine Supermax this or that. It is not an exaggeration to say that—counting this Mickey Mouse —there were maybe twenty radios on board, if you count Dick's ten. But the Panasonic was the dreamboat, with digital readouts, the whole business. Probably Van spent a cumulative twenty-five hours trying to get it to perform. He had tables giving information about where, and when, and at what frequency, reports would be broadcast giving a vessel an idea of what lay ahead of it on the plotted course.

The easy way to say it is that the Panasonic didn't work. That much is certainly true. And, of course, it relied ultimately on the same aerial on which our delinquent radiotelephone relied. On board the *Sealestial* there were considerable resources of electronic and engineering talent. If you throw into the pot everything Allen knows, everything Reggie knows, add David, plus a mite from Van, Dick, and from me an unpredictable but occasional capacity to descry from a written instruction an actual meaning, you had quite a lot.

Not enough. Primary blame, one supposes—not having conducted an inquest—falls on technology: the signals simply didn't come in at the predesignated moments at the predesignated channels. But having said as much, it is necessary to communicate the full meed of the amateur sailor's frustration at the forbidding bureaucratization of the language of the sea.

Hugh Kenner had on several occasions made an interesting point on the subject. He had made it directly to me, and indirectly to Hewlett-Packard's Ken Newcomer: namely, that it really does make sense, when writing instructions for the use of people at sea, to recognize that some of them are in small boats, and then to imagine conditions at sea for such folk. After all, the QE2, if really confused about the weather directly ahead, can always wire the Privy Council or whoever and get satisfaction. Aboard such vessels as the *Sealestial*, typically the circumstances are less auspicious. It is very black outside, the winds increasing in velocity. We have just taken a reef in the mainsail, checked out the barometer but found no significant movement. One watch member is at the wheel, the second approaches the radio, having first consulted Van's radio log. He stares, to see what is available at this moment, in order to get an idea of what lies ahead.

I did this one night and I quote verbatim what the Admiralty List of Radio Signals, 1972, shot back at me:

"This volume should be corrected each week"—those of us who confess our sins less frequently than once a week marvel at the suggestion that every single Friday, on the way from the office to the country, one should check with the Admiralty List of Radio Signals, 1972. You turn to the relevant page, page 149 in our case, where is advertised, "*Transmission from St-Lys, Special Marine Weather Bulletins and Storm Warnings.* TIME: (*messages in French*): *30 m. past two successive* EVEN *hours, immediately before the traffic lists. If necessary, a repetition is made at the first* EVEN *hour in which the watch keeping schedules of single-operated ships in Zone A. (8.510: 'Not on Sundays or holidays.')*" There are those for whom the above is translatable into English, but they are rare; and the probability is high that they maintain their special cerebral sensitivities by insulating themselves from tumultuous situations at sea, with a fractious radio in their hands, salt water whistling past their ears, minor and major objects crashing about them and, over it all, the sound of radio static.

Moral? Teddy Tucker's is simple. What he says is characteristically fatalistic: *Go where you want to go, and take your chances on the weather.* Teddy is very tough, and very lucky, and very ingenious. My own position is down the middle. Forget trying to tease out of the weather the kind of information that might prove critical to a racing sailor. Take, in a cruise, what comes—but try to make certain that you and a man-eating hurricane are not headed on converging courses. And this means that you need either a Weathermax (luxury stuff) or a reliable radio with one or two frequencies that will actually talk English to you, and tell you what you need to know. You are, in my experience, better off tuning in constantly to one or two very good stations stateside until about Longitude 55°, then go to England and count on them to tell you if something ominous is coming up. If so, and your radio works (try to see to it that it does), *then* call the Hurricane Center and keep track of the storm or hurricane, and make entries, every hour, of your barometer reading.

Having said as much I confess that if I were tomorrow to set out on the identical journey I would not know offhand which frequencies to recommend. What I *would* do, the third time out if ever I should go again, is talk to one or two captains of the regular freighter runs. Ask them. The kind of thing they tell you—what frequency to keep your radio tuned to—isn't likely to show up in the yachting magazines. Or in the books of dilettantes.

It's possible to get cross, every now and then, with Bermudians, but safe to generalize that they are really the friendliest people in the world. Their anxiety to be helpful seems to rub off on anyone who spends time there, as witness the wonderful amiability of the people at the U.S. Naval Base, to the operations center of which Van directed our taxi when we were on our way to St. George's to board the *Sealestial*. He desired from the meteorological officer projections of the weather, and from an obliging young man we got Xerox copies of four sheets predicting the area isobars four days down the line, a high-pressure escort, beginning that very day, in the direction we were traveling. These bits of paper are by no means easy for the amateur to read: I have a terrible time with them, and devote as much attention to the expression on Van's face as to the efforts to transcribe what the stigmata are trying to say to me. The rule of thumb, we all know, is High Pressure is Good, and Low Pressure is Bad. But the rule of thumb is qualified by what it is that the sailor is in search of—namely, wind. Not too much wind, mind, but wind enough to sail by. So that—particularly if you were racing—you would avoid heading directly into the center of a high, lest you find yourself windless. You would be willing to make considerable sacrifices in geographical distance in exchange for propulsion: that sort of thing. In any event, we left with four pieces of paper that suggested the going would be easy for the four foreseeable days in the future, which indeed it was.

I say we left, but not quite without incident. At the reception area, maintained by a young sailor whose dress and all-American features might have been crafted by Norman Rockwell, and whose posture behind the reception desk was disconcerting only because he'd have looked more natural coming in from the sea, towing a rescued grandmother, I espied a clock. A most tantalizing clock. Exact-time nuts are clock-conscious, and there is nothing more challenging to our machismo than a clock that asseverates its own correctness. This particular clock was the more provocative because it asserted not its correctness to the second, but to the three seconds. It is easier to ignore the magazine cover that promises to display the most beautiful woman in the world (routine hyperbole) than to dismiss the cover that promises to display the woman than whom no one has discovered two more beautiful women.

I looked at my watch, the pride of my life (when it works, this being one such moment, or at least was, as of that morning when I checked it against our radio). I paused, and addressed the young man.

"Excuse me, but are you saying that the time on the clock there is in fact correct within three seconds, plus or minus, for Greenwich Mean Time?"

"Yes, sir."

"Well," I said, studying my wristwatch carefully, "in fact, you are twenty-five seconds off."

"No sir. I think you will find that *you* are twenty-five seconds off."

What to do? Should I go to *Sealestial*, five miles away at St. George's, bring in my $36 Radio Shack WWV time-tic, and *ram it down Jack Armstrong's throat?* That, I thought, would be to commit the sin of pride; so I motioned to Van that we should be off. But I brooded on the subject. Twenty-five seconds. Four seconds equal one mile. So that our naval base was giving out the time, misleading people, to the extent their navigation depended on it, by six miles. I tried to crank up a sense of civic obligation, but I was too hungry, and so we simply went on to St. George's, told the taxi driver that no, the dark-gray World War II submarine that squatted on the water like a dozing lamprey eel *wasn't* our sailboat—the next boat, with the two masts, all the sails, and the people, was our sailboat; boarded; asked Danny—to check on myself—to check my watch time; and it was right. If our ICBMs land six miles north of Red Square, I've got a scoop.

That night, the first night on the leg to the Azores, I took star sights with the usual frustrating results. But I felt that I was on the verge of Discovery, and lo, this was correct, as I have revealed, forever liberating the legions who have suffered over the ages from the problem of bringing in the stars. The next morning was Sunday, and on this occasion Danny and I did meet to pray together. We sat in the stateroom looking at "suggested passages" in the index of the Bible, and Danny nominated "Separation from Worldliness," which certainly suggested our condition, twenty-four hours out from Bermuda with a destination two thousand miles away.

"Having therefore these promises, dearly beloved, let us cleanse ourselves from all the filthiness of the flesh and spirit, perfecting holiness in the fear of God. . . . Love not the world, neither the things that are in the world. If any man love the world, the love of the Father is not in him. For all that is in the world, the lust of the flesh, and the lust of the egos, and the pride of life, is not of the Father, but of the world." How true this was—is—and how wonderfully apposite, in its current inapplicability. At that moment Danny lusted most awfully for the flesh and the spirit of his beloved Gloria. And I was most fearfully grateful to the Lord for things of the earth, the sea and the skies, and a tight hull, the sails above me, and my companions who made them function, and proud of this spirited company. But the purpose of prayer, surely, is to stress the great divisions between the material and the supernatural condition, not to gloss over them.

The second night out I shared the watch with Christopher, and we got around to talking about the book we were committed to produce about our journey. I had decided on *Atlantic High* as its title, having spent some time looking for a word—like airborne—

Reg, Christopher, Tony, Van, WFB, Danny, in Faial.

that was intentionally ambiguous. Mark Dichter told us he had heard that Roy Disney (nephew) had poured a prodigious sum of money into the production of a feature film based on the Ensenada race, a California staple. Roy Disney is a committed yachtsman who (a coincidence) bought the broadcasting company I had served (there is a difference of opinion on how well) as board chairman. At least six times a year, in my travels, I run into people who say to me, "I saw Roy Disney the other day and told him I'd be seeing you and he said to say hello." After a considerable accumulation of these greetings I suddenly found myself wondering why Roy did not bother to convey his own greeting. But then, why haven't I? So: "Hello, Roy! I liked the title of your feature film—which one day I hope to see—so very much that I leaned on your title (*Pacific High*) for my own book. Hope you enjoy it."

Christopher asked if I had a subtitle in mind; I told him I didn't, but hoped to come up with one. *Airborne*'s subtitle was a pre-emptive strike. It was: "A Sentimental Journey." There is sentiment in that book, and I didn't want the reviewers to say it first. It worked. Van came into the cockpit. Our pace was absolutely steady, the moon and stars were out, and we were going very nearly at hull speed, propelled by a wind suddenly turned warmer than what we had experienced, inducing me to slide my sweater off while I balanced the wheel on my knee. Van overheard the last part of our conversation and said why didn't I use as a subtitle, "How to Survive at Sea with Only $650,000 Worth of Equipment"? He proceeded to pollute the water, mutter good night, and go back to his cabin. He was still reading when, a few minutes later, at watch change, I myself went to bed in the bunk directly below his. He was chuckling, a copy of *Encounter* on his stomach. "Here," he said, "is a quote from a sign in an Istanbul hotel: 'To call room service, please to open the door and call room service.'"

Christopher had said after Van went below that he, Christopher, was greatly struck by the congeniality of the crew, and I reflected on the philosophical proposition: If A likes B, C, D, E, and F, and they like A, does it follow that B will like C, D, E, and F? . . . etc. Van had never met Tony or Christopher; Tony didn't know Van or Christopher; Christopher didn't know Reg, Van, Tony, Danny; Danny didn't know Tony or Christopher. A metaphor survived in the memory from the column I had written the previous morning—namely, the dialectic between intimacy and loneliness. It was so at the South Pole. I was there for only five days in midsummer (January), but beginning in April the sun would disappear, to rise again only in October. Six months of darkness, isolation: no traffic whatever with the rest of the world; a community reduced from its summer-size complement to about one hundred people. How did they get on? I am not ready to generalize on the subject, but it is objectively true that on our voyage no one was getting on the nerves of anyone else; and so it would be, on through the trip. Whether they will remain friends doesn't, really, matter.

The centrifugal forces that lead people away from each other—the hectic anonymity of New York; different professions; different extra-marine interests—all these argue for separation. But in the loneliness of the sea there is a bond. It is highly attenuated, by comparison with the bond that binds men in combat, but it is there, as the element of combat is there.

12

Dick is of course correct that you cannot easily leave shore or, having done so, leave your concerns entirely behind. I belong to a club in California whose motto is "Weaving spiders, come not here." Indeed the (quite extraordinary) Bohemian Encampment begins with a rococo ritual in which the members witness a pageant wherein worldly concerns are first corporealized, and then eliminated. It is called the "Cremation of Care," and came to us right from the golden age of Victorian optimism. Bah humbug; it was at the Bohemian Grove that I first saw Ronald Reagan and George Bush pawing the ground as they greeted each other; two years later they plighted their troth so happily. And so forth.

Danny, as we know, was absorbed in thoughts of his girl. Poor Reggie was struggling to adjust to a divorce and a (temporarily) wrecked professional life. Van worried (to the extent Van can do so, buoyed as he so regularly is by the piquancies of life, and ricocheting surefootedly off its bizarre juxtapositions) because his spirited wife's unhappiness at leaving London was something much greater than merely not wanting to leave A to return to B because she had got used to A; her resistance was truly organic, and Van worried about it. Christopher can probably be said to have brought his professional worries on board quite intentionally, and his discharge of those duties was as industrious as anything I have ever beheld—it would not have surprised any of us if, sometime after midnight, Christopher had thrown himself overboard, so as to be able to photograph the rescue party. Tony—one never quite knew whether the expression on his face was that of Hamlet facing life's tortured ambiguities, or merely reflected an internal biological dialectic on whether he could have a second helping of chile con carne without becoming queasy. I had my concerns, but as a most practical matter, I had my unanswered mail.

I have found over the years that unanswered mail is no problem at all for some very nice people, for instance Whittaker Chambers, James Burnham, and John Leonard—a prophet, a philosopher, a critic—who somewhere along the line decided, with significant exceptions, not to acknowledge correspondence. Chambers wrought architectural masterpieces, to those to whom he elected to respond, and probably sent out ten times as many words via the post office as ever he sent to his publishers, whether at *New Masses*, Time Inc., Random House, or *National Review*. James Burnham courted anonymity, notwithstanding the grand and justifiable claims he made on the attention of those who cared about what he (chronologically, the first to do so) called *The Struggle for the World*. Leonard—who came to *National Review* at age twenty, freshly kicked out of Harvard for the kind of endearing delinquencies that, in John's case, will surely, a century or so hence, cause a half-holiday to be declared at Harvard on the anniversary of Kicking John Leonard Out—developed a personal eccentricity not readily fathomable, particularly when old friends write him letters that, in circumstances commonly accepted as civilized, "require" a reply and are greeted by silence, unaffecting his cheery voice when he answers the telephone.

In any event, I have always felt a compulsion of sorts to answer mail. Let me begin by affecting no distortion. My mail does not come in (I assume) at anything like the volume of Mick Jagger's or—at an entirely serious level—Walter Cronkite's. But it comes in in awesome volume. I answer the mail in part because I desire to do so, in part because, as editor of a journal of opinion of ambitious political-intellectual reach, I feel I should do so; in part because my journal, and to a degree my ideology, are mendicant in their posture toward the various tribunals that judge us and the readers that sustain us. I write now not long after a man who long ago publicly declared that his favorite magazine is the magazine I edit has been elected President of the United States. Not bad. I do not regret answering *his* letters over the years. But, mostly, the letters aren't from people who have in mind the presidency. They are an infinitely interesting breed, and their motivations are diverse.

Some people write letters compulsively—a lady I knew (R.I.P.) wrote me about ten pages every week for a period of about twelve years, until I wounded her by coming out for the decriminalization of pot, after which she reduced the flow by about one half. There are, as I say, those who 'simply will not write letters (I am married to one, more's the pity: because those few letters she has forced herself to write are memorable). In between, where most people are found, there are the Utilitarians (they write only to accomplish a finite purpose); the Supplicants (they write to get something from or out of you); the Professionals (they write out of a sense of duty, and in order to effect something or set something right); the Critics (they write to tell you what's wrong—and, occasionally, what's right—about you and your world); and there are the miscellaneously motivated.

Since the volume of mail received by editors is very great we need to develop a style of our own. The key is brevity—there is no way to indulge the dilative impulse and get on with the business at hand, not unless you are prepared to be severely discriminatory— i.e., send Jones a very long letter, and ignore the next twenty. But there are different ways of being brief, and a decent respect for the feelings of mankind argues for the development of non-peremptory brevity. "Dear Mr. Jones: I return your manuscript, which is unusable," is a world away from "Dear Mr. Jones: The answer is a most reluctant No," though the word count is exactly the same. Granted, my rejection formula does not achieve the oriental plenitude of the Peking publication whose editor returned a manuscript to a British economist with the note, "We have read your manuscript with boundless delight. If we were to publish your paper it would be impossible for us to publish any work of a lower standard. And, as it is unthinkable that in the next thousand years we shall see its equal, we are, to our regret, compelled to return your divine composition, and beg you a thousand times to overlook our short sight and timidity."

Reggie at the helm, in rough weather; Reggie adapting to a change in weather. Below, Christopher Little's camera is fastened on the spinnaker pole (note guy line).

I settled down in the huge armchair in the owner's stateroom, and raised my foot to the vertical bar to provide balance from the ship's pitch. On the floor, to the right, the growing mound of letters answered. On the left, in the large canvas case, the pile on which I would whittle away. I had breakfasted, talked with the duty watch about sails and strategy, calculated a Dead Reckoning (DR) position, checked to see what time the sun would cross the meridian so as to have ample notice before taking the indispensable noon sight. I brought in the battery-operated cassette player, and inserted a tape. . . .

Among the pending requests is one from a young editor of madcap inclinations. "Would it be convenient to get together for a chat or drinks during that period [when he would be in New York]? Would it be convenient to tape you on the Corporation Song during that period? This is of course an important matter, for I have always seen myself as a defender of high culture." This particular writer, founder and editor of the *American Spectator*, has the habit of catapulting himself into higher forms of inanity from paragraph to paragraph. He did not let me down this time: "As a defender of high culture, I enclose a copy of one of the latest songs we have added to our repertoire. It is so beautiful that on the first night Kapellmeister Von Kannon led us in it we were all moved to uncontrollable sobbing. It indeed qualifies somewhere between the sublime and the beautiful, probably the ridiculous." Answers to such letters are necessarily genial, and it is prudent not to attempt to reply in kind.

A doctor in Montana, a devotee of classical music and the traditional Roman liturgy, is shocked by a recent experience. "I attended the First Communion of the first-born of a friend whom I had delivered into the world and as the child walked solemnly down the aisle the organ played 'Raindrops Keep Falling on My Head.'" Could I, he asked, tell him how to get in touch with the orthodox liturgists in America? This was not difficult to do, there being only about three of them left.

A regular correspondent who does not let a week go by without sending along a rainbow or two he has happened upon in his discursive reading, or else trapped from the stream of his reminiscences, complains that he cannot find the word *"negritude"* (used by me in a recent column) in a dictionary. I reply, *"negritude* is the French word for blackness, and has attached to it the same kind of thing that attaches, in an entirely different context, to the word machismo." That query was harder to handle than that of another correspondent of the week who demanded to know the meaning of the word "querencia," which he said *he* could not find in any dictionary. This greatly worried me and before leaving New York I actually put in a call to Barnaby Conrad, who taught me the word in one of his books on bullfighting a million years ago. As I waited for the long-distance operator to track him down, I thumbed through Webster's Third: and there it is, big as life *"querencia: . . ."* My answer, I think understandably, had a touch of the drill sergeant's: "See Webster's III." I didn't even furnish the page number, though I probably would have done so if the letter writer's tone had been a little less peremptory.

A reporter, calling attention to a book diligently unreviewed by the press, wrote: "I'm sending you a copy with hopes you might be motivated to read it and if so moved to comment." Book writers, including the author of this book, are incapable of learning that the one thing an editor can least afford to do is promise to read *any* given book (time required, depending on the book and on the reading speed of the reader, 6–16 hours). The reply is necessarily evasive.

Every editor *begins* life by resolving *never ever* to agree to read book manuscripts. No one succeeds completely. In this case however, it is a protégé who wrote first at age fourteen to ask exactly what was meant by the right-wing shibboleth against "immanentizing the eschaton." Finally I found the time to read one hundred pages. Courage! (He is young and very sensitive.) "It needs total overhauling. If ever you are in the mood for it, come see me and I'll spend an hour and a half with you and show you the kind of thing that needs to be done just to the first three or four pages in order to electrify them. I hardly consider myself a master—but in one respect my advice is extremely good: I am the most easily bored man in the universe, and under the circumstances a good

---

Always there is the mail to answer.

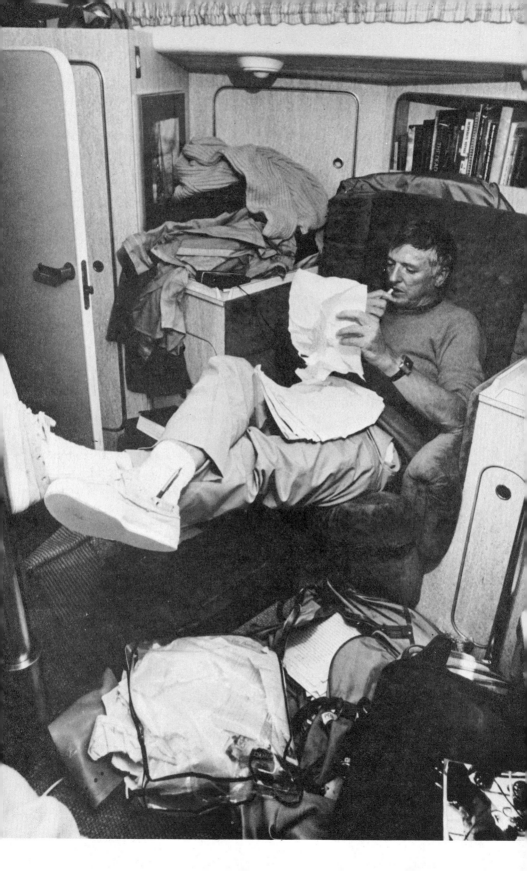

litmus test on the question whether the attention is conscripted. You *must* command the reader's interest and attention—much faster than you now do."

One is invited, once or twice a week, to join committees. It is sometimes very hard to say no—as the shrewd letter writer clearly knows, and, accordingly, his invitation is quite other than merely perfunctory. ". . . we [have] decided to organize a new university in a manner that excludes, from the beginning, elements that have contributed to the decline of higher education." How can you resist associating yourself with anything that noble? As follows: "I do not believe I am sufficiently qualified to serve as a consultant, and I know that I do not have the time to try, which I greatly regret." And to another invitation, a formulaic reply: "I resolved several years ago not to join any non-social organizations, resigning even from several I had belonged to for years. I find it inhibits my freedom as a journalist. I know you will understand that I wish you well with your important enterprise." It is quite true that you wish him well, less than true that you *know* he will understand your declination to join him.

The big enemies are: 1) youth (some of whom you cannot bring yourself to say no to) and, 2) other editors. In the latter category, along comes Mr. Slick himself. He gets away with it by being possibly the nicest man in the whole world. He sends you the current issue of his magazine in which it just happens that there is a rave review of your most recent book *written by Mr. Slick himself!*, collapsing your first line of defense, since most writers will commit matricide for a good, understanding review, an understanding review being one in which you are mentioned in the same breath with, say, Melville. Mr. Slick maneuvers by invoking Duty. "Enjoying the sea, you should give something back to the sea, something to honor the shades of earlier voyages. We are the way to do that—the best way, I am bold to say. And the way to help the cause [*Sea History* is devoted to] would be for you to dash off a piece for our next issue."

"Dash off" is a form of professional flattery; it goes a long way.

"I will be glad to repay your kindness . . ."

Reggie comes in, sorry to interrupt me. . . . No sweat, what's up? . . . Do I know where Captain Jouning keeps the batteries? Allen is taking a snooze. Reggie is trying to fix the radio, and wants to try out a fresh set of batteries. . . . No, I don't know where the ship's supply is, but I know where *my* supply is, and Reggie knows that I arrive on board pursuing the autarkic imperative of self-sufficiency. Thoreau defined freedom as the increased knowledge of what he could do without. I tend to define it as the increased knowledge of what I shan't need to do without. I opened the bottom left drawer on the dresser and gave Reggie his six Cs. . . .

My guess is that everybody who has dominion over any kind of press space spends considerable time answering letters from convicted felons. This one tells me that Tony Scaduto, the same author who in a widely noticed book a few years ago "proved" that Bruno Hauptmann was in fact innocent of killing the Lindbergh baby, for which crime he was electrocuted in 1936, *believes* in the innocence of the writer, whose address is "The United States Penitentiary, Lewisburg, Pa." The writer quotes back at me a line from a recent column by me, to wit: "As for those who believe that the Edgar Smith case [he was finally adjudged guilty—by his own confession; I had spent a quarter of a lifetime arguing his probable innocence] warrants a vow to accept the ruling of any court as factually definitive, it is necessary to remind them that this year and every year an innocent man will be convicted. Edgar Smith has done quite enough damage in his lifetime without underwriting the doctrine that the verdict of a court is infallible." I once asked Truman Capote to read Edgar Smith's book, *Brief Against Death*. He did so, and then I asked him:

"Do you believe Smith was guilty?"

Capote answered, "Yes."

"Why?" I asked.

"I never met one yet who wasn't."

That cynicism has its charm, *but one must resist it*. On the other hand, one is so easily conned. So I wrote, copy to the prisoner: "Dear Mr. Scaduto: I have a letter from Mr. ———, a copy of which I enclose. If you have written anything on [his] case, I'd be glad to read it. Yours faithfully." Speaking of conmanship, there is a letter from Rubin (Hurricane) Carter. He is the gentleman-pugilist who is always being convicted of killing someone. A few years ago he persuaded half of Broadway to sponsor an appeal for a new trial. He won it and, stepping out of jail, angrily denounced his persecutors. He got his new trial, on his own terms: and, verily, a brand-new jury sent him right back to jail, convicted of first-degree murder.

Hurricane wrote to remind me that *before* his legal victory, I had agreed to meet with him to hear his story—a commitment that became moot when he won his (temporary) freedom. He wished to revive that commitment, and wrote euphuistically, ". . . being fully cognizant of that old idiom which speaks to the fact that neither a wise man nor a fool can clearly see where they are going if they're always looking backwards at where they've been—I must ask you what are the chances of rescheduling our meeting of yesterday for today? . . . I just had to ask you that because of yet another age-old idiom—that being, 'He who bemoans the lack of opportunity forgets that small doors often open up into large rooms.'" I reflect, on reading his typewritten letter, that the availability of typewriters in the death house at Trenton resulted from the only objectively successful political campaign I can ever remember having mounted. But—sigh—I am disinclined to believe that Hurricane Carter was twice cheated, though temperamentally disinclined to shut the door *absolutely* tight. "Please forgive the lateness in answering your letter. It would be easier for me to answer it if you would be specific in advising me what it is that you wish to talk to me about." I swear, if he answers simply, "What do you think, shithead—a prison break"— I know myself, and I'll be on the next train to Trenton; maybe a one-way trip.

In which event I would lean all the harder on my professional associates. What a pleasure when *they* need *you!*

My accountant had read that Milton Friedman might give professional economic advice to the government of Israel. Since my accountant, in addition to being the *Pithecanthropus erectus* Anti-Socialist man, is also the Original Zionist, the prospect of working *for Friedman* in behalf of *Israel* is quite simply overwhelming. Like the professor in Randall Jarrell's novel who loved Greek and loved the thirteenth century: "If the thirteenth century had spoken Greek, it would have killed him not to have lived in it." Of course, I comply with a recommendation to Milton Friedman, and take the occasion to congratulate Milton on his book's longevity on the best-seller list. Just two weeks earlier, I had spoken at an affair in Washington at which Milton was the other speaker. I remarked that I had greeted my old friend at the reception by embracing him, which embrace he did not fully requite, permitting me to ask huffily, "What does the King of Sweden have that *I* don't have?" Milton blushed, just as, I am certain, he did when he was handed the Nobel Prize.

There are the correspondents who Never Forget. Where is the book I was writing on Ortega y Gasset? I had practically forgotten about the book. The correspondent encloses an eleven-year-old New York *Times* clipping from which she had gleaned the information. . . . A mad artist, wonderfully talented, sends me an engraved invitation to attend an opening at which he will exhibit a piece of sculpture commissioned by me. "I would truly love to be there, but alas the mountain will have to be shipped to Mohammed." (The exhibition is in Honolulu. The invitation to attend it is an invitation to take an eleven-thousand-mile trip.) . . . A student wishes to know with whom he might commune, on transferring to Georgetown, of harmonious sympathies. The writer employs a device at once banal and effective. "If this letter does not reach you personally, I won't be dismayed, for I imagine that your letter-readers, or a secretary, might be able to find such information. Sincere thanks for any help you—or someone else there —may be able to offer." It is not any longer safe to suggest that, at Georgetown, merely because it is nominally a Jesuit-run institution, he might look up the Holy Ghost and expect to find that He has tenure there, so I give him the name of an old conservative crony who has survived the academic purges. . . . A pretender to a formidable European crown laments the ignorance of so many Rhodesians of the strategic realities, and wonders if some money might not be raised to pay the passage of a few scholars who might go to Salisbury to tutor the leadership: but already it is too late. Mugabe is by now established.

Could I have your comment on . . . ? Probably the single most frequent gambit. This one does it in spades: ". . . I would be happy to hear your views and criticism on [the] subject. Do you believe that the time is right for ESOTs? How do you feel about ERISA, and the TRASOP, where capital-intensive companies are allowed an additional tax credit of 1% with an ESOT? How about AT&T's recent adoption of an ESOT? Do you see the proposal making dividend payments to ESOTs tax-free as the beginning of the end to double taxation of dividends? Can you help Mr.

Kelso, Senator Long, and small business (the primary beneficiary of ESOTs) in the promotion of the ESOT concept?" What *can* you reply? ("I'm glad you prodded me on the general subject . . .") You stand up, and go out on deck where everything is bright. Reggie (having given up on the radio) and Tony are playing Ghost. I consider asking them, in grave accents, their opinion of ESOTs and TRASOPs, but good nature arrests me.

Ah, but then you too are always asking favors. Dinah Shore *must* place on her program my wonderful harpsichord teacher. I sent Dinah the videocassette of my teacher, ages ago—"Miss Shore will look forward to viewing it." Six months go by. Silence. I call her from Switzerland; she promises she will dig into it immediately. Six months go by. Silence. I send her a telegram. She replies! "I received your wire last night. Please forgive me. Everybody fell in love with Ms. Norell on the cassette and they are busy making plans for all kinds of introductions and productions on the show. I guess they communicated their enthusiasm to everyone *except* Ms. Norell and you. That is my fault. I apologize. I'm still in a state of lovely shock at a long-distance person-to-person call from Switzerland! I'll bet even Cyrus Vance calls station-to-station these days. You know how President Carter is. I hope your book is finished and satisfying. I also hope to see you soon. Love from your closet groupie—Dinah." *Dinah!* aaaahhhh! But a complementary gallantry? "FORGIVE MY IMPORTUNITIES, BUT IT DID TAKE EIGHTEEN MONTHS. BUT ALL THAT IS FORGOTTEN IF JUDITH NORELL GAVE YOU PLEASURE, WHICH IS THE HIGHEST AMBITION OF MY PUBLIC LIFE. WITH LOVE."

In the category of letter writers who desire to do you a favor there are also categories. There is the letter that suggests a formulation that would be useful to you. The letter of simple amiability ("I wanted to encourage you" and its converse). There is the hot tip, or even hot scoop, letter. . . .

Did I know that a new edition of Whittaker Chambers' famous book *Witness* was coming out soon, a professor at the University of Wisconsin writes? "I call the circumstances to your attention since it might be an occasion for coverage in one of your columns." A simple reply will do nicely: "Thanks so much for the tip. We will act on it."

A student at Stanford University sends me his term paper,

which is about me and my writings. He says I have been very useful to him, and I thank him for saying so. His essay is, as I put it in my reply, "interesting, and well put together, but strikes me as somewhat fragmentary. Perhaps that is inevitable." You can hardly be blamed if it was inevitable, right?

A scholar at the University of South Carolina lassoing a Ph.D. has taken to sending me illuminating letters on the general subject of economic theory. These are elaborate enterprises in wrought-iron thought. "First," he begins this letter, "a Diversion on Economics and Ideology: Without standards of self-enforced intellectual honesty, there could be no science. Economics, being eminently suspect, demands rigorous adherence to a code which restricts the economist to the following line of questioning: Is any given hypothesis capable of being falsified (and thereby tested)? Is any given theoretical or empirical result analytically correct and logically consistent? What, then, are its economic implications?" There is no way to reply in reciprocally nutritional coin. . . . "I am as ever indebted to you . . ."

A professor at Yale writes that he has submitted a letter to the New York *Times* which is as yet unpublished, the thesis of it "my solid belief that if we do finally abandon the Republic of China for Peking, the USSR will move into Taiwan. They have every good reason for doing so." And that is consistent with the letter from a board chairman who participated recently at a weekend conference at which was also present a high U.S. official recently in China. This gentleman confided that his "experience with Mao as well as the existing Chinese leaders, in spite of formal agreements and their rhetoric, has made very clear that there is to be no pressure on resolving the Taiwan issue. In fact, as G—— put it: 'They say . . . relax . . . take four years, take ten years, take 100 years.'" That one is worth running down, and I make a note to do so. A month later, "G——" is nominated for the vice-presidency of the United States; four months later, he is elected.

The wife of a scholar friend, who is herself a scholar, writes to enclose a book of essays on Dante's *Inferno*. The introductory essay, by herself, alludes to the use of Dante's symbols by Whittaker Chambers in *Witness*. I forward the collection to a Dante scholar at Yale, an old friend. I am reminded of a piece of (excusable?) mischief I got into, intending that old friend a favor.

The year was 1965, and I was in the apartment of Mr. and Mrs. Henry Luce—Mrs. Luce wished to talk about the forthcoming tenth-anniversary dinner for *National Review* that she had agreed to chair. Harry Luce was out at a Council on Foreign Relations dinner and would be back in an hour or so. Mrs. Luce was called to the telephone, and I idled in the study where, on the coffee table, I spotted some galleys. I picked them up. Next week's book section, *Time* magazine. *The whole of the book section devoted to a single volume!* Written by my old friend at Yale. Two hours later, when I left the apartment, I rushed to the pay telephone at the corner, not waiting, even, to get home, ten blocks away. I reached him: Guess what's being reviewed in next week's *Time* . . . Rave review! . . . *Devoted an entire section to it!* . . . My friend, an unexcitable type, managed a little trace of excitement. "Perhaps I should call the publisher in the morning?" he asked. "Perhaps you should call him tonight, and perhaps you should get a bottle of champagne! . . ."

There. I am glad, after all these years, to have got that indiscretion off my chest. It's time for the noon sight. Will resume tomorrow.

A professor at St. John's in Brooklyn, commenting on my response to John Kenneth Galbraith's *The Age of Uncertainty*, wishes I would devote more of my attention to the work of Cobden, who he says was the primary intellectual force for the repeal of the Corn Laws. Right ho. A classmate (who because we did not know each other at Yale addresses me, "Dear Mr. Buckley") has come across my novel *Saving the Queen*, and spots the portrait of a pompous and fastidious dean to whom my roommate, early on in freshman year, gave as his excuse for missing a class, "Diarrhea, sir," earning immunity against any further summons ever after. "I won't bore you with an account of the atrocities [that dean] committed in my case, but I am very happy that he will be remembered in print accurately. In fairness, he probably was stupid rather than malicious." Actually, I rather liked the old codger.

A former official of the USIA writes to tell me he was *personally* present when an official of the State Department, during the Nixon years, announced that the U.S. Government would do nothing to challenge Soviet inroads into Africa, so that our present policy does not surprise *him*. And every now and then—the voice from the ideological underworld. This letter informs me that Goleniewski, a Polish defector who served with the Glowny Zarzad (intelligence), and whose testimony before British and U.S. intelligence has never been impeached in any particular, testified that a Soviet spy ring was formed in 1948 "named ODRA—its purpose . . . to penetrate U.S. and British intelligence. One agent, according to Goleniewski, coopted by this ring was one Sgt. Henry A. Kissinger, code name BOR. In a 1954 update, this same Henry Kissinger was found working at Harvard University, while moonlighting for the CIA. Thus the former Secretary of State stands accused, by the greatest known defector to the United States, of being a Communist agent as late as 1954."

Well, that certainly is a story. I reply, "Though I think it extremely unlikely, there is no reason to exclude the theoretical possibility that Kissinger might have been a Soviet agent in 1954. I didn't know him in 1954. I met him in 1955, and can confidently tell you that by then, if he had been a Communist, he had defected. Thank you for writing." Probably my correspondent will put me down as a naif or, more probably, an unindicted coconspirator. But for the fun of it I must remember, next time I write to H.K., to address him, "Dear BOR," and see what happens.

Most letter writers consider themselves sovereign over at least one preserve of facts, however tiny; and woe to the man who steps carelessly onto it. Others are anxious after your ideological purity, and correct you primly, like a teacher picking up a solecism in a student text. Some express outrage, in whatever is the appropriate conjugation. . . . And then there is the occasional posy. Criticism, after all, includes analytical *approval*.

Anthony Lewis of the New York *Times* writes about a review in *National Review:* "[The author] suggests that the only countries I would criticize in terms of human rights are South Korea, Chile, and the United States. Even with full allowance for the fun of exaggeration, that is a contemptible lie and he knows it." The reviewer is grown-up and responsible, and I shall let him handle Mr. Lewis's ire, though I shall keep a paternal eye on the arguments—after all, I am editor of the journal in which a tort was allegedly committed.

The president of the University of Michigan at Flint writes to say that his guest as visiting lecturer, Alan Paton, thought that I devoted too much time to asking economic questions when we met at Flint, to tape an hour of "Firing Line" on the South African question. "Alan Paton's interest in the theory of economic systems is very limited. He answered questions in this area because they were asked—but these questions do not rouse his deepest interest. Now one might argue that if they didn't, they should. But that is another matter. He loves his country and all of its citizens—both black and white—very deeply and is anguished to contemplate what lies ahead if Christian charity does not prevail in that troubled land. He said to me on two separate occasions that he regretted not clarifying and asserting to you the motivating force behind his own will to change the country before it is too late—that it is the gospel message as he understands it. This is not to say that he believes that capitalism is inherently hostile to gospel values or that socialism has anything spiritual to be said for it." How gentle, and how fluent the analysis. I reply (hastily), that "since [Paton] believes that economics is the instrument by which African blacks are most likely to experience relief, I thought it relevant to bring the subject up."

I have the impression that four out of five subscribers to *National Review* who let their subscriptions lapse succumb to the invitation (it is really a publisher's ruse) to give their reasons why. One highly literate reader says about *National Review:* "I read the magazine as if hearing story after introductory story from an after-dinner speaker who sits down before coming to any point. Too often I feel as if I've been listening to comments in the losers' locker room rather than hearing a philosophy articulated. Why not legitimate poetry, ancient, modern, rather than the consolation-silliness of the verse that is published? Who selects the letters for publication? Do you really need filler? Is this the readership company I'm to see myself as joining? More bewildering are the cute replies, the demeaning buffoonery. I think of Ali making faces last night, the shame of Pindar, and of De Gaulle's comments on the students in '68. You seem insistent on taking away the seriousness you offer in other sections. . . . Why not a full issue on Nozick and Rawls themselves, a symposium; or on Kenner. Now there is too much of the expensive playground to the product. Partisanship is merchandised skillfully, but little more. We are

*A pump hoses up fresh water for a variety of purposes. Danny,
sobering up before assuming watch captainship.*

mirrored, informed, rather than educated." I replied—I fear, too
brusquely—saying, "The kind of publication you want would be
read by you and a dozen other people. Which is not to say that it
shouldn't exist. You might undertake it." He deserved a politer
reply. But *time*. . . .

Speaking of time, there was talk at dinner that during the past three days, during which we had powered, there being no wind, the six-hour daytime watches have dragged. Why not, Tony suggested, bring in a dogwatch for two hours' duty, one to three, shortening the two long watches by one hour each? I countered that during that period lunch is served, so that all hands are on deck in any event, and that since when we power we tend to use the autopilot, being "on-watch" as distinguished from "off-watch" is a purely psychological burden. I can't remember when last my analytical powers so closely approached sheer poetry. It was greeted by dumbfounded amusement, followed by acquiescence, followed by cheering, followed by a flat refusal by Van to pass me the wine, advising me that the psychological burden of doing so was too heavy. . . .

Was it Katharine Brush who wrote the short story about the attendant at the ladies' room in the night club? The story, in any event, is appropriate to the editor. In the story a dozen women, coming and going in the course of the evening, powder their noses and exchange comments in the style of Clare Boothe Luce's *The Women:* brilliant, frothy, mean, generous, trivial, melodramatic. The attendant, a middle-aged woman, tends abstractedly to the needs of her wards because she is preoccupied. Whenever the room clears, she rushes back to her *True Story* pulp magazine, experiencing therein great, exhilarating draughts of Reality—which she never noticed was taking place right about her, evening after evening. People of expansive impulse tend to write you their thoughts, describe their reactions, document their pains and pleasures: as an editor, you are the attendant.

"Alice," who writes me frequently, was brought up in a most unusual household. Her father was—is—a pornographer. Now her young brother is receiving an award from the nation's most select concentration of artists and writers, and Dad goes along, perforce, to the ceremony. "The only book I know my father's ever read is *Exodus*. He was completely out of his turf, which is a condition my father never likes to find himself in, and it wasn't like you could say, 'Come on, Dad, cheer up. . . . Look, there's John Updike!'" There is a short story there.

A Belgian-American toolmaker, Gus Renson, a worker in the

tradition of Eric Hoffer, writes me perhaps his three-hundredth letter, this one on the eve of his retirement at sixty-five. "Circumstances beyond my control made this week's paycheck the largest ever. Worked $1\frac{1}{2} + 1\frac{1}{2}$ hours overtime during the week, all day Saturday and twelve hours Sunday (double time). Could have declined, it's optional, but with all that time for resting coming up, opted for the work orgy. I think today's Americans have more cause for rebellion than at the time their forefathers dumped those tea sacks. Gross for sixty-four hours? $560. Net $342. For a change, on this rush job, I was paired with a shopmate called Pee Wee who, occasionally (i.e., without sneer from less serious mates), allows personal pride to prevail. An apotheosis of sorts for me: total cooperation, anticipating the other guy's next move, readying his machine and needed tools, coming up with astute solutions when stumped temporarily; a joy, I could have kissed the sonofabitch. Why can't it be like that all the time? When we got through Sunday at 7 P.M., we both felt secretly that we deserved applause." And, on the heels of that concupiscent brush with the Puritan ethic, he lets me have a nice taste of the dirty old man, in his native French of course. He notes the address in Paris of the publishers who brought out my novel in French. "Librairie Arthème Fayard. Arthème, you can hardly reek more from La Belle Époque. Dig the quaint location too: 'rue des Saints-Pères.' Once the den of rubicund padres switching from *enluminures* to green Chartrooze with the greatest of ease? Or flagellants wearing T-hairshirts with the picture of Joan of Arc imprinted in batik? Ah words, ah names. *Je ne puis me rappeler sans rire ma visite à Avignon en 1961 où je découvris un square entièrement consacré aux plaisirs de la chair* (awright, *you* never got lost in a strange city)? *Le nom de l'endroit: Place des Corps Saints.*" It's letters like that I want to be writing when I retire.

An old sailing buddy, Mike, puts it on the line. Look, he is negotiating with Mr. Nightingale, who fancies himself a *great* composer, and will send me a cassette of one of his songs. For an advertising account for Mike, would I acknowledge the cassette appreciatively via an inscribed book? I listened to the cassette—causing some concern in *Sealestial*'s saloon—did my duty, and wrote to Mike: "I put it on to your friend. I inscribed my book to him as 'The new Noel Coward.' It's all very well for you to get an account, but has it occurred to you that I might go to Hell?"

And from my most indefatigable and versatile correspondent, first a translation of the letter written to Charles Lindbergh by Einstein in 1939, requesting that Lindbergh meet with Dr. Leo Szilard. Background: A couple of years ago I reviewed a book for the New York *Times* on Lindbergh, written by Brendan Gill. In it Gill reports that so many people wrote to Lindbergh that many of their letters still repose in the Yale University archives, unopened; for instance, a letter known to have been written by Einstein. I remarked this in my review and much later received from Yale, repository of my own material, an indignant reaction. The mystery letter is nicely catalogued, thank you very much, and enclosed is a copy. But it is in German, in which I am illiterate. My friend Sophie translates. Here is the world's greatest scientist hinting to the world's greatest aviator (and America's most dedicated political isolationist) that a scientific insight has been achieved which . . . "Most honored Mr. Lindbergh: May I ask you to be kind enough to receive my friend Dr. Szilard and to consider carefully what he has to tell you. The subject he has to present to you may seem fantastic to a man not involved with science. But you will surely soon be convinced that a possibility here presents itself which must, in the public interest, be carefully kept in view, even though the results hitherto may not appear too impressive to the naked eye. With highest esteem and friendly wishes, Yours, A. Einstein."

Sophie comments, "My God, what lovely restraint, care, modesty, sweetness, and what shaking in one's scientific shoes behind all that impeccable cool." She recalls an editorial mission to an already ailing Leo Szilard, some twenty years later, to induce him to write his memoirs for her firm. All she came away with was a short story he outlined for her (published later, elsewhere) based on the premise that the Russians had won World War III, and that he would be able to needle people in conversation without their being able to put their finger on just where and how they had been pricked. "Better the firing squad than such a castrate life, he decided." She signs, "*Ave atque vale, con amore.*"

On and on, about six hundred letters answered and enclosures scanned, working two or three hours a day in my stateroom, in that huge, sybaritic armchair—Dr. Papo's ultimate touch. But I must quote one more, because it came in from Tom. Tom Wendel will be joining us in the Azores, where we lose Van. He is a historian, and the clipping he enclosed must have special appeal to a historian. I dropped everything and took it up on deck to give the watch extraconventional relief.

The letter [to the San Francisco *Chronicle*] was headlined:

WHERE DRAKE LANDED

Editor—The loquacious Scott Newhall has made a gallant leap from ignorance to certainty in his uninformed article of May 12, "Where Drake Landed—Exactly."

True, as he had insisted, one should take the mariner's approach to a resolution of the controversial anchorage. Still, if he had been aware of my recent research—"Portuguese Pilotage on the First English Entry into San Francisco Bay, 1579"—as published this year in the *Boletim Sociedade de Geografia de Lisboa* [Tom had written in: "Can you imagine missing that?"] he would have realized that N. de Morera, Francis Drake's second Portuguese pilot, had taken the conn of Rodrigo Tello's 15-ton *fragata*, manned with an English crew, to escort the *Golden Hind* through the Golden Gate Strait to her careenage site near Corte Madera Creek.

FREDERICK BENDER
San Francisco

13

I suppose if you are a professional captain, eventually the landfall becomes routine stuff, even as—I guess—the symphony conductor, after thirty or forty years, coming home in the evening, picks up the evening paper. . . .

Wife (preparing snack): "What did you play tonight, Arturo?"

"Huh? Oh . . ." (yawn) "Lemme see. Mozart's Fortieth, Mahler's Fourth, and Stravinsky's Rite. . . . No, no cucumbers (burp), been (burp) burping since those onions at lunch. Did the Redskins win?"

But I'll have to have many more landfalls before achieving insouciance. So after Allen spotted the great Pico, barely distinguishable from the surrounding clouds, it felt rather good when I left the helm to go to the chart, to call for a change of a mere five degrees in our course to take us down between the islands to the port of Horta.

What followed was one of those exasperating things that have a way of happening on boats. The night was moderately, though not immoderately, clear. We dallied, though not for more than fifteen minutes, when someone spotted what looked like a whale about three miles off our port beam. My instinct is to head in the

The (dead) whale.

opposite direction from whales, who have been known to be
frisky in the vicinity of small boats. But after studying this one
through binoculars* we concluded that it was quite dead; so over I
steered to take a close look.

We circled the great creature slowly, taking lots of pictures.
The light was failing rapidly, and the whale was surrounded by
the pinks of the sun, and pink from its own oozing blood diluted
by the Atlantic Ocean. Two sharks, at least, were visible, chewing

---

* (Beard-McKie—"Binoculars: *Entertaining shipboard kaleidoscope which when
held up to the light reveals interesting patterns and designs caused by salt spray,
thumbprints, and scratches. Uncapped, its lenses may also be employed to collect
small amounts of salt from seawater through evaporation.*")

at the great hulk. The jawbone alone, had we had the means of salvaging it, would have fetched us over two thousand dollars at Horta, and no dollars in the United States, because whale teeth are among the things you're not allowed to import, lest they move from scarcity to extinction.

Anyway, our ghoulish poking done, I resumed course confidently awaiting the three telltale lights to usher us in: one of them dead ahead, one on the island of Pico to the right, the principal (range, fifteen miles) light to port, on the western tip of the island of Faial. In due course we discerned three lights—indeed, six lights. But no one of them corresponded in characteristic to any of the lights described on the chart. Could we have caught an aberrational view of Pico? But we had got our heading, all right. Well, could there be a strange and fierce current that might have taken us down, south of Pico? Or up, north of Faial? Such things occur to you, so much do you rely on lights. Allen and Reggie were working on the radar, trying to coax life into it, and I kept doggedly on the course I had pre-plotted.

Eventually (about 11 P.M.) it became clear that we were indeed coming in on Horta, at a respectable distance south of the island. A head current kept down our speed, and there was no wind. I had that morning confided to Diane and Judy that I estimated we would tie up between midnight and one. I note with amusement an entry in Tony's journal:

"Reg finally coaxed us in with a skillful blend of radar, chart reading interpolation, and a little local knowledge from Allen. The breakwater had Bill stymied for a second because a row of lights on shore appeared to him as a solid wall right where we were telling him to steer. Was it his contact lenses playing tricks or was he just a little plastered?" I smiled on reading this because I automatically cut the booze to a submetabolic level of consumption when I am coming in for a landing or otherwise maneuvering. I had not always done so. I am as grateful for the experience in 1960, at Cape May, as I am for an experience at a casino in New Orleans the summer of my freshman year. It was in New Orleans that, in a single trauma, I lost what had been a (to be sure, short) lifelong compulsion to gamble. My roommate and I lost everything we had been given (by generous parents) to see us through the summer, and I was reduced to acting as a guide-chauffeur, taking visiting Shriners, gathered for a leisurely convention, around Mexico City and as far away as Taxco. Today I can walk through a casino like a eunuch through a harem.

The night Nixon and Kennedy first debated, Van and I, with Peter Starr and Mike Forrestal, set off down the Hudson River to take my cutter *The Panic* to Annapolis, where it would winter. We'd race it up to Newport in the spring. We experienced the not unusual crisis when, with a light southerly wind on the nose, our engine conked out opposite the Statue of Liberty. Mike deduced (correctly, as it turned out) that the engine had got too cold, the result of our having overcompensated by opening full the water intake after we had retrieved the boat from Maine, where the temperature of the outside water requires a smaller volume for the engine cooling system. He predicted that in an hour or so, after the condensation dried, it would start up again; and in an hour it did, while we tacked quietly out toward Ambrose Lightship, listening to the debate over the radio and concluding (as did most people who heard, rather than saw, the debate)—even Mike, a Democrat of indomitable loyalty, who would soon serve in Mr. Kennedy's administration—that Nixon had won it.

In any event, our engine functioning, the wind turned into a brisk easterly and we made absolutely record time, putting in at Cape May exactly twenty-four hours later. There we had resolved to spend the night, proceeding the next day up the Delaware and over to Annapolis. Ah, but that was before dinner at the marina restaurant's bar.

After dinner Mike was treating us to—stingers. And to stories of the boat he had chartered the preceding summer in the Baltic, and the terrible crewman who came at him one night with a knife! Resulting in—a fight to the finish! It was Mike or the Baltickian—one or the other had to go—and with a *huge* effort Mike finally kicked him overboard, and he gurgled down into the cold, dark, deep: good riddance, I said, and Van and Peter cheered, and the man at the bar said, "*Another* round of stingers?"

That was the moment when I said, "Why stop tonight? Let's sashay through the canal, and on into the Delaware and have a nice sail?" Everyone thought that a quite superior idea, and ten minutes later we were on board *The Panic*, and three minutes after that, aground. I decided to winch us out of our difficulty, threw out a heavy anchor with a long line, and winched in the line with the greatest of ease, because I had not properly fastened it to the anchor. Now we had no alternative but to sleep, until the tide rescued us. That was the last night I permitted alcohol to get in the way of my duties aboard a boat, heartily though I endorse the uses of wine and fine spirits at sea. What I have developed, after some very close calls, is super skepticism when you aren't one hundred percent sure of what lies directly ahead, when coming into an unfamiliar harbor.

But suddenly the logic of the breakwater became plain, and the eyes settled down and, rounding, I felt the confidence of Superman, spotting a narrow opening alongside the crowded quay, to which I took the *Sealestial* for—dare I say it?—a perfect landing at 0100. Then the champagne, and a little walk, up and down the long wharf, so crowded with boats of every variety. It was too late to go out on the town, and in any event we hadn't been properly cleared by Immigration. So we just walked a little, on land for the first time in eleven days. We had sailed 2,150 nautical miles, approximately the distance from New York to Denver, and we felt just fine. It would have been perfect except that the next day, Van would leave.

14

~~~~~~~~~~~~~~~~~~~

When we reached the Azores we found waiting for us, in the hotel suite I had reserved, a case of champagne together with a telegram, written of course in the cablese that had been Dick's staple for so many years:

"EYE TRULY SAY THAT EYE DAILY THOUGHT ABOUT THE MERRY BAND EYE LEFT BEHIND IN BERMUDA AND MISSED YOU ALL AS WELL AS THE SEA THAT SURROUNDED US. ALONG WITH ITS BEING AN EPIPHANY FOR ME, THE FIRST LEG OF OUR TRIP PROVIDED ME WITH A CREDENTIAL IN ISRAEL VERY FEW OTHER INQUIRERS HAVE EVER HAD. THANKS TO OUR VOYAGE TOGETHER, THE PRIME MINISTER AND HIS CABINET VIEWED ME WITH THE KIND OF DISTANCE EYE PROFESSIONALLY WELCOME. THEY HAD NEVER BEFORE MET A JEW WHO ARRIVED IN ISRAEL FROM A SAILBOAT UNLESS HE WAS FLEEING FROM SOMEONE, WHICH EYE PLAINLY WAS NOT EXCLAM.

"SAIL ON. BE WELL. EYE DEEPLY MISS YOU ALL AND EVERY-THING."

The following day was busy and we occupied ourselves with the usual chores. Tony's special commission, this time around, was to find some edible bread, which we hadn't had since leaving St. Thomas. What we brought from there was so mangy and bleached it might, with a drop or two of water have been served as vichyssoise. In Bermuda, Van had gone to the biggest and best bakery in Hamilton and ordered twenty-seven different kinds of bread, of every size, shape, and color, whose only common denominator was that they were every one of them tasteless. Tony secured for us, at Horta, and again at São Miguel, heavenly bread, which is the way bread tastes before you take the flavor out of it. Years ago Murray Kempton remarked that the United States had succeeded in taking all but a bit of the flavor out of our bread, and when we were through developing the peacetime uses of nuclear energy, we would succeed in getting *that* last bit of flavor out. Actually, *pace* Mary McCarthy, whose King Charles's head in her penultimate novel was the tastelessness of American bread, America is teeming again with edible bread.

We took a little tour of the island which included an inspection of the only functioning windmill I have ever seen; I mean, it was not a Disney World reconstruction, but a genuine survivor, with the old grandparents inside making flour, and the blades turning at a fantastic velocity, rather like propellers on an airplane. We drove past the forlorn northern end of the island, which in 1957 was smothered—the lighthouse included—by a great eruption that buried tens of thousands of acres in a sooty ash. That was the explanation for the mysteriously missing lighthouse signal, though it is no explanation of why a new lighthouse, somewhat to the south, didn't reproduce the antediluvian signals; and certainly no reason why charts purchased in 1980 should not have been corrected for what happened in 1957. From the ashes we drove back into the lushness of Faial to the airport, leaving Van there, all of us feigning stoicism at his departure; and on to dine at a little restaurant recommended by someone Tony had run into during his bread-searching—one Otto, as we called him.

A native place—and there, seated with friends in the far corner of the thoroughly utilitarian restaurant, was Otto (Othon Rosado Silverra), whose mission in this world is to serve. He dashed over

In real life the blades turn so fast they are barely visible. Christopher's camera was set at ¹⁄₁₀₀₀.

to describe the kitchen's alternatives, translate our orders, and expedite the service. Basically it was roast meat, potatoes, wine, and vegetables—every item superior in every respect.

We were to see more of Otto who, it turned out, was by profession a scrimshander, which is a fellow who takes whales' teeth and carves designs on them, as in the days of yore when sailors, spending two or three hundred days on boats without sight of land, sought out means to divert themselves. We were invited to see Otto's collection the next morning, amassed during the winter for a single purchaser who had bought the yacht *America* and would soon come around to collect the scrimshaws. Wonderful pieces, two or three dozen, of various sizes and decorations. Otto was working in his atelier, the size of two pullman berths.

He is active, to be sure, in every capacity, but a specialty is his ham radio, and as he sat at his workbench etching figures on his

*Horta, Faial. Packing Van off to the airport. Note visiting yachts'
equivalent of the tourists' initials, painted on seawall.*

whale teeth (the teeth are covered in black tincture of sorts, and
after the etching is done, they are buffed by an electrical device
that looks like the revolving bushy things you shine shoes with,
and the dye remains only in the little cracks, and you have your
scrimshaw), he diddled with his radio. Throughout the operation
he was interrupted by calls on the radio, of which he kept dutiful
record in his logbook, patching in calls here and there, uttering
pleasantries to his friends in half a dozen languages.

He invited us, as we waited for the three scrimshaws we had
commissioned and for the earrings for Tony's girl and for Gloria,
to survey his scrapbooks. There were six of them, and on the odd
pages were pictures of beautiful yachts, opposite which was an in-
scription, of which a typical one would be, "To Dear Othon:
How can we ever repay you? If you hadn't stood by us during
those terrible weeks, everything would have ended for us. Come

to us in Newport. Come to us in Palm Beach. Come to us in Monaco. Forever yours, Gloria Merrill Vanderbilt Auchincloss Gibson"—but literally dozens and dozens of people whom, over the years, Otto had apparently taken in hand, quietly attending to their problems, ordering their meals, getting their boats fixed, arranging their communications, making them a scrimshaw or two for peanuts. If I had had handy a picture of *Sealestial*, I'd gladly have added to his collection, but Otto is overburdened with gratitude.

We headed for the boat, hoping to recapture an afternoon five years earlier at a bight on Pico Island. The wind was bracing at first, from the east, which suited our southerly purposes perfectly, but—unaccountably—I slid past the deserted village I was looking for, and we settled instead for an undeserted village, of probably a hundred fishermen. We threw out the anchor and set out for a two-hour walk up the steep hills, during which Tony spoke of his immediate plans, and of his intention to sell the hacienda on Majorca he and his cousin had inherited from his great-aunt, a friend who first gave me Tony's name as a qualified sailor. It is unlikely anyone had ever before parked a yacht in this little half-bay. The natives were typically five feet two in size, and friendly: they insisted we ride their burro, and the children giggled, in their rumpled white cloth skirts and pants, and ran off to hide.

Danny would cook again, and as he laid on the coals, two fishermen approached us in their dory. I called for Allen to ask whether he wished to purchase fish. Only on the condition, he indicated to the fishermen with gestures, that they clean the fish first, which the two men—one of them young, the other perhaps his father—proceeded industriously to do, devoting half an hour to the enterprise.

What followed will live in the annals of humiliation. Allen took the fish—twenty of them—and asked how much did we owe them? The answer came back, with smiles: "Nada." Nothing. The news was flashed to me below, and I said that they must be given a twenty-dollar bill, if necessary tossed to them in their boat in a receptacle of some sort. After much arguing, they consented to take the money—but only after handing up a bottle of white wine. They left then, waving. But ten minutes later they came back. This time they did not reduce their speed as they approached our stern. They rounded us closely, in elegant stride, and having sig-

Reggie at Faial, practicing for the Democratic Convention.

Trying to pay for Portuguese obsequies. Danny with fish, Allen with wallet.

naled to Danny, standing astern tending his coals, to prepare to catch something, tossed over to him a bottle—and, waving and smiling, sped off. They wished to make us a gift of a bottle of brandy, and would not, this time, expose themselves to the ignominy of being offered money for it: I mean, what would these Americans, on returning home, otherwise say about Portuguese hospitality?

We drank the brandy, after Danny's chicken and the roasted fish, and felt truly welcome. At ten, we hauled up the anchor and set out the 150 miles east to the island of São Miguel, which favorable winds put us in sight of at eight in the morning, when I took the helm, remaining with it—such is my inclination on nearing land—until, shortly after noon, we pulled alongside the quay at Punta Delgada, the busy little harbor with the wide Mediterranean avenue arcing opposite the great breakwater, marred now by an abortive skyscraper-bound hotel. Begun since we were last there, it had never been completed, serving now only to profane the city's silhouette. It is a scar on an otherwise engrossing and stately harbor, once much busier than it now is, when the cruise boats don't even call—there being, really, no cruise boats left that cultivate the Atlantic, let alone the Azores, which from my brief knowledge of them are, quite simply stated, the most beautiful group of islands in the world.

Again we had a suite reserved, to act as headquarters, from which everyone received what Tony calls in his journal "our petites commissions." I knew I would need a little official cooperation here, as my vacation from column writing was over; so before leaving the United States I had telephoned Hodding Carter at the State Department and asked him please to inform the Consul General at Punta Delgada that I was the nicest person Hodding knew who would be voting for Reagan. Whatever the message, it worked, and Consul General Ruth Matthews, whose charming husband Glenwood is a retired Foreign Service officer, took wonderful, motherly care of us, which included conveying two invitations, one to lunch the following day at a picturesque, flower-besotted villa a few miles from town, the second to join for cocktails, that very night, the captain of the *Knorr*, an official ocean-research vessel from our Oceanographic Institution at Woods Hole, Massachusetts.

Doing this turned out to be very convenient, because moments after leaving *Sealestial* to go to the hotel, our vessel had been evicted by the harbor police—we were occupying space reserved for commercial traffic, and there was no place to go . . . except? Allen Jouning approached the skipper of the *Knorr*, identifying our vessel. Might we berth alongside? Not as easy as all that, because already aberth, alongside the *Knorr*, was the U.S. Naval ship *Wyman*, so that the permission of a second captain had to be got; but all this was in fact accomplished by the time we showed up, at seven, for cocktails.

While the others attended to their chores, I took a rented car and went to the airport to meet Tom Wendel. Meeting a plane in the Azores (or catching one) is half a day's activity, because the planes are regularly late, though not predictably enough to make it safe simply to arrive late. No matter—I had brought with me four back issues of *Time* and *Newsweek*, which I would need to go through thoroughly before resuming my profession as a seer. Besides, waiting for Tom is itself a pleasure because, eventually, Tom arrives; and when you first see Tom—or when you last see him, or for that matter any time in between—it's good for uninterrupted laughter. We have primarily in common that we find the same things funny, and he is one of those people whose laughter is catalytic. Moreover, we know each other's reactions so well that we often skip right over the normal catalyst, and simply begin laughing right away.

You would not, from the above description, have any intimation that we are both *very serious men*. I am, among other things, the kind of person who gives Commencement Speeches, in the unlikely event this is not known about me. Tom is a very serious historian, an authority on Colonial history, author of a life of Benjamin Franklin. When I first knew him at Yale I half expected that he would become a performing pianist, so gifted was he; is he. His father, a businessman of great civic spirit, widely admired and beloved, in 1957 was officially designated as the "First Citizen" of Portland, Oregon, and when Tom graduated from Yale, the senior Wendel had it all set for young Tom to follow in the family footsteps and, if memory serves, had a little vice presidency or whatever cut out for him in the department store. Tom summoned all his courage—he practiced for weeks—for the dread moment.

"Dad, I'm not going back to Portland to business."

Stunned silence. "What are you going to do?"

São Miguel. From left to right: Sealestial. *The U.S. Naval Ship* Wyman. *Largely obscured by the* Caribic, *the Oceanographic Institution's* Knorr.

"I've accepted a job as an American history teacher at Putney School."

"What is the Putney School?"

"It's sort of an advanced preparatory school in Putney, Vermont, for boys and girls, very good academically."

"What will they pay you?"

"Fifteen hundred dollars."

"Fifteen hundred dollars every what?"

"Fifteen hundred dollars every year."

Stunned silence. "Tom, have you no . . . pride?"

We lost touch with each other during most of the fifties and early sixties, but I rejoiced to get a note from Charlotte, Tom's superb wife, the development director of the museum at San José at whose university Tom teaches, advising me ten years ago that Tom was coming east for a sabbatical during which he would live at Swarthmore. He brought his two boys, Hal and David, in their early teens, and one afternoon, with Clare Boothe Luce and Pat, the lot of us boarded the *Cyrano* on the East River and sailed to Stamford—which I think was about eighty-five percent of Tom's sailing experience when, learning finally that Van couldn't make it on through, I wondered who might be the next best thing, and happily thought of Tom.

He had been much excited by the invitation. His older son Hal, a senior at the University of Washington, an avid sailor, a tournament tennis player, had taken to writing letters to the student newspaper, copies of which Tom would from time to time with paternal pride pass along to me. "Dear Bill [Tom had written me in May]: I am not at all sure that you are thrilled by having another example of my son Hal's prose—but just in case, I quote a bit of it. At least it's not another letter to the editor:

" 'I'm still exceedingly jealous over your upcoming adventure. In fact so much so, I've been ripping my hair out [Tom is nearly bald] and reading up on Benjamin Franklin. I have also been attempting to develop a potbelly [unfair: Tom's stomach is flat]. As you can surmise, I'm trying to impersonate you so I can go. I guess regardless of what I do, Buckley is sure to see right through my disguise. First, he will undoubtedly say, "My gosh, Tom, how did you get so handsome?" I'll have to quickly, and I might add slyly, reply, "Well, Bill, you've heard of the fountain of youth? . . . I drank the whole thing." ' "

Just as Charlotte is a born helper, Tom is a born helpee (the immutable division, taxonomized by the late Sir Arnold Lunn, to assert the principal, extra-sexual cleavage in human beings. Marriages don't work, Lunn said, when helpers marry helpers, or helpees, helpees). At any rate, my office undertook to make Tom's travel arrangements, which required that he go to Boston after pausing at my office to pick up a sack of mail for me, fly thence to Santa Maria in the Azores, wait there four hours, and take that flight down to São Miguel where I now awaited his arrival. Tom's reply relayed a vague skepticism about the proposed arrangements, in the tone of, "Why-can't-I-just-fly-from-New-York-to-São-Miguel?"

MEMO TO: Tom Wendel
FROM: Captain Bill

It is not plain to me what it is that you have against Boston. If you would like to persuade TAP Airlines to institute a flight from New York to the Azores in the place of their existing flight from Boston to the Azores, you are most welcome to do so.

The Captain most politely rejects the suggestion that it is more convenient for him to transport First Mate Wendel's gear from New York to Puerto Rico to St. Croix to St. Thomas to Bermuda to Horta to São Miguel than it is for First Mate Wendel to transport same from Boston to the Azores. Next question?

Eventually Tom arrived. I drove him straight to the *Sealestial*, introducing him to those who were there and turning over to him Van's bunk in my stateroom, which Reggie, though senior, had gallantly volunteered to give up in deference to the predictable nervousness of the New Boy. We went, then, to the *Knorr*, which, particularly below, looks like a boat that began small, but was added to, section by section, warren by warren, trying to keep up with the desperate pace of U.S. technology. Actually, it was launched as late as 1968, 245 feet long, displacing 2,000 tons, with fuel enough for sixty days at sea. Eventually we were deposited by our guide in a cozy room, the captain (and his wife's) state-room-living room, the kind of room you would expect to find inhabited by a clubbable couple given to much reading and eclectic collecting. It required something of a production to come up with the requisite number of chairs to accommodate Captain Emerson Hiller's hospitality. I think Tony and Christopher sat on the floor, but the conversation was convivial, and soon the tall craggy Yankee master of the research vessel *Knorr* got around to the adventure of three and one-half weeks earlier. . . .

The next day I got from Captain Hiller the transcript of the log of his vessel for the dramatic day. I reproduce it, with high regard for the spareness of the style by which dramas are routinely recorded on shipboard:

R/V KNORR
At Sea
24 May 1980

KNORR departed St. George's, Bermuda at 1630 (+3) [This
parenthesis, and others like it, are for the purpose of indicating
what adjustments are necessary in order to transform local time
into Greenwich Mean Time (GMT)] 23 May 1980 for work
site in Lat 24° N, Long 45° W.
Master's Statement Re: Rescuing man in lifeboat this date.
24 May 1980

0035 (+3) Full ahead at ten knots steering 117° T.
            Flare sighted by 2nd Mate about 2½ miles on port
            beam.
            Course changed to 020° T and Master called.

0040   Master on bridge.
0042   Course changed to 030° T.
0045   2nd red flare observed. Between flares white light
            observed.
0046   Course changed to 040° T.
0050   Various courses to pickup life raft with one man on
            board.
0100   Raft alongside and man climbs ladder without
            assistance.
0117   Raft brought on board with heavy crane.
0120   Full ahead 117° T.

0145   Advised US Coast Guard, Portsmouth, Va.
0230   Advised Bermuda Harbor Radio.
            Requested airlift to take man to Bermuda—100 miles
            to N.W.
            Airlift not available and man agrees to remain
            on board to Azores.

Rescued Man's name: François Erpicum   27 years old
Address: 107 Ave des Martyrs   4620 Fléron, Belgium

François's Statement: Sailed from St. Martin Isl. in Windward
                         Islands 12 May 1980. At 0300* (+4)
                         heard odd ringing sound outside, went
(*19 May 1980)   on deck and at that moment something

232

shook the boat. He went into cabin and found it half filled with sea water. Launched his six-man rubber life raft and boat sank, stern first almost at once.

Boat: NANESSE 30 foot sloop of fiberglass.
D.E. Position of sinking: 31°30′ N 63° W

Position of recovery: 31°45′ N 63–04° W
Time in raft: 4 days 21 hours
Man in good physical condition. No adverse effects.

/s/ E.H. Hiller
E.H. Hiller

The above, as I suggested, is a denatured account of what whoever kept the log appropriately designated as the "saga" of M. François Erpicum, of Fléron, Belgium.

Priscilla Hiller—tall, stately, warm, passionate on the subject—told the story more graphically. Erpicum, by profession a marine biologist, was married. In the fall of 1979 his young wife died of cancer. François thought to distract himself by undertaking a spartan single-handed sailing voyage to the Caribbean, returning in the spring. All had gone (to the extent one can use the word about sailing boats at sea) so to speak routinely; until the night of May 19, seven days out, on the course from St. Martin to Bermuda. It was at three in the morning that he was struck; by postmortem conjecture, one minute later he was in the water—that quickly did his sloop go down. The log does not record that it happened that a gallon plastic container of fresh water was perched conveniently on the navigation table. François, instantly evaluating the terminal chaos below, grabbed it just before plunging aft to release his emergency life raft, throwing it into the raft.

François's raft carried one dozen flares. By the night of May 24 he had expended all but two of these. Toward dusk that very evening he had spotted a vessel off at a distance, and taxed himself on whether to let fire with his penultimate flare. But what reason was there to suppose that this time he would be seen, when he hadn't been the other times? With singular discipline he desisted, hoping for the juxtaposition of the vessel, and nighttime. He was delirious with joy, he later reported most persuasively, when he saw definite movement in response to his flare fired shortly after midnight; and so he fired off his final flare almost by way of celebration, because he knew now that he would live.

He was, on retrieval, in fairly good physical condition, considering that he had been five days on a life raft. That one gallon of water was important. His life raft was providentially of the kind that carries canopy shelter from the sun. Moreover, if capsizing at sea is the sort of thing that's going to happen to you, better that you should be a marine biologist than, say, a Chaucer scholar. François had contrived to seduce some ocean crabs, which he had greedily eaten.

The important thing, of course, was that François Erpicum was alive.

But what *had* happened?

Captain Hiller and John Arens, the captain of the adjacent naval vessel, declined to speculate on which one of the (only) two plausible alternatives they inclined to. The first is that the little sloop had been hit by a whale. These things do happen, as acknowledged above. But they are very very rare, because whales don't like to bump into boats, and are born with sensory mechanisms fine enough to prevent such things from happening.

The second alternative is that François's sloop was hit by a submarine.

But if a submarine knocked the keel off a boat even as small as thirty feet, wouldn't the submarine know it?

Silence from the officers I put the question to.

The answer is: Yes. A submarine has more electrical capillaries coursing about its carapace than a human being, and will as predictably record impact as the human body would a pinprick.

But then why didn't the submarine surface and rescue the poor victim?

A good question, for which no one was volunteering an answer. It ran through everyone's mind, of course, that an American or a British submarine would have done exactly that.

A Russian submarine? Better that a sailor, nationality unknown, perish at sea, than pick him up and permit him to descend into the Stygian mysteries that comprise those vessels that slink, unseen, about the oceans of the world, coiled to do things far more unpleasant than merely leave one young man gasping for life in the middle of the Atlantic. . . .

234

Well, there it is. Someday a generation hence, some researcher, going through old submarine logs in Vladivostok or wherever, may stumble across an entry for 0300, May 19, 1980; 31°5′N, 63°W: "Collided with small vessel. Vessel sank. Survivor XX-XXXXXXXXXXXXXXXXX (BALANCE OF ENTRY EXCISED, BY ORDER OF NAVAL SECURITY COUNCIL)."

The adjacent vessel was about the same length (286 feet), but could stay out at sea a full ninety days. The *Wyman* was built to conduct hydrographic, oceanographic, and geophysical surveys, and my own feeling—almost but not entirely unfounded—is that there is a whole lot that is secret that goes on aboard the *Wyman*, but let it go; you would *never* find out if it were so, not from teetotaling Captain John W. Arens, recognized as the foremost expert in the West on Arctic scuba diving; a sky diver: paratrooper; racing-car driver who headed a demolition team dur ing the Korean War; about whom nothing unpleasant could be said, save that when they all came aboard the *Sealestial* for our lit-tle cocktail party, Captain Arens took one look at Dr. Papo's chair, that monstrously comfortable thing I sit in when I write let-ters, and announced, in accents threateningly realistic, that he in-tended to *steal* it *that very night*, substituting a facsimile made of papier-mâché. When, the following day, moments before we cast off on our last leg, Captain Arens slipped a bulky envelope into my hand containing, I correctly supposed, technical literature on his ship the *Wyman*, I received it with routine obeisance. But I would learn that it contained, also, a very beautiful and magnani-mous personal tribute, which I shall not publish, but will always cherish.

After dinner at the hotel following Captain Hiller's cocktails we all felt, I think, a joint suspension, an unrootedness, a carefree lan-guor. There would be no watches that night, and the following day our responsibilities were light. We found ourselves strolling through the park, toward the boardwalk. Jutting out of it is a mini-park given over to amusements, rather like the country fairs in America a generation ago. The central activity was the Dodg'em arena, and we all clambered in, each with his own Dodg'em. To my astonishment Tony proved to be too young ever to have driven a Dodg'em, and so he was easily victimized until he began to catch on. Maybe because his face is so cherubic, I decided to make Christopher my special victim, and managed a few first-class collisions, which I wish he had photographed. I told him, as we wandered over to the shooting gallery, that it was a pity each car didn't come equipped with an Impact Meter, so that at the end of the round a winner could be proclaimed, which winner, I suggested, would clearly be me. He did not demur. At the shooting gallery we were given BB guns of sorts to shoot at collapsing ducks, candle flames, the lot. I was an infantryman during the longest year of my life and offered free lessons to anyone who desired them on the proper way to hold a rifle, but since Reggie was proving more accurate than I in snuffing out the candles, my ministrations were received lightly. A young and street-wise Portuguese, whose English was picturesquely imperfect, offered to take us to the town's special delights, and we dispatched him to bring us beer, which we sat lazily and drank, in the city park—the first time I have sat in a city park, that I can remember, since my nurse used to take me to one in London when I was six. It was very pleasant, and our Portuguese cicerone kept describing, with increasingly voluptuarian imagery, the objects that lay at his command. But—I speak for myself and those responsible elements with whom I mingle—a sudden but quite unmistakable fatigue seized us, and we ambled over to the hotel. We forgathered in the lobby the next morning to go with the Matthewses first to inspect their brand-new, solid-wood, stormproof residence; then to John (Canadian) and Liz (English) Gladwin's beautiful villa where a half-dozen expatriates joined us.

In the Azores, notwithstanding the unpleasantness of the political spring of 1974 in Portugal, there is a special sense of security, though the islands suffer from progressive emigration by skilled workmen. The English-speaking colony there is heavily influenced by people who otherwise live either in Bermuda or in St. Croix, and the consensus is that in St. Croix, what with the burgeoning Caribbean nationalism, life is becoming dicey. The patio outside the villa is bursting with flowers—can there be, in all the rest of the world combined, as many flowers as on the island of São Miguel? John took me through the house and showed me the sextant of his grandfather, who in 1880 at age sixteen shipped out from Halifax on a whaler, and next saw land 247 days later, when the boat pulled in to Saigon. Saigon! Two hundred and forty-seven days at sea! I said to John it was hard to make appropriate comment, but could only say that I very much hoped his grandfather liked the sea.

The following day, Sunday, had been designated our sight-seeing day. Danny and I went to Mass at ten, and I was glad I didn't understand Portuguese, because the priest was very hot under the collar about something, and I was in no mood to contemplate my sins. Then, in two small rented cars, we began the enchanted trip. You go to the west of the island, rising through curved roads to about five thousand feet (I brought along my altimeter). Then you look down on what was once a crater and is now the most beautiful valley in Christendom, with the lake in the center, the greens of pastureland emerald in their brightness, the graceful trees lining the country roads, the little white village. We had resolved to swim, and descended to the lake's edge, but finding no place ideally designed to protect us in our nudity and not wishing to get our undershorts wet, we decided to postpone the swimming until after lunch, and with much effort found our way back over the mountain edge to the west-east road on the northern shore, itself a continuing spectacular.

We had been told to look for a restaurant called Cabalho Blanco. It was harder to find the Cabalho Blanco, setting out from Punta Delgada, than it was to find the Azores, setting out from Bermuda. But we did find it, and the busy lady serving the Sunday crowd turned out to be an assistant to Ruth Matthews during the weekdays, helping her mother run the restaurant on weekends. If challenged on it I will hold my wrist unflinchingly over a burning flame: the fried fish we ordered at the Cabalho Blanco is the finest, in taste and preparation, available anywhere, a proposition on which there was a quite unusual consensus. We traveled east, found an exciting beach with great breakers, swam in our shorts (the beach was public), dried off as best we could, and returned to Punta Delgada, because that evening at seven the *Sealestial* was having a party! To it we had invited the ranking people on the two naval vessels, the Gladwins, the Matthewses, and the Queen Mother of Punta Delgada, who is Mrs. Bunny Olsen, a name that Fortune had tossed our way, via Tony. She lives in a picturesque penthouse apartment opposite our hotel, and part of the year in a converted windmill in Horta, and the rest of the time in St. Croix.

We reminisced at some length about Charles Blair, killed two years ago when his airplane, ferrying passengers from St. Croix to St. Thomas, failed, landing Charlie and six passengers in the water where a wave knocked him out, drowning him and three others.

Charles F. Blair, Jr., had been the leading pilot for Pan American, and for three years after we purchased our property in Stamford, Connecticut, Charlie and wife (number two) rented our garage apartment. Charlie was half Gary Cooper, half Clark Gable. In 1948 he won the Harmon Trophy, which is given to the aviator who that year has made the most spectacular achievement (Charlie flew single-handed over the North Pole, a remarkable navigational feat at that time) and there was a picture in his little apartment of President Truman handing it to him. He flew Pan Am's prestigious Flight #1 to London every Monday, on the old Boeing Stratocruiser—sleeping quarters, Pullman style, all first class—and back Tuesday, with nothing to do until the following Monday.

Nothing to do, my behind. He would disappear on Wednesday and go to Georgia where, he said, he was doing a little moonlighting, training pilots for Eastern Airlines. He *was* doing a little moonlighting—for the CIA, I discovered many years later: training Francis Gary Powers and his colleagues to fly U-2s over the Soviet Union.

We saw Charlie only once after he left Stamford. It was seven or eight years ago and Pat and I were at the pool, and a familiar figure, tall and handsome, strolled down. We were glad to see him, and he chatted, perfectly relaxed, for at least half an hour, then said suddenly, "Oh, my wife Maureen is in the car—okay to bring her down?" Down he came with Maureen O'Hara, whom he had married a year or two earlier; together, now that he was retired, they were going down to St. Thomas to start up a local airline.

Bunny said the story didn't surprise her a bit, that Charlie was thataway with his wives, and that Maureen became so fixated about his casual coming and going that, during the last six months he served Pan Am, she bought a first-class ticket on every flight Charlie commanded. There were pictures of Charlie everywhere in her apartment.

The guests inspected every corner of *Sealestial* with gasps of joy and admiration, even from the wizened captains of our ultramodern research vessels. The girls had prepared nice hors d'oeuvres, and we served assorted booze, and white wine. I proudly

Walking on Pico: Tony, Dan, Reg, WFB. BELOW: Pulling away from Punta Delgada, full speed toward Gibraltar.

Preparing to reef.
FOLLOWING PAGE :
Day five, easing up.

showed off my computers; I was pleased that Allen had on display the scrimshaw I had ordered for him (Allen communicates to you by little gestures of this kind). We had made a dinner reservation at what was said to be the gourmet center in the Azores, the *Chez Shamin,* so the problem was to bring on an emigration. I devised a plan that so pleases me, I think I shall institutionalize it, though it is not really a good idea to give it too much publicity. I whispered to Christopher, and he got the attention of the milling crowd of fifteen to twenty by banging on a bottle. *"Everybody on deck for a group picture, please."* Everyone submits readily to the discipline of any photographer, so all of them climbed up the companionway to the forepeak, by the boarding ladder that rose to the *Wyman.* Christopher climbed halfway up the ladder to focus his camera on the crowd. I said, "Now, everyone look as though you had just gotten the news that Ronald Reagan had won the national election!" Christopher snapped the picture. I am anxious to see it, because to half the guests President Carter was commander in chief, and to the Matthewses he was chief employer. But the smiles were good-natured of course—and at that point there was nothing to do but say goodbye and leave. Ken Galbraith and I have in common what strikes some as a disadvantage, but isn't, really: namely our plainspoken bias, which gives a harnessing energy to our work. It is a terrible pity that he uses his talents to such subversive ends.

Except for one scene at the restaurant, the meal was splendid. The rather self-important young owner served us an excellent red wine which, however, was too damned warm, and I told him so. He proceeded to give me a lecture about the proper temperature for red wine. I was nine years old when my father, after deep researches, installed year-round air conditioning in his wine cellar, a practice I duplicated in my own cellar about the time the man from whom I was receiving a lecture was given his first popsicle, so I overreacted, embarrassing myself and my companions, I'm sure, though they mention the incident very calmly in their journals, and are *united* in believing that, on the issue of the wine's temperature, I was *dead right.*

I went directly back to the hotel. The others sauntered. Tony writes in his journal, "On the way back, Reg, Chris, and I were in one car, so we stopped at the village before Punta Delgada and joined in the festivities of some obscure saint. In the middle of the

Punta Delgada. Swinging, aboard the Sealestial.

village on the only street, a band had been set up which was pumping out some dreary martial music. There were lights, and a little stall for an auction, and people weren't doing much but looking at each other a little depressed. So Reg started working the crowd and I followed in. We soon had a rag-tag bunch of urchins who seemed mesmerized by Reggie's size and tricks, and whatever else he does."

The following morning I wrote the last two of the three columns I needed to telephone in to New York, and at twelve Danny picked me up to drive me to the *Sealestial* for the last leg of our journey. There was great underground amusement aboard our vessel because (Danny swears to the truth of it) late the night before, after the meal, and preparing to retire, Tom Wendel began questioning Dan. The ship's company, slouched about the saloon, reading, drinking, heard the conversation in the cockpit.

"Danny, when you are 'on watch,' what is it that you watch *for?*"

Danny, whose sense of humor is highly developed, is incapable of sarcasm with anyone who is being entirely ingenuous. He explained that you watch out for things like other ships, changes in wind direction, sails that blow out, men who fall overboard, that sort of thing.

"When you are on watch"—Tom, the scholar, persevered—"do you have to go outside?"

Danny told him that someone was always "outside," but that the second watch member frequently went below, to make a log entry or fetch up some coffee or whatever. How Van and Dick would have enjoyed it all.

I like to take off on a boat not more than five minutes after boarding it, and this time we very nearly made it, but for a slight delay caused by Allen's retrieval of our passports from Immigration. The wind was blowing us into the *Wyman*, so we had to spring ourselves out, a nice maneuver involving a spring line (a line from the stern of the boat to a bollard forward on the "dock"), and reverse engine until the bow, there being nothing else it can do given the vector of forces, eases out: then rudder amidship to permit you to move out straight ahead, so that your stern doesn't scrape against whatever you were tied up to. Thirty seconds into the harbor and I headed the boat into the wind, Allen and I having decided we would depart like true sailors. In two minutes the mainsail was up. In another two, the genoa; the wind was blowing smartly from the north, and within three minutes we were passing by our two naval vessels at hull speed, waving at everybody in sight, trying, even, to catch sight of a red handkerchief or something from Bunny at her penthouse apartment. Tom was utterly elated as, just past the harbor entrance, I set my course east, the girls brought out the wine and soup and sandwiches, and, traveling a half mile south of the island, we spent the next two hours watching São Miguel slide by, with all its greenery, its vine-yards, the noble houses, the fincas, the sheep. The high cheer of Tom was precious, because moments after we slid past the lee of the island I had to call for a reef in the mainsail. Before the evening was out, I called for a second; and then a third reef. We blew out the main genoa that night and rigged a topsail and a staysail. We were embarked on one hundred hours of the damnedest, steadiest, hardest, most sustained wind I can remember. I knew, I knew, that the ocean would not let us get away with the cotton-candy stuff we had had that last week reaching the Azores. I was right. But then what else is new.

15

~~~~~~~~~~~~~~~~~~~~~~~~~~~~

Toward the beginning there is exhilaration. "Log 465," Danny made his entry, "wind gusting to 30, seas—rolling chop, speed 8.8, making terrific headway, love it. What a way to begin a watch, blow a sail, reef main, put up headsail and topsail, bring aboard dinghy, get soaked and enjoy Chris Little's happy expression. He finally got his action shot."

But there are exasperations, including the episodic failure of the Indians to follow your instructions. . . . "One purpose of a watch captain," Danny, too diplomatic to upbraid his watchmate directly, addressed his admonitions to the logbook, "is to assume the safety and procedures of his watch and when asked to secure oneself with a life harness, please do so." And, lest he sound too hortatory, a propitiatory ending. "I thank thee."

On the state of health of his confederate, Danny was succinct. "Log 433.6. Tom's a ghost." And, a little later, a reappearance. "Log 442. Wind up again to 20 knots. Tom's a ghost."

Tony, as is customary, was more detailed in describing exactly what happened:

Trouble forward. The sheet pulls right through the clew of the genoa. Retrieving it (below) is strenuous. Opposite (top): Aft, the reefing of the mainsail begins. Below: Reg and Danny coordinate lowering of the halyard and winching in the clew outhaul. The objective is to reduce the mainsail uniformly.

"At 2100, we double-reefed the main. Experienced difficulties:

"1) Topsail sheet prevented main boom from going out to supply sufficient luff.

"2) Topping lift parted.

"3) Double-reef clew outhaul stuck, so that winching it in proved very difficult, resulting in *protracted experience*."

Let me explain the new procedure for reefing the mainsail—so to speak, the third-generation reefing procedure of my lifetime.

When I began sailing, you lowered the mainsail completely when you wanted to reef, made all the adjustments, then raised it. This procedure, for racers, was an awful concession—all that time without the propellant force of the mainsail. There evolved the idea of roller reefing, and in a matter of years, if you didn't have it —well, it was as if you didn't have winches. Now the idea was to permit you to specify the extent of your reef. Instead of having to sacrifice one eighth the area of your mainsail (a single reef), or one quarter (a double), or one third to one half (a triple), you could contract your sail by exactly as much as you desired.

How? By redesigning your boom, making it circular, stripping it of all accretions of hardware, and winding the sail around it. Where the boom joins the mainmast (the gooseneck), instead of a simple locking device, you installed a worm gear that when cranked causes the whole of the boom to revolve. One man would stand at that winch, slowly turning the boom, while a second man would lower the main halyard, *pari passu*. As the sail comes down, naturally the aftermost corner of it comes progressively closer to the mast. Perhaps a clearer way of stating this is that the foot, which is the base leg of the triangular mainsail, shortens. Typically at the moment of reefing there are great pressures on the mainsail. When using the old method of reefing, it was required that the new clew be disciplined—that is, brought down close to the boom and stretched tight along it. Indispensable, else the reef points holding the unstretched sail to the boom rip out under the force of the wind. In roller reefing this is no problem because the boom is using up the unwound sail, and the original clew outhaul keeps the sail structurally sound.

We did this for years, and it worked, though somehow it was never as facile as advertised, and often things went wrong. The strain on the roller reefing device was always very great.

The new system—and the *Sealestial*'s new mainsail was devised to use it—went back in the direction of the first, with this critical improvement. If you decide, let us say, to take a single reef, you find, already passed through the single-reef cringle (a clew grommet becomes a "cringle" as you travel up the leech or hypotenuse of the sail), a light line. By reaching for this and attaching it to a durable line, say three-eighths Dacron, you have, already strung out, ready for use, the new clew outhaul. That line now comes from the cringle down to a corresponding sheave on the boom, and forward to a winch on the mast. The decision having been made to take a single reef, two men can handle the job. The second lets down the sail as the first winches in the reefing cringle, simultaneously bringing down the new, corresponding tack and engaging it to the gooseneck. When he is satisfied that the reefing cringle is good and tight, and after the tack is secured, the second man tightens the halyard. You have now an area of sail, no longer in use, fluttering about but not doing anyone any harm. At your leisure, you take the little lines (reef points) sewn into the sail every twelve inches or so, and tuck in the unused sail by tying the lines around it, as though furling.

Experience (ah, experience!) showed us that when it is extremely windy, it is a good idea to throw the instructions overboard. In this case: let the mainsail down completely. Bring in the clew reefing cringle without wind pressure; attach the new tack without wind pressure—then raise the sail, the helmsman having brought you into the wind to help eliminate all wind pressures. No doubt racing boats would disdain this alternative, and their crews are practiced enough to reef without snag. When cruising, with men inexperienced in your particular boat, you are best off lowering the sail.

It was now blowing very hard. "Wow!" one entry reads, simply. Another: "Log 616. Speed 10.15. Winds now gusting to 45 knots! Very cold and wet. Reg and CSVL [Christopher] somewhat happy and extremely exhilarated." Ah, but inevitably, "Log 627. Speed 10.25. Winds 30–35 with higher gusts. Cold, wet. Novelty eroding with each wave that breaks over my head."

Meanwhile, below . . . "Bill and Tom," Tony wrote, "took the usual 8–12 and we all suffered through a horrid night. I don't care what it was like on deck, because down below I didn't get any sleep at all. Torrents coming in the hatches all over. The waves found totally new places, and all sorts of shelves to get into. Every fifteen minutes after a new inundation you could hear screams and groans coming from the other cabins as beds became progressively wetter and tempers ever shorter. After a series of really bad bangs, I wanted to go on deck to tell Bill to shape up, because he was ruining my sleep, but I decided he couldn't do too much about it. So he was luckily spared my scorn and wrath." Close shave, that.

Tony rose for his watch: "Coming on deck was a shock. The motion had been very pronounced down below, but I was not prepared for the size or steepness of the waves coming down toward us. They glistened in the bright morning sunlight, and had those rows and streaks of foam made by the wind that you get with the 'over 35 crowd'; I mean over 35 knots wind. Danny was steering pretty robustly to keep control, and I was chomping at the bit to get my hands on the wheel. And when I did, what bliss. I had been thinking that my 2–8 of the evening before was going to be my last real sail of the trip. But no! There's more where that wind comes from. We estimated the big ones between 15–20 feet, and I don't care, by my standards that's big. You can get in trouble in that sort of stuff."

Tony meditated on the vessel's virtues, reaching conclusions slightly at variance from his original ones: ". . . Thundering along at 10 plus knots, the whole thing vibrating and hissing, luckily not banging into waves, but riding easily over them. With Dave helping out Allen, I managed to get in a few really long tricks, steering more than the three hours of the watch which I am entitled to. This is really my idea of what a passage should be. The waves requiring some real steering, picking a route out through the waves bearing down on us, and trying to keep the bow and the stern from getting pushed around too much. What continues to impress me is how *Sealestial* feels like a dinghy under these conditions. The response is phenomenal, and it's exhilarating."

But the discomforts were not always transcended: "The action was starting to get a little boring by dinnertime, and we had to eat below. I was having my usual discomfort readjusting to the sea once more, but I was able to enjoy the leisurely dinner. Unfortunately, it was quite obvious that Tom was not. He would stretch out on the settee, closing his eyes and chewing, contemplatively and at great length. I could imagine the effort with which he had to talk. I guess he had been pretty well sedated by Bill's various anti-seasick tablets so he was O.K. But then he started to press his luck. Bill, who believes that there is a magic pill for just about every ailment, suggested that Tom counteract the soporific with a 'Ritalin' or something which was a mild stimulant. No. His stomach, I think, became a raging battleground, and he lost."

Poor Tom. It was a dreadful initiation. His journal had begun with a grandiose sense of well-being, including amicable characterizations of his companions. "Tony Leggett, sailor, preppy, Harvard grad, traveler, and banker-to-be—an altogether fine young man; Danny Merritt, upbeat, agile, ready and eager for anything, fine sailor; Chris Little, teddy-bearish, youngish professional photographer—amusing and knowledgeable . . . the immensely professional jack-of-all-things-navigational skipper, Allen, and his young helper-athlete—competent, muscular young man originally from New Orleans who did the derring-do necessities at mast-top, for example. Reggie—bibulous, sentimental, wise about the sea, friendly to the point of attracting crowds where'er he goes, including and perhaps especially children."

Then the departure: ". . . the casting off and smooth heading to seaward was spine-tingling. This, thought I, was living." The succeeding sentence, for Tom, foretold it all. "From here on I will not try to trace events day by day."

Much much later: "For at least half the voyage, I felt slightly nauseated."

So it was, for four days. At the end of which, sometime after dinner, Allen, who speaks infrequently, sniffed the air, ducked a great wave that splashed across the deck, and said quietly, "Tell you what ah think. Ah think tomorrow, this time, we'll be under power." We all smiled; but at 1800 the following day I said, "We're doing only 5.5 knots. Let's have some power," and there was great rejoicing for lo, we had a prophet in our midst. Two hundred miles to go. The ordeal was not, however, at an end.

16

~~~~~~~~~~~~~~~~~

Tom is asleep above me, and I can hear the waves from my bunk, but the moon just eludes me. The voices of the helmsmen on watch can't be heard. I am protected from falling out of bed by canvas leeboards. When the port side of the ship is the windward side and you are heeled over hard, as we have been now for two days, you need to extricate the lee straps from under your mattress. They come conveniently equipped with snaphooks, so that you need only find the corresponding eyes under Tom's bunk and hook them in. Every time, you pause to consider alternative ways of proceeding. The first is to snap in both ends (the canvas is about three feet long, protecting you from somewhere just under your armpits to below your hip) and then grope your way through the upper or nether aperture until you are in full possession of your bed. Or, you can secure the lower end, sliding your body in quite easily; but you then have to contrive to snap on the upper end when your whole body is being directed by gravity to put its full weight on exactly that part of the canvas that you need to stretch tight in order to fasten the hook. Extreme exertion, combined with isometric control, permits the latter, and I chose this way in, this time around.

It has been a mysteriously unsatisfactory day. The conditions of course are hard. Tom, simply put, is miserable. But Tony is preternaturally silent, and I fear he is sick. Even Reggie and Christopher are rather more dutiful than lusty as they go about their business. Only Danny is, as ever, zestful, twice coming to me in the morning, on instructions interrupting my paperwork, to tell me he thought I might snatch the sun through the clouds. Because although the conditions are stormy, the visibility is good, and for perhaps twenty percent of the day we had glimpses of the sun, even as now the moon is fitfully out, causing the monstrously wonderful shadows that augment the savagery of the waves as they thunder past us, so that sometimes you are plunged from near midday visibility into utter darkness.

All the meals were strictly utilitarian. We were given deep bowls, with a gruel of sorts. That and bread and cheese and wine. At that, we spilled much of what we were given. Allen has taped a two-by-four down the length of the table, but it isn't high enough to serve as efficiently as one of those fiddles Tony speaks of. It will resist only that in which the center of gravity is low. Coffee in a heavy mug, yes; wine filling a plexiglass goblet to the brim, no.

Suddenly I realized what uniquely characterized this day. We had had no music. Early on, the ship's cassette player broke down, but my battery-drive Superscope, with its two extension speakers, is every bit as good, and we have had it on several hours a day. I had contrived to confer on Tony the high rank of Curator of the Cassette Collection (mine) which has seventy or eighty hours of music, half of it baroque, a quarter this and that, mostly piano; and then some non-rock jazz, splendid swing music. When the young generation decides it will perish from this earth if it does not soon hear again the Mint Funks, or whatever it is they listen to nowadays, there are plenty of those in the ship's collection, to say nothing of the private collection of David. Last night, hoping to bring a little cheer to poor, prostrate Tom, I told him that during our watch, after I did the navigation, we would hear a private concert given in my house by Fernando Valenti. Tom and Fernando were classmates at Yale. I did not know Fernando then. But seven or eight years ago Fernando wrote to me, having seen Rosalyn Tureck on one of my television programs. We became friends, I reintroduced him to Tom, Tom in due course persuaded his university at San José to come up with the budget for a resident harpsichordist; and now Fernando lives nearby.

Tom and I regularly refer to him as the "greatest horticulturist in the world." It was six or seven years ago that Fernando flew back from a concert tour in Europe, called and asked himself out to the country. We welcomed him but told him we would all be going out that evening for dinner with Mike and Jan Cowles, along with another houseguest, Carl. I called Jan and told her we had an unexpected visitor, Fernando Valenti, "whom *Time* has called the greatest harpsichordist in the world," and might I bring him along? Of course; but when dinnertime came Fernando said he was simply too exhausted to go anywhere, so we set out with Carl, and a half hour later, at Mount Kisco, found ourselves in the company of twenty interesting people. Carl, however, was continually mystified because the guests, particularly the women, kept addressing to him such questions as: "Can I mix my hydrangea with my poppy?" to which Carl would reply that nothing would please him more than to give good counsel in the matter, but in fact he had no idea what if anything would happen if you mixed a hydrangea with a poppy, and after a half-dozen such questions, fired at random, I did a little discreet sleuthing to discover that dear Jan had announced to her guests that I would be bringing along the world's most famous "horticulturist."

In any event, Tom looked forward greatly to hearing the concert I had recorded, and he stretched out on the cockpit while I stuck my little cassette player in one of those plastic zipper bags, which nicely protected it, all along the way, from salt spray. Fernando had played in the little music room I have in the country, whose humidity is controlled, which saves me from having to tune the harpsichord twice a week. He played the C Minor Partita and the G Major Partita, and then a string of Scarlatti sonatas of such compounding beauty they are, at his hands, almost unbearable to listen to, like Beethoven's last quartets. Tom's own harpsichord is a duplicate of my own, so that the entire experience was intimate in every way. Music showed no powers to soothe the savage sea, but Tom felt distinctly better, for an hour or two, and was quite voluble on the strengths of Fernando as a harpsichord player. I told him that when he was well again, I would play him the cassette I made of a magnificent piano concert by Rosalyn Tureck, whom I love, and who the year before had volunteered as a birthday present to give at my house the same concert she would be giving the following Tuesday at Carnegie Hall. I was quite dazzled by it all, and introduced her to the twenty or thirty friends I brought in by recalling one of those two-liners that were making the rounds when I was at college. He: "Do you want to go into my car and hear Guy Lombardo and the Royal Canadians?" She: "I didn't know you had a radio in your car." He: "I don't. I have Guy Lombardo and the Royal Canadians." That was how I felt that night.

Bad omen, no music. What do people do when there is no music? I suspect they don't notice. Four years ago I had I think the most exasperating musical experience of my life. I embarked on the QE2 as a lecturer, New York–Fort Lauderdale–Curaçao–Caracas–Salvador–Rio: four lectures in return for room and board, which suited me just fine because I had a novel to begin. I kept the good music channel on and the first morning heard César Franck's D Minor symphony, which is okay to listen to, once a year. That afternoon I heard Franck's D Minor symphony; also that evening, four times the next day, three times the following day, till I thought I would go crazy. I remember expressing my frustration by killing off one or two extra-nice people in the opening chapters of my spy book. But what was going on? Finally, in frustration, I called the radio room and said: "I have heard Franck's D Minor symphony perhaps one hundred times in my lifetime, eighty-five of those on this trip. Are you short of inventory?"

"You don't like it?"—the symphony was stopped in mid-movement, and some Mozart slid in.

"Is that better, sir?" I expressed great gratitude; but two days later, would you believe it, they were back to César Franck. I would keep my set on, and when the opening chords were struck, would rise, turn off the set, and forty minutes later turn it back on. I got my exercise that way, relieving me of the responsibility to do my daily calisthenics. I thought surely we would pick up from the crowd (1,500 passengers) a mutinous hum; but so help me, I found no one with whom to share my misery.

Well, tomorrow would be another day, as the saying goes. Certainly there were no indications of any change in weather. The barometer hadn't budged in days—hadn't tipped us off, as a matter of fact, to what we were in. Presumably we were still in the same Azores High, but in a part of it that was windy. I missed, also, our daily swims, though the rain and the waves kept us well laundered, besides which there is a splendid shower by the master stateroom. The sights have been irregular, and this afternoon we spotted a Portuguese warship and spoke it (*v.t.*). The reply: "We ahrr Portugal. You ahrr what?" I suppose if we had said we were Mozambique they'd have declined cooperation, but we gave our flag, and asked if they had a position, and after a few minutes' silence they gave us one. Either we were six miles south of where I had us, or they were six miles north of where they placed themselves. I had had a noon sight, and was not lightly going to give ground on the subject, though those northerly winds were probably giving us considerable set and leeway, and I cranked our course north by three degrees. I'm not worried about where we are. As a matter of fact, I thought, turning off the reading light, I wasn't really worried about anything. The *Sealestial* was built without any notion of being overwhelmed by such seas as come at you with winds of forty miles per hour, and was proving it very nicely.

The next day was just as bad, but it was on the evening of it that Allen made his remarkable prediction. It is hard to describe the joy that comes to a sailor when after a particularly long blast, the weather clears. I swear, it's like V-J Day. You just want to go out and be happy. There were still swells at 6 P.M., but the wind was down to seven knots. For the first time since leaving the Azores, we ate in the cockpit. The moon was perfect, the stars were out. The music was on. Everyone had a snort, and wine besides. Tom was fully recovered, and once again was finding everything funny, including imitations of him during the preceding three days (Reggie's was superior. To do it right, you must lie flat on your back, and look straight up, and put your hand over your eyes. The tone of voice must be funereal. "I'll have one saltine. No! Make that *half* a saltine. Thank you"). And the whole of the next day was more of the same, with just enough wind to sail by.

FOLLOWING PAGES:

Tacking across the Strait of Gibraltar. Tony forward, WFB at helm.

I began to make calculations. As I've suggested, I don't like to end a big trip at anticlimactic hours. At the rate we were going, we'd pull into Marbella at about two in the afternoon, and that is no damn good for celebrating. Rather like being married at six in the morning. So, said I studying the charts, I have a proposal. Let's go into Gibraltar, get off the boat, have lunch there, look around for an hour or two, then reboard and sail up the thirty miles to Marbella. My proposal was greeted with cheers from all sides, and I knew how Magellan must have felt when he said, "What do you say we pop around the world?" That night was especially animated, we played poker followed by a little wild Red Dog, and when the chips were counted, the whole exercise resulted in an entirely tolerable redistribution of wealth, a modest amount of it in my direction.

You must not ever count on uneventful endings to ocean passages. For every day I have finished a race or cruise in calm circumstances, I can think of two that have been turbulent.

The next morning the breeze was on the nose, and before I came on deck, Tony had hardened up the sails; and now, the wind having veered directly east, we had given way, heading about 110 degrees. We had run into what they call in those parts a "levanter," namely a tough wind that comes out of the Mediterranean from the east, and has a swooshing funnel effect in the Strait of Gibraltar, which after all is only nine miles wide at its closest point.

I took the helm, and hung on to it for six hours, enjoying it all, though it was fierce and salty. By now we could see the southern st of Spain—and the northwestern tip of Africa. The navigation this point would be visual. Consulting the Coast Pilot, I ed that after high water in Gibraltar, the current flows east to beginning four hours after high tide in Gibraltar, until the gh tide. So, all we needed to do was find out what time was e in Gibraltar.

ensued a search through every paper and document on Sealestial. We came up with stuff that would have per- to navigate up the Amazon, around Patagonia, into orts in Micronesia; but no tide tables for the Mediter-

So I asked Allen to try Radio Gibraltar, which he did. *This is Whiskey Oscar George 9842 Whiskey Oscar George 9842 calling Radio Gibraltar, calling Radio Gibraltar.* Nothing. By now we were coasting along the shore of Africa, with a good view of the wind-harried dunes, including a relatively new-looking tanker that had missed the turn by a mere quarter mile and was now abandoned, on its side on the rocks. There is a spectacular lighthouse there, at a point east of which the Barbary pirates took sanctuary for so many years. Now we were abeam of Tangier, and I suggested we try Tangier Radio, with which, however, we had no better results than with Gibraltar. Okay, I said, let's try the hand-held radio with which we had successfully communicated with several vessels during our passage. There were great tankers and freighters of every nationality and size steaming east and west across the Strait. All we desired was the simplest datum—namely, What time was high water in Gibraltar?

We tried it in English, in French, and in Spanish: just the bare question. There was a sullen muteness in all that traffic: hard, really, to understand, because ships at sea tend to be civil to one another. I tacked about again, to starboard, pointing now to the Spanish coast about ten miles west of Gibraltar, and thought: what the hell, we'll stay on this course. If the tide is favorable, it will waft us into Gibraltar. If it isn't it will blow us west with the wind, and worse fates are imaginable than spending a night in a southern Spanish bay, *reculer pour mieux sauter* and all that sort of thing.

The triple-reefed main was augmented by a storm jib, because we had blown out the staysail and topsail, so we added engine power and moved tight into the wind at a full nine knots.

Within one hour, we knew we had gambled—and won.

Two hours later, without tacking again, we were suddenly surrounded by hills—we were in the Bay of Gibraltar, and the time was four in the afternoon. Too late for our lunch plans, but not too late, I thought, for a little *tour d'horizon*, and so, with the binoculars, I got the lay of the land and brought the *Sealestial* through a crack in the breakwater, only to run into a frenzied harbor pilot on an armed launch, directing us away from the southern end we thought to tour. "Probably Limey off-limits naval forces," Allen commented. I was glad to experience the sinews of Western military strength: but thirty seconds later we heard the crack of a gun. It was not a fusillade, let alone the beginning of the third

We made it. Top, Danny, Gibraltar. Below, WFB, Danny, Tom Wendel, Tony, Reg.

world war. It was a blank cartridge signaling the start of a children's dinghy race. We had been escorted out of an area in the bay reserved for ten-year-old kids on the days they race. Oh well.

So we took in other parts of Gibraltar, passing the fancy hotels serenely, looking up at the mountain where all the monkeys are cosseted, passing a dozen freighters tied up, loading and unloading. The girls were handing around some wine, and I took some and said, "Well, gentlemen, shall we proceed to Spain?" The consensus was affirmative, and so we moseyed out of Gibraltar and, to our surprise, found that the levanter had entirely dissipated, leaving us waters so placid, one would not have thought they had experienced wind in a week. We rounded, and I set the pilot on automatic, with a heading for Puerto Banús, whose light we would in any event pick up within a couple of hours. I don't remember ever seeing such pinks and blues as we saw that night, quietly proceeding at a mere thirteen hundred rpm so that there would be no noise to contend with. Every few moments, as the sun went down and the moon blared up, the color combinations changed, and we saw deep mauves, every color every painter ever used, when painting in a tranquil frame of mind; such a frame of mind as our own. Dinner was served slowly and consumed slowly, and there was barely time for coffee, brandy, and cigars before we saw the light and closed down on our destination.

I had seen it before, and remembered sending Danny in a dinghy to delineate absolutely the angular little channel by which you enter the huge facility at Marbella. I remembered it, and we crawled in, and instantly spotted two flashlights signaling us in a direction where, through the glasses, I could make out an unoccupied section of a dock, about the length of the *Sealestial*, and so I gave my last command: "Fenders, port side." I approached, did a figure eight to test the current, and we slid in. Betsy and a friend had just then (at midnight) arrived, expecting an all-night vigil. Betsy and Christopher had eloped only last November.

There was great commotion at the Immigration dock during which we all endeavored to place telephone calls to America, on the understanding that doing so would not interfere with our consumption of champagne, which Van had sent ahead in copious supply and Betsy had taken care to keep chilled. I don't know why, but suddenly I felt an impulse to pull out. I did so without ceremony, walking, champagne glass in hand, back along the lifeless dock, toward the boat. I stepped gingerly over the lifeline, grasping the shroud with my left hand: the other hand was not available, as there was still the champagne glass. The boat, mothballed in moonlight, was dead. Everyone was ashore, telephoning, reveling, roistering. There was no breeze, no sound. I walked aft to the stern cockpit and maneuvered down the stillness of the companionway to the master cabin, flicked on the reading light, dropped my pants, shoes, and socks with a single downward motion, and slid between the sheets. For the first time in seven days, no need to fasten the canvas leeboards that had kept me, during those screeching moments of heel, from being tossed onto the floorboards. I picked up my journal and began to write. The dozen words I managed I cannot, at this moment, decipher. They are illegible. But I know what they say. Know what they express. Gratitude.

Our destination, Puerto Banús.

Entering the Strait of Gibraltar: Tony discovers Africa.

BELOW: *Here the sky and sea play the role of a mirror depicting the ship and the photographer.*

"I don't remember ever seeing such pinks and blues as we saw that night."